MINISTRY HAS ITS MOMENTS

A JAMES DYET COLLECTION

JAMES DYET

Ministry Has Its Moments
Print Edition
© Copyright 2021 James Dyet

CKN Christian Publishing
An Imprint of Wolfpack Publishing
5130 S. Fort Apache Rd. 215-380
Las Vegas, NV 89148

www.christiankindlenews.com

This book is a work of fiction. Any references to historical events, real people or real places are used fictitiously. Other names, characters, places and events are products of the author's imagination, and any resemblance to actual events, places or persons, living or dead, is entirely coincidental.

All rights reserved. No part of this book may be reproduced by any means without the prior written consent of the publisher, other than brief quotes for reviews.

eBook ISBN 978-1-63977-070-0
Paperback ISBN 978-1-63977-071-7

IT'S A GOD THING

AND OTHER POPULAR CHRISTIAN MISCONCEPTIONS

To daughters Sherrie Escue and Heather Whiting and son Brian. They never wandered from their biblical beliefs and never lost their sense of humor.

1
IT'S A GOD THING

IN SPITE OF THE POPULAR BELIEF THAT MEN ARE FROM Mars and women are from Venus, many couples get along quite well. Some even stay married for more than sixty years. But any couple can tell you some differences never change.

Take shopping, for example. A man shops only out of necessity. He may be down to his last dress shirt and its collar is frayed. So he hops into his car, drives to a department store, walks briskly to the dress shirt display, finds his size, picks up a shirt, pays for it, hops back into his car, and returns home. It's a guy thing.

When a woman goes shopping, it isn't necessarily because she needs something. For her, shopping is a happening. It's like visiting a free museum. Upon entering the store, she looks for sales signs. If a sign at the Petites display announces "50% Off," she heads straight toward it. The "50% Off" draws her like a magnet. It doesn't matter that she is six feet tall. After shuffling pants and tops around in rack after rack, she moves on to another attraction, and another, and another.

Another difference: When have you seen two men shopping together? Women, on the other hand, often shop in twos or threes. And when one finds an item she likes, she shows it to her friend. Immediately, the two launch into a litany of girl talk. "So cute!" "Precious!" "How darling!" Can you imagine those words coming out of a guy's mouth?

And another difference: A husband and wife can eat lunch together at the same restaurant but each one's focus is entirely different. His attention is riveted on the food. Hers is fixed on the couple at the next table. He is hardly aware there is a next table. After lunch, she tells him what each person at the next table was wearing, what they ordered, what they were talking about, and what their after-lunch plans were. She isn't nosy, just observant. It's a woman thing!

We have grown accustomed to hearing, "It's guy thing" or "It's a girl thing," and I suppose we can live with these remarks and the differences that prompt them. Recently, however, a spin-off comment has slipped into our Christian vocabulary and I think we should bid it farewell. "It's a God thing" seems to explain every good turn of events that pops up in the Christian life.

Perhaps you have heard this expression in response to a situation like one of the following:

"There I was, driving 65 miles an hour down the freeway, when the front left tire blew out. I couldn't control the steering. Before I knew what was happening, I found myself skidding into the grassy median. I thought for sure I would crash into oncoming traffic but my car stayed in the median and stopped just inches short of a culvert. A couple of motorists saw what happened and stopped to check on me. They said they were sure I was going to end up in a wreck and be killed. I told them I thought I would get killed too. Now, as I look back on what happened, I know my survival was a God thing!"

"Kim and I know every fertility specialist in the city and every one of them said the possibility of our getting pregnant and having our own baby was about nil to zilch. But you know what? They were wrong. Four months from now, we'll be singing 'Rock-a-Bye-Baby' to our own little guy. It's a God thing!"

"Greg and I had dreamed about owning a five-bedroom two-story house on a wooded lot backing onto a lake but it was only a dream. We don't play the lottery, so there was no way we could come up with the money for our dream home. But the strangest thing happened. Last week the CEO called Greg into his office. It seems he had been getting good reports about Greg's ability to schedule products and ensure their quality. So he told Greg the company plans to build a second company in Oshkosh, Wisconsin, just a mile off Lake Winnebago. Here's where the story gets really good. The CEO wants Greg to be vice president of production and quality control at the new facility at a starting salary of $180,000. Dream house on the lake, here we come. It's a God thing. Oh, one more God thing—an exciting Bible-believing church is under construction right down the road from Greg's new workplace."

"The health clinic called Maryann and asked her to

return for another mammogram. The first had revealed a suspicious spot on her left breast. Maryann was worried. Did she have cancer? Surely God would not allow that to happen to a mother of one-year-old twin boys! She was too young and far too energetic to have cancer. She worked out every day, ate right, and pushed the boys in a twin stroller every day around a big neighborhood park.

The second mammogram followed by a biopsy confirmed the presence of an aggressive cancer. Both Maryann's physician and her surgeon explained her options. It seemed a radical mastectomy was the best option. A thorough pre-op examination would tell the full story.

Amazingly, the pre-op exam revealed no abnormality—no spot, no lump. Everything was suddenly normal. The medical staff could not offer an explanation. But Maryann could. "It's a God thing," she said with a bright smile."

Obviously, God cares for his children and causes good things to happen in our lives. But would the individuals mentioned in the preceding stories say, "It's a God thing" if the outcomes had been quite different? Let's revisit each story and turn the tables around.

"There I was, driving 65 miles an hour down the freeway, when the front left tire blew out. I couldn't control the steering. Before I knew what was happening, I found myself skidding into the grassy median. I thought for sure I would crash into oncoming traffic but my car stayed in the median and slammed into a culvert. I lost consciousness. When I came to, I was in Memorial Hospital. A neurologist told me I had been in a coma for three weeks. An orthopedic surgeon explained he had performed three surgeries to repair my shattered kneecaps, a broken right leg, and a broken pelvis. I might begin physical therapy soon, he said, but I might never walk again without assistance. Guess I'll have to get used to crutches and then graduate to a cane." A God thing?

"Kim and I know every fertility specialist in the city and they all said the odds of our getting pregnant and having our own baby were nil to zilch. We hoped they were wrong, but after eight years of trying to get pregnant, it seems they were right. Looks like we'll never get to sing 'Rock-a-Bye-Baby' to our own little guy or girl. Friends say we should adopt a child, but we simply don't want to." A God thing?

"Greg and I had dreamed about owning a five-bedroom two-story house on a wooded lot backing onto a lake, but it was only a dream. Last Friday, Greg got called into his manager's office. It seems the company's profit line has dipped every year for the past five years, so the company decided to lay Greg and a bunch of other middle managers off. The boss told Greg to clean out his desk and go home. Now what are we going to do? Greg received only one month's severance pay and jobs in his field are almost nonexistent. We can kiss our dream house goodbye. We may not even be able to pay the rent on our apartment much longer. Instead of living a dream, we're now living a nightmare!" A God thing?

The health clinic had called Maryann and asked her to return for another mammogram. The first had revealed a suspicious spot on her left breast.

Maryann was worried. Did she have cancer? Surely God would not allow that to happen to a mother of one-year-old twin boys! She was too young and far too energetic to have cancer. She worked out every day, ate right, and pushed the boys in a twin stroller every day around a big neighborhood park.

The second mammogram followed by a biopsy confirmed the presence of an aggressive cancer. Both Maryann's physician and her surgeon explained her options. It seemed a radical mastectomy was the best option.

That was ten months ago. Maryann had the surgery and hoped to resume normal, energetic life. Her husband has been supportive, and the twins are now walking and acting like most two-year-old boys. But Maryann is troubled. Cancer has returned and is attacking both her liver and her brain. In all likelihood, she has only three or four months to live. When she dies, she will leave behind a grieving husband and two lonely, confused little boys. A God thing?

When my two brothers and I were wee laddies, our Scottish mither (mother) gave us cod-liver oil regularly. We screwed up our noses and turned our heads every time she put a spoonful of the stuff near our mouths, but our faither (father) would order: 'You get that knocked into ye or I'll break baith [both] your legs." Strict child protection laws didn't exist back then and a swig of cod-liver oil seemed more desirable than two broken legs, so my brothers and I downed what was supposed to be good for us.

Sometimes we Christians screw up our noses and try to turn away from distasteful circumstances. We can't possibly imagine that our loving heavenly Father wants us to experience such distasteful things as pain and suffering, financial hardship, or loneliness. Such "bad" things certainly aren't His things, are they? In other words, when good fortune enters our lives, we say it's a God thing but when ill fortune invades our lives, we say the Devil is out to get us.

Perhaps we need an attitude adjustment.

The apostle Paul didn't get wealthy; he got welts. In 2 Corinthians 11, he reported, "I have ... been flogged ... severely.... Five times I received from the Jews the forty lashes minus one. Three times I was beaten with rods, once I was stoned" (v. 23-25). His life was never smooth sailing; he experienced rough seas and shipwreck (see Acts 27). He never spent a day in a penthouse; however, he spent many nights in prison. No one ever threw him a party; most of his friends deserted him (2 Tim. 4:16). Instead of everything coming up roses for Paul, he received a "thorn in [the] flesh" (2 Cor. 12:7). His only stocks were iron stocks that secured him in prison (Acts 16:24). When his life ended, he wasn't rolling in money; his head was rolling across an executioner's floor. Yet this same man, Paul, trumpeted the truth that "we know that in all things God works for the good of those who love Him, who have been called according to His purpose" (Rom. 8:28).

This amazing truth comes alive when we understand God's purpose for us is to conform us "to the likeness of his Son" (Rom. 8:29). If we truly want to be like Jesus, we must experience friction and buffeting. Tough times can help make our hearts tender, our lives pure, and our faith strong. The apostle Peter taught us to see trials as having greater value than gold. They refine our faith and prove its genuineness (1 Peter 1:6-7). James even advised us to "consider it pure joy" when we "face trials of many kinds" (James 1:2). He urged us to anticipate the results of such testing—spiritual maturity (v. 3-4).

Long before Romans, 1 Peter, and James were written, men like Job, Joseph, and David learned to view "all things" as fulfilling God's plan for their lives.

If the expression "It's a God thing" had been circulating in Job's day, some of Job's friends might have used it to explain his enormous success. His ranch spread far enough to make Texas cattlemen envious. His flocks and herds dotted the landscape like ants on a discarded slice of watermelon. He and his wife owned a number of homes and enjoyed the good life. Their seven sons and three daughters thrived on the rich land, so did his many ranch hands. Everything was as close to perfect as it could be, including Job's spiritual life.

But, suddenly, that good life turned ugly. Lightning strikes, a tornado-force wind, and marauders reduced Job's livestock to nothing and killed most of his ranch hands and all of his sons and daughters. Then Job's health went south. He experienced excruciating pain and crushing emotional distress. His so-called friends credited all the bad events to sin in Job's life and his wife rubbed salt on his wounds by telling him to curse God and die. No one said, "It's a God thing!"

The rest of the story vindicates Job. He maintained his faith. He testified he would still hope in God even if God were to slay him (Job 13:15). He looked beyond life on earth to life in the glory of the resurrection, believing he would behold his Redeemer with his own eyes (19:25-

27). When all the trials finally lifted, Job's view of God's character and ways was richer and fuller than before the trials rained down on him. Troubles had not made Job bitter; they had made him better. They had given him a better understanding of his mortality and humanness and a greater appreciation of God's majesty and wisdom.

The whole story of Job's suffering includes a behind-the-scenes look at spiritual forces. We learn that Satan, the Devil, whined to God that Job worshipped and obeyed God only because God had blessed Job so abundantly. He claimed Job would curse God if God swept away everything from Job (1:11). God knew Job better than Satan knew Job. God knew trials would only validate Job's faith and draw Job closer to him, so he allowed Satan to assault Job. However, he restrained Satan from taking Job's life. The drama ended with a defeated Satan, a vindicated Job, and a victorious God!

We may not like trials but they serve us well. When we are flat on our backs, we are looking up! We pray with a sense of urgency and we search the Bible diligently for reasons and promises. Patience builds stronger roots of faith and the fruit of the Spirit flourishes in our attitudes and actions.

Nearly a third of the book of Genesis is devoted to the story of Joseph. When he was a youngster, he received a multicolored coat from his father. It distinguished him as Dad's favorite of the twelve sons. He also received a couple of dreams from God that predicted he would be prominent. According to the dreams, Joseph's parents and brothers would pay him homage. Joseph could have summed it all up as "It's a God thing." But he didn't!

As he grew older, Joseph encountered trouble on top of trouble. From a purely human perspective, it seemed like his life was caving in like a poorly constructed building struck by a 6.5 earthquake. His brothers nearly killed him but sold him into slavery instead. He was taken far from home by traders to Egypt and sold to a high-ranking military officer. The officer's wife tried desperately and repeatedly to seduce Joseph; when her efforts failed, she framed him, charging him with attempted rape. Joseph received a prison sentence and Egyptian prison life was extremely tough.

Who would call any of Joseph's "tragedies" a God thing? But years later, when all his "tragedies" were only memories and Joseph was the Pharaoh's right-hand man, Joseph reconciled with his brothers and declared: 'You intended to harm me but God intended it for good" (Gen. 50:20).

Get the picture? It's better than the best Kodak moment. God designs everything in our lives for our good and His glory.

If you have spent much time reading King David's psalms, you will get an enlarged copy of this grand picture. He wrote most of his psalms after experiencing persecution and deprivation. They originated from desert caves and other hiding places, not from the comfort of a royal palace. They rendered praise to God during hard times as they acknowledged his presence and provision.

Even Psalm 23, which begins on a tranquil note, reflects on God's presence and provision in hard times. Have you noticed the use of the third-person pronoun in verses 2 and 3? David wrote: "He makes me lie down in green pastures, he leads me beside quiet waters, he restores my soul. He guides me in paths of righteousness for his name's sake." Suddenly, David reflected on trouble and trials and switched to the second-person pronoun. "Even though I walk through the valley of the shadow of death, I will fear no evil, for you are with me; your rod and your staff, they comfort me. You prepare a table before me in the presence of my enemies. You anoint my head with oil; my cup overflows" (v. 4-5).

There's no doubt about it, we can look upon tough circumstances as launching pads to a closer relationship with the Lord. So why should we single out only what we see as a fortuitous turn of events as "a God thing"?

Something else to consider: The construction "It's a God thing" employs "God" as an adjective, and an adjective is less important than the noun it modifies.

How would you like to be referred to as an adjective modifying a thing? It would certainly depersonalize you. Saying, "It's a Mary or a Craig or a Dan thing," makes Mary, Craig, or Dan less important than the "thing" referred to. Therefore, it seems to me the adjectival use of God's name diminishes respect and reverence for Him.

By contrast, God's name deserves our highest esteem. We should not mention it lightly or thoughtlessly. Exodus 20:7 commands, 'You shall not misuse the name of the Lord your God," and Jesus taught us to hallow God's name (Matt. 6:9). We may not intend any disrespect for God's name when we say, "It's a God thing," but unintentional error is error, nonetheless.

Here's a sure way to gather a crowd. Stand on a busy sidewalk and stare into the sky. Before long a crowd of pedestrians will join you. Everyone in the crowd will peer into the empty sky to find what you are looking at.

Because many Christians are followers—groupies—they quickly pick up on popular expressions, even empty ones like "It's a God thing." Soon a big crowd is exclaiming, "It's a God thing."

Isn't it time to drop this unscriptural expression and leave mob mentality behind?

2

IT TAKES TWO OR THREE GATHERED TOGETHER IN JESUS' NAME

IT WAS THE SAME OLD SAME OLD. LIKE EVERY WEDNESDAY evening at seven, Jack and Carol Woolford, Debbie Morgan, Molly Jefferson, and Pastor Bill and his wife, Sue, had arranged several chairs in a circle in the church's basement and were quietly awaiting the start of the weekly prayer service. The downcast expression on Pastor Bill's face spoke volumes. Clearly, he was discouraged by the congregation's lack of interest in the midweek prayer service. Jack peered around the room, wondering once again why so many members chose to stay home. They must be addicted to TV, he thought. Then he glanced at Pastor Bill. Sensing the pastor's discouragement, he intoned, "I don't know why our group is so small but the Lord promised that where two or three are gathered together in his name, there he would be in the midst of them."

Jack was probably more aware of the absence of the many than he was of the presence of the Lord in the midst of the few but was his observation valid? Did he correctly apply the promise of Matthew 18:20 to the situation at hand or was he off the mark? And just what does it take to acquire the Lord's presence?

Did Jack correctly apply the promise of Matthew 18:20? The context surrounding this verse holds the answer.

If you read Matthew 18:15-20, you will discover at a glance that this context doesn't relate to a midweek prayer service. The situation it describes isn't nearly as chummy as a prayer service. Quite the opposite! The situation bristles with tension and crackles with conflict. It involves sin, an offended believer, one or two witnesses, and a congregation's decision to excommunicate the guilty party. Jesus was preparing his disciples for leadership in the first-century church. Knowing that personal conflicts would arise in local assemblies of believers, he counseled, "If your brother sins against you, go and show him his fault, just between the two of you. If he listens to you, you have won your brother over" (v. 15).

Generally, believers ought to be able to settle their differences quietly, peaceably, and agreeably. After all, they belong to the same spiritual family, share common beliefs and values, want to please their heavenly Father, and understand that love covers a multitude of sins. The counsel Jesus gave in verse 15 ought to mend a broken fence, shouldn't it?

Of course! But sometimes only the offended person wants to repair the fence. While he works to put the boards back into place, the person who caused the damage keeps kicking them out.

For example, Kip had an affair with Hank's wife, Caitlin. It all started as a flirting session between the two in the choir room. Then, after a choir practice, Kip and Caitlin went out for coffee. Soon, they were meeting for more than coffee—at a motel. When Caitlin could no longer live with her stabbing conscience, she confessed her sin to Hank and asked for his forgiveness. She said she had called off the affair with Kip, but he would not give up. Instead, he was pleading with her to stay in the illicit relationship. She also expressed a willingness to confess her transgression before the whole church and ask for forgiveness.

Caitlin's shocking news stunned and angered Hank, but he found the grace to forgive her. Then, he decided to confront Kip. At first, Hank railed against Kip, but then he calmed down and urged Kip to confess his wrongdoing and break off all communication with Caitlin. He even offered to forgive Kip if he would admit his sin and agree to leave Caitlin alone. However, Kip showed no remorse. Instead, he cursed Hank and threatened to punch out his lights if he raised the subject again.

Now, what was Hank to do? Jesus' further instruction dictates: "But if he will not listen, take one or two others along, so that every matter may be established by the testimony of two or three witnesses" (v. 16). Obviously, Jesus valued the Old Testament principle of establishing truth at the mouth of two or three witnesses. He honored Deuteronomy 19:15: "One witness is not enough to convict a man accused of any crime or offense he may have committed. A matter must be established by the testimony of two or three witnesses."

Hank took the next step. Accompanied by three members of the church board, he confronted Kip about the affair and begged him to leave Caitlin alone. At first,

Kip denied the accusation but denial turned to rage. He admitted the affair but once again threatened to rough Hank up if he didn't stop hounding him.

Hank and the others could only regret Kip's adamant spirit. Shaking their heads almost in disbelief, they walked away.

But the story doesn't end there. Jesus counseled that if a sinning brother refuses to listen to witnesses, they should "tell it to the church" (v. 17). Although no local churches existed when Jesus spoke these words, the word translated "church" can be applied to a church. The word means "assembly" and usually referred to an assembly of Jews, but it can also refer to a future assembly or congregation of church members. So in a church business meeting, Hank and the three witnesses reported Kip's sin and the steps they had taken to restore him. They also reported that Kip had resisted every effort on their part. Prayerfully, the church determined its course of action. It officially contacted Kip, urged him to repent, and explained that he would be dropped from membership if he refused to comply.

Kip remained obstinate and unrepentant.

Having followed every step to restore Kip without resolving the conflict, the church dropped him from its membership. It had done what Jesus instructed: "If he refuses to listen even to the church, treat him as you would a pagan or a tax collector" (v. 17). Jesus would affirm the church's action, whether it resulted in forgiving and restoring a repentant member or excommunicating an unrepentant member (v. 18). He guaranteed, "If two of you on earth agree about anything you ask for, it will be done for you by my Father in heaven. For where two or three come together in my name [under my authority and meeting to protect my reputation], there am I with them" (w. 19-20).

Church discipline is almost as extinct as dinosaurs. Why? Perhaps, we just don't have the stomach for it. It is unpleasant business. If we discipline an unrepentant, sinning church member, he will simply join a church across town, we reason. So what have we accomplished? Worse still, he may have relatives and friends in the church. If we take disciplinary action, they may get upset and leave the church. Perhaps, we fail to exercise church discipline because we misapply Jesus' promise to be with us when two or three have come together in his name. If we properly applied his promise, we might be confident that he is in charge of the disciplinary process instead of fearing a negative backlash.

Is Jesus with us only when we gather to exercise church discipline? No! He is with us all the time and everywhere we go but we should not use Matthew 18:20 to prove the point. We can appeal to many other Scripture verses to attest to his abiding presence.

Jesus taught his disciples that he and the Father make their home with whoever loves and obeys him (John 14:23). When asked about our permanent residence, we give the address of our home. "Home" indicates permanence and comfort. Unlike a guesthouse or a hotel room, our home belongs to us and in turn gives us a sense of belonging. We furnish it for our personal enjoyment. It is a place where we can settle down and feel comfortable. So our hearts are Christ's home. He dwells there permanently. We may not always furnish our hearts to His liking but He doesn't leave. However, we would do well to turn the designing and decorating over to Him.

When Jesus commissioned his disciples to proclaim the good news throughout the world, he promised, "And surely I am with you always, to the very end of the age" (Matt. 28:20). How, then, can we doubt that he is with us?

Seated next to a guest speaker, the pastor of a rather emotional congregation whispered, "Surely, the Lord is with us this morning. I can feel his presence."

Recalling Jesus' promise to his disciples when he commissioned them to proclaim the good news worldwide, the guest speaker assured the pastor, "The Lord is with us, whether we feel his presence or not."

Indeed, He is with us—and not just when we meet as a church to exercise discipline.

3

GOD WANTS YOUR FAITH, NOT YOUR DOCTRINE

AT THE AGE OF TWENTY-TWO, I WAS EAGER TO ENTER MY first full-time pastorate. Pastoral training at Moody Bible Institute was under my belt and so was a major in religion at Houghton College in New York State. My pastoral experience was limited but varied. I had preached at Pacific Garden Mission in Chicago every Sunday morning during my last two and a half years at Moody. Also, I had opened a closed country church near Houghton College and had served as its pastor until I graduated. Because I held Canadian citizenship and was in the United States on a student visa, I had to return to Canada when Houghton College handed me a diploma. Five days later I entered another institution—marriage—and moved back to St. Catharines, Ontario, with Gloria, my bride from Virginia, at my side. I could hardly wait to become a full-time pastor and I was sure my congregation would welcome strong doctrinal sermons.

Within a couple of months, I received an invitation to preach at a small town about twenty miles north of

Toronto. The church needed a pastor and had learned of my availability from the interim pastor of my home church. It would be an understatement to say I poured prayer, zeal, and Theology 404 knowledge into a trial sermon. I planned to deliver a never-to-be-forgotten message on pneumatology, the doctrine of the Holy Spirit.

The special Sunday arrived. The sun was shining and birds were chirping. Crimson and yellow roses flanked the sidewalk entrance to the old church building. Its freshly coated white frame reflected the sun's rays. Everything was picture perfect. But once inside, I saw the positive picture turn negative. All it took was a sign in the foyer: We have no creed but Christ. No law but love.

Hoping against hope that the sign was simply a warm, fuzzy alert to visitors that the church was nonthreatening, I asked the first person to greet Gloria and me, "Does your church have a printed doctrinal statement?"

Attempting a smile, he replied, "No, we don't. We don't think doctrine is important."

As I think back to that experience, almost everything after the conversation in the foyer left a blip in my mind's memory. I can recall two things, though: (1) When Gloria and I walked to our car after the service, the sun had slipped behind a dark cloud, the birds were chirping off-key, the roses were drooping, and (2) I did not receive a call to be the church's pastor.

A DECADE LATER, I received a church profile and a pastoral candidate form from a suburban Chicago church. The congregation had built a reputation on strong interpersonal relationships and its profile announced that it was "seeking a pastor who knew what he believed."

Aha! I'm the man, I thought. I may not know everything, but I do know what I believe.

I read on. "We want a pastor with settled theological beliefs but we would strongly object to any attempt to persuade the congregation to his point of view. He will serve primarily as a resource person."

They don't want a pastor; they want a librarian, I mused as I filed the mailing under "Churches out of the Question."

The 1960s and 1970s witnessed popular gimmicks and giveaway contests in a segment of evangelical churches. Hoping to attract crowds and boost Sunday school attendance, those growth-minded churches gave away everything from trinkets to travel vouchers to students who brought the most visitors to Sunday school in a specified period of time. In their zeal for numbers, some pastors promised to swallow goldfish or preach on their church's rooftop or skydive into the church's parking lot or let students smash their faces with cream pies if Sunday school attendance reached a high goal. Although the dog and pony shows piled up new names on the Sunday school rolls, the additions soon rolled away to other churches in search of something that would help them grow spiritually. Many who promoted "the circus and carnival" growth methods eventually saw the method's weakness and, in time, the circuses and carnivals closed.

During the gimmicky era, a Christian education director in Louisiana was concerned that his congregation lacked Bible knowledge. Somehow, he succeeded in persuading the church's board to bring a few curriculum educators, including me, to his church. The senior pastor balked at the series of training workshops my colleagues and I had arranged for the Sunday school workers. He told those attending the Sunday morning service that Bible teaching wasn't for every church. His church, he said, was a soul-winning church, not a Bible-teaching church, so he wanted his Sunday school teachers to avoid implementing what they would hear from us about how to teach the Bible. After the admonition, he presented two live chickens to the person who had brought the most visitors to Sunday school the previous week. Obviously, his pluck outstripped his politeness.

Is our postmodern era better informed about Bible doctrine? Is there a strong desire today to know and apply Bible doctrine? I don't think so. It seems to me that many churches are being swept along in a landslide of emotionalism and care little about doctrine. Exceptions exist, of course, but often what matters is how people feel about themselves, their worship experience, and the church's programs. The popular buzz is, "Where is the best worship in town?" Long gone is the question, "Where is the best Bible teaching?" Is it any wonder Bible colleges and seminaries express their disappointment with incoming students' Bible knowledge test scores? Are we surprised that a paltry number of Christians carry a Bible to church? Why carry a Bible if there is no reason to open it?

Worship is truly important. The Bible instructs us to "worship the Lord in the splendor of his holiness" (Ps. 29:2), and Jesus assured us that God's "worshipers must worship in spirit and in truth" (John 4:24). Our worship, therefore, involves the prompting of the Holy Spirit in accordance with truth.

But what is truth?

A relativist would answer, "There is no absolute truth."

A postmodernist would say, "Truth is whatever you believe it is."

Jesus referred to God's Word as truth and asked his heavenly Father to sanctify us (make us holy) by the truth (John 17:17). And that's why Bible doctrine is so important. Doctrine is simply the teaching of God's Word, which, when properly understood and applied, makes us the kind of people God wants us to be.

What would we know about God and his purposes for our lives if it were not for what we have learned from the Bible? The Bible's teaching—doctrine—communicates everything we need to know about him and his will that we cannot gain from natural revelation. Nature shows that God is highly intelligent, mighty, orderly, purposeful, and benevolent, but only the doctrine of God given in the Bible reveals his love, grace, mercy, faithfulness, transcendence, triune being, eternality, omnipresence, righteousness, forgiveness, holiness, justice, immutability (unchanging character), and truthfulness.

How would we know to respond to God in faith by trusting in Jesus as our Savior if it were not for the Bible doctrine of salvation? How would we know we could trust him to guide our lives if it were not for the Bible's teaching about his wisdom, care, and abiding presence? How would we know what a righteous God requires of us if it were not for the instruction the Bible imparts?

How would we know what a wise and loving heavenly Father has planned for us if it were not for the Bible's teaching about the future?

The Greek word didache, translated "doctrine" in the New Testament, derives from the word didasko, meaning "I teach." Didache in the New Testament refers to the body of teaching—the truth—that Jesus and his apostles communicated to believers. Understandably, the believers who witnessed the formation of the church on the day of Pentecost "devoted themselves to the apostles' teaching [didache]" (Acts 2:42). Who can question the reality of the early believers' faith? Based on the apostles' doctrine, the early believers' faith was strong enough to attract thousands to Christ, forge a bond of close fellowship, endure severe persecution, and launch a vigorous relief program. Their doctrinal learning produced dynamic living.

The ancient Greeks associated didache (teaching) with on-the-job training or the teaching of skills. The word also meant to demonstrate a theory. Geometry students, for example, had to prove each theorem they had studied. Similarly, a working faith demonstrates that we have learned Bible doctrine.

Before becoming an apostle, Paul was Saul of Tarsus, a young firebrand persecutor of the church. He despised Jesus of Nazareth and all his followers. Acts 9:1 depicts him as "breathing out murderous threats against the Lord's disciples." He lived to eradicate the name and message of Jesus from the earth. Like so many religious zealots, he had funneled his devotion to religious tradition into hatred. His theological wires were crossed and red-hot sparks were flying wildly as he journeyed from Jerusalem to Damascus in search of followers of Jesus.

With arrest warrants in hand, Saul salivated for the taste of martyrs' blood and he didn't care whether it flowed from the veins of men or women.

Nice man? Of course not! But he was sincere about what he believed. Unfortunately, he was sincerely wrong. His skewed doctrine (teaching) produced rabid conduct. Looking back on that period of life, Paul wrote in Galatians 1:13-14: "For you have heard of my previous way of life in Judaism, how intensely I persecuted the church of God and tried to destroy it. I was advancing in Judaism beyond many Jews of my own age and was extremely zealous for the traditions of my fathers."

Did you catch the word "traditions?" If Saul of Tarsus had heeded the Old Testament Scriptures, he would have learned the doctrine of Christ and the need to love God supremely and others as oneself. Faith in the Old Testament prophecies about Jesus Christ would have prepared Saul to believe in him just as a number of devout Jews waiting for the consolation of Israel believed in Jesus (see Luke 1 and 2). But Saul allowed traditions to block truth.

Everything changed dramatically, though, when the risen Christ stopped Saul in his tracks on the road to Damascus. His glory blinded Saul but Christ's grace flooded his heart with light. Saul believed in Christ and submitted his life to him. Soon after his conversion experience, he was alone in the Arabian Desert, learning the doctrines of grace from the Holy Spirit. He had entered the desert with a load of traditions on his back; he left with the gospel of grace in his heart. Emerging from the desert, he was ready to teach doctrine and lead a godly life.

Paul knew by firsthand experience that faith and

doctrine are inseparable. Before his conversion, he had placed his faith in traditions and operated his life like a steaming locomotive running downhill off the rails. After his conversion, his faith, joined to correct doctrine, kept his life on the track God had set for him. He testified in 2 Corinthians 4:2 that he and his fellow workers set forth "the truth plainly" and commended themselves "to every man's conscience in the sight of God."

The Lord used the apostle Paul to write thirteen New Testament letters. Most of those letters were addressed to churches, while a few were addressed to individuals but all are rich in doctrine and strong on application. A quick survey of Paul's letters clearly reveals that they summon us to show our faith by implementing doctrinal instruction.

The link between doctrine and the implementation of real faith in Paul's letters is unmistakable, but it leaps at us from 2 Timothy 3:15-17. Paul credits the holy, God-breathed Scriptures as able to make us "wise for salvation through faith in Christ Jesus," to smooth the rough edges of our lives, to educate us "in righteousness," and to equip us "for every good work."

Where would we be without God's truth? How useless our "faith" would be if it did not spring from the soil of Scripture?

Paul wasn't the only apostle to link doctrine and real faith. The apostles Peter and John did the same thing in their letters. In his first letter, the apostle Peter instructed his persecuted readers about how suffering fulfills God's purpose—to approve and strengthen personal faith (1:3-9). Building on this theme, Peter identified Christ's sufferings as the perfect example of accepting God's will (2:21-24; 4:12-19). He also wrote about the glory Christ entered into after suffering and encouraged his readers to anticipate the glory that awaits all believers in heaven (5:10).

Writing 2 Peter, the apostle Peter taught that God has given believers everything they need to lead a godly life (1:3) and urged his readers to add noble virtues to their faith (v. 5-7). He also instructed his readers about the end-times and exhorted: "What kind of people ought you to be? You ought to live holy and godly lives as you look forward to the day of God and speed its coming" (3:11-12). Having focused their sight on eternity, he reasoned, "So then, dear friends, since you are looking forward to this, make every effort to be found spotless, blameless and at peace with him" (v. 14).

All who argue that prophecy is unimportant place themselves at odds with Peter's inspired comments. An awareness of what lies ahead prods our faith to implement God's provisions for the present and to anticipate the fulfillment of God's plans for the future: "In keeping with his promise we are looking forward to a new heaven and a new earth, the home of the righteous" (2 Peter 3:13). In the meantime, we ought to "grow in the grace and knowledge of our Lord and Savior Jesus Christ" (v. 18).

The apostle John linked truth (doctrine) and practical Christian living. Throughout his first letter, he identified the evidences of real faith as a righteous lifestyle and love for God and others. In 1 John 3:1-2, he focused his readers' attention on the amazing love God had lavished on his children and promised that we shall see Christ and be like him when he appears. Tying together the truth of the Lord's coming and the importance of becoming Christlike, John wrote, "Everyone who has this hope in him purifies himself, just as he is pure" (v. 3).

Who hasn't known someone who professed to be a believer and later succumbed to false teaching and joined a cult? Who hasn't witnessed someone's profession of faith and subsequent slide back into his or her former sinful lifestyle? Faith that is not anchored in doctrine leaves a person as vulnerable to the winds of false teaching and the currents of immoral conduct as a ship adrift on the high seas is vulnerable to destructive winds and swirling ocean currents. But the person who anchors his or her faith in sound doctrine stands firm in the face of every onslaught of error and temptation.

Is it any wonder the apostle Jude urged his readers to "contend for the faith [Bible doctrine] that was once for all entrusted to the saints" (Jude v. 3) and concluded his letter by challenging them to "build yourselves up in your most holy faith" (v. 20)?

I am sure no one has ever seen a boxcar pulling a train. Engines pull trains. Like a boxcar, faith is incapable of taking life in the direction God has mapped for it unless it is connected to the engine of biblical truth. Truth empowers our faith and takes it where God wants it to go. Believers and congregations cannot go wrong by linking doctrine (biblical truth) and faith.

4

BEWARE THE UNPARDONABLE SIN!

EVERY THANKSGIVING EVE, THE PRESIDENT OF THE United States pardons his main course—a turkey—usually assigning it to a petting farm where children lavish plenty of TLC on it. The tradition started with Harry S. Truman and has become popular. More serious, of course, are presidential pardons or the granting of amnesty to such notorious figures as the Whiskey Rebellion rebels in 1795, Confederate rebels in 1868, Richard Nixon in 1974, Tokyo Rose in 1977, Vietnam draft resisters in 1977, Caspar Weinberger in 1992, Edwin L. Coxjr. in 1993, and Marc Rich in 2001.

We may wonder why a president would grant a pardon in a given situation but we cannot question his authority to do so. Our main concern focuses on pardon for our own offenses, the vast majority of which seem trivial but are troubling, nonetheless. Will my wife forgive me for coming home late from bowling or for playing golf on my day off instead of doing yard work? Will my husband forgive me for refusing to attend his company's Christmas party? Will my mother-in-law forgive me for the mean thing I said against her in a moment of anger? Will the boss forgive me for calling in sick, only to run into me at the ball game? Will the pastor forgive me for falling asleep during last Sunday's sermon?

Finding forgiveness for such offenses brings genuine relief, doesn't it? Forgiveness works like a soothing salve for the soul. But, even if a spouse or mother-in-law or boss refuses to forgive, our guilt may diminish with the passing of time. But some offenses are so heinous that those who commit them believe they can never be forgiven or relieved of heavy guilt. They believe they have committed the unpardonable sin. Do they have legitimate reason to worry?

Jesus referred to a sin that cannot be forgiven in Matthew 12, Mark 3, and Luke 12. He said: I tell you, every sin and blasphemy will be forgiven men, but the blasphemy against the Spirit will not be forgiven. Anyone who speaks a word against the Son of Man will be forgiven, but anyone who speaks against the Holy Spirit will not be forgiven, either in this age or in the age to come. (Matt. 12:31-32)

I tell you the truth, all the sins and blasphemies of men will be forgiven them. But whoever blasphemes against the Holy Spirit will never be forgiven; he is guilty of an eternal sin. (Mark 3:28-29)

I tell you, whoever acknowledges me before men, the Son of Man will also acknowledge him before the angels of God. But he who disowns me before men will be disowned before the angels of God. And everyone who speaks a word against the Son of Man will be forgiven, but anyone who blasphemes against the Holy Spirit will not be forgiven. (Luke 12:8-10)

It's A God Thing

These words carry a heavy message that resonates with authority and involves the eternal destiny of the soul. If we examine the context in which Jesus spoke about the unpardonable sin, we will understand what he meant. Hopefully, this understanding will clear up some common misconceptions and allow those who hold them to escape an unbearable sense of guilt.

I asked members of a biblically literate congregation to write what they believed to be the unpardonable sin. Their answers varied. Here are the most frequent responses:

- rejecting Jesus as Savior.
- saying Jesus is not the Son of God and dying with that belief.
- suicide.
- cursing the Lord.
- mistreating your spouse.
- denying Christ and his finished work; s. attributing the work of the Holy Spirit to Satan.
- lying about your faith to others.
- continually rejecting Jesus until your heart becomes too hard to respond to him.
- lying about what you believe so others will accept you.
- taking the Lord's Supper unworthily.

As you can see, these interpretations cover a broad spectrum but they can't all be right. Before we examine the biblical context in which Jesus spoke of a sin that will never be forgiven, we can dispense with several interpretations listed above as viable interpretations.

The Bible says very little about suicide and it never indicates that suicide bars a person from heaven. Samson committed suicide by collapsing a pagan temple onto the heads of his enemies, the Philistines. He even prayed that the Lord would let him die with the Philistines (Judg. 16:30). The Bible doesn't indicate that the Lord barred Samson from heaven because he took his own life.

King Saul committed suicide by falling on his own sword after Philistine archers had wounded him critically. He chose suicide because he wanted to escape death by torture at the hands of the Philistines (1 Sam. 31:1-4). Again, the Bible does not say that suicide disqualified him from life in heaven. After Saul committed suicide, his armor bearer also committed suicide by falling on his own sword (v. 5), but no comment follows that suggests suicide doomed him eternally the Bible records three other suicides, two without any comment about the suicide victims' eternal fate, and the third with an earlier reference indicating he was not a believer. The two are Ahithophel (2 Sam. 17:23) and Zimri (1 Kings 16:18). The third is Judas (Matt. 27:5; Acts 1:18), identified as "the one doomed to destruction" (John 17:12).

When God struck a jail in Philippi with an earthquake at midnight, cell doors flew open, freeing Paul and Silas and other prisoners. Believing his charges had escaped, the jailer became so alarmed that he drew his sword and prepared to kill himself (Acts 16:25-27). Only Paul's shout, "Don't harm yourself! We all are here!" (v. 28) curtailed the suicide.

Those who believe suicide is the unpardonable sin might label the Philippian jailer an unlikely, perhaps disqualified, candidate for salvation. However, he followed Paul's advice to believe in the Lord Jesus and became a member of God's eternal family (v. 34).

So, as heinous a sin as suicide is, it is not the unpardonable sin. Neither is the sin of cursing the Lord. Many Christians admit to having had a foul mouth prior to their conversion to Christ. They used not only coarse language but also profane language. They violated the commandment "You shall not misuse the name of the Lord your God" (Ex. 20:7). Nevertheless, when they turned in faith to the Lord, he forgave all their sins. He gave them not only a new life but also a new language. Now instead of profaning his name, they praise it.

But what about the belief that mistreating one's spouse is the unpardonable sin? Obviously, the mistreated spouse may find such treatment unpardonable but who hasn't mistreated his or her spouse at one time or another, apologized to the spouse, and asked for and received divine forgiveness?

Is the unpardonable sin the sin of lying about your faith or denying your faith so others will accept you? Of course not! Peter denied his Lord three times in the presence of wicked men in order to save his skin but, after rising from the dead, the Lord forgave Peter and subsequently equipped him for outstanding leadership in the first-century church. Keep in mind that this man who had denied his Lord was the same individual who later proclaimed Christ to a multitude of Jews and drew 3,000 of them to Christ.

Those who believe the unpardonable sin is the act of partaking of the Lord's Supper ought to rethink their position. How many religious people with a tradition of partaking of the Lord's Supper when they were unregenerate eventually heard the gospel and became believers? Consider, too, that if the Lord imposed the penalty of eternal condemnation on believers who partook of the Lord's Supper unworthily, his promise that believers will never perish (John 10:28) would lack credibility.

So what is the sin that can never be forgiven? Obviously, all who die without having believed on Christ as Savior do not receive forgiveness beyond the grave. Hebrews 9:27 testifies, "Just as man is destined to die once, and after that to face judgment."

Several conditions existed when Jesus commented that "whoever blasphemes against the Holy Spirit will never be forgiven; he is guilty of an eternal sin" (Mark 3:29). First, Jesus was physically present as Israel's legitimate King. Second, Jesus had performed an indisputable miracle. Third, the Pharisees accused Jesus of performing miracles by the power of Satan.

Let's examine each of these conditions.

5

JESUS WAS PHYSICALLY PRESENT AS ISRAEL'S
LEGITIMATE KING

THE OLD TESTAMENT HAD INSTRUCTED ISRAEL TO anticipate the arrival of her messianic king and his kingdom. Psalm 24:7, 9 instruct, "Lift up your heads, O you gates; be lifted up, you ancient doors, that the King of glory may come in." The prophet Isaiah pointed the nation to a redemptive day when the Prince of Peace would "reign on David's throne and over his kingdom" (9:7). He also called on the nation to "see, a king will reign in righteousness" (32:1). Daniel prophesied that "the God of heaven will set up a kingdom that will never be destroyed, nor will it be left to another people" (Dan. 2:44). Zechariah encouraged Israel to anticipate the coming of her King: "Rejoice greatly, O Daughter of Zion! Shout, Daughter of Jerusalem! See, your king comes to you, righteous and having salvation, gentle and riding on a donkey, on a colt, the foal of a donkey" (Zech. 9:9).

These prophecies were fulfilled in part when Jesus came to earth. As King David's most prominent descendant, he was born "king of the Jews" (Matt. 2:2) and offered himself to Israel as her King (see Matt. 21:1-5). However, the nation rejected her King and called upon Governor Pilate to crucify him. But when the governor's soldiers nailed Jesus to a cross, they placed a sign above his head that announced in Aramaic, Latin, and Greek, the king of the Jews (Matt. 27:37; John 19:20). Offended by the designation, Israel's chief priests protested to Pilate. They demanded, "Do not write 'The King of the Jews,' but that this man claimed to be king of the Jews" (John 19:21). Obviously, they knew Jesus had presented himself to the nation as her king but they had scorned him.

Someday, the Old Testament prophecies of a messianic king reigning over Israel—and the Gentiles too—will be fulfilled completely. Jesus will return to the Mount of Olives, smite his enemies, enter Jerusalem, and establish his government (see Zech. 14:1-5, 16-17; Acts 1:11-12; Rev. 19:11-16).

The gospel of Matthew, written to present Jesus to Israel as her rightful King, teems with references to the "king" and "kingdom." We should not be surprised to find Jesus speaking about the kingdom and the unpardonable sin in close proximity in Matthew 12:25-32. (See appendix E. I believe, in fact, that neither King Jesus nor the kingdom God promised to Israel is present today on earth.)

6

JESUS HAD PERFORMED AN INDISPUTABLE MIRACLE

EXAMINING THE CONTEXT IN WHICH JESUS SPOKE ABOUT the unpardonable sin, we learn that he had healed a demon-possessed man (Matt. 12:22). The event was one of many miracles he performed in the power of the Holy Spirit as evidence that he was Israel's Messiah. The apostle Peter testified that "God anointed Jesus of Nazareth with the Holy Spirit and power, and ... he went around doing good and healing all who were under the power of the devil, because God was with him" (Acts 10:38).

Jesus was conceived of the Holy Spirit (Luke 1:35), anointed by the Holy Spirit (3:21-22; 4:18-21), and filled with the Holy Spirit (4:1, 14). Israel should have recognized by Jesus' miracles that he was her messianic king. The apostle John, a Jew, constructed the gospel of John around eight of Jesus' miracles to prove that Jesus was the Christ (the Messiah) and to incite saving faith in him. He wrote in 20:30-31, "Jesus did many other miraculous signs in the presence of his disciples, which are not recorded in this book. But these are written that you may believe that Jesus is the Christ, the Son of God, and that by believing you may have life in his name."

You may recall that God promised Israel many centuries before Jesus was born that he would raise up a prophet like Moses (Deut. 18:15, 18). He said that he would put His words in that prophet's mouth and that the prophet would tell the people everything he would command him. God included a warning with this prophecy: "If anyone does not listen to my words that the prophet speaks in my name, I myself will call him to account" (v. 19).

Think back to the burning bush event. God spoke to Moses from the midst of a burning bush in Midian and commissioned him to redeem the Hebrew slaves from Egypt. With the commission came the supernatural power to perform signs and wonders not only to persuade Pharaoh to release the Hebrews but also to convince the Hebrews that Moses was God's authentic prophet and deliverer.

Centuries later, Jesus arrived in Israel as God's anointed prophet who declared God's words and brought redemption to the nation. His miracles clearly validated his credentials. Some members of the nation believed when they heard His words and observed His miracles but the nation as a whole rejected His teachings, His miracles, and His deliverance. The nation's leaders were especially adamant in their rejection of Jesus.

The apostle Paul, who had risen to the top of Jewish ranks because of his knowledge and zeal for Mosaic law and the traditions of the Jews, wrote that the "Jews demand miraculous signs" (1 Cor. 1:22). Interestingly, after Jesus pronounced the eternal sentence that accompanies the unpardonable sin, some Pharisees and teachers of the law said to him, "Teacher, we want to see a miraculous sign from you" (Matt. 12:38). Had they not already seen Jesus perform miraculous signs? How many more would it take to convince them that he was the Messiah? Obviously even miracles in profusion would not soften their stony hearts!

So the unpardonable sin involved the physical presence of Jesus on earth, presenting himself as Israel's King and performing indisputable miracles. These conditions do not exist today.

The Pharisees Accused Jesus Of Performing Miracles By The Power Of Satan

AS WE HAVE SEEN, Jesus performed miracles by the power of the Holy Spirit. The eyewitnesses to Jesus' miracle of the exorcising demons from a blind mute (Matt. 12:22; Luke 11:14) did not dispute this fact. As a matter of fact, they were so astonished that they entertained the thought that Jesus was the Messiah. "Could this be the Son of David?" they asked (Matt. 12:23). This miracle, like all the others Jesus performed, clearly testified that Jesus was indeed Israel's Messiah.

However, upon hearing the eyewitnesses' question, the Pharisees countered that Beelzebub, the prince of demons, had possessed Jesus and empowered him to drive out demons (Matt. 12:24; Mark 3:22).

Beelzebub, the Greek form of the Hebrew name Baal-Zebub, meaning lord of the flies, was commonly used in ancient times as a synonym for Satan, the Devil.

The Pharisees were attributing the work of the Holy Spirit to Satan and therefore were guilty of the sin of blasphemy against the Holy Spirit (Matt. 12:31). The Spirit had testified by Jesus' miracles that the Messiah and his kingdom had arrived (Matt. 12:28; Luke 11:20) but the Pharisees had rejected both. By doing so, they jeopardized their eternal destiny. Jesus warned, "Anyone who speaks against the Holy Spirit will not be forgiven, either in this age or in the age to come" (Matt. 12:32).

Having placed the warning about the unpardonable sin in its biblical context, we can see that it related to Israel when her messianic king was on earth, offering his kingdom and validating his royal credentials by performing miracles in the power of the Holy Spirit. This sin cannot be committed today.

Nevertheless, a sin persists today that cannot be forgiven. It is the sin of rejecting Jesus Christ as Savior. The invitation to believe in Jesus as Savior and receive the gift of eternal life extends to all who have fallen short of God's standard of righteousness (Matt. 11:28; Acts 16:31; Rom. 6:23; 10:13), but death stamps "Canceled" on the invitation.

A dying thief received the gift of eternal life by believing in Jesus. Saul of Tarsus, an accomplice to Stephen's murder, a persecutor of believers, and an enemy of Christ, received eternal life when he believed in Jesus. Some of the Corinthians had been sexually immoral, idolaters, adulterers, male prostitutes, homosexual offenders, thieves, greedy persons, drunkards, slanderers, or swindlers, but they received a new and eternal life by believing in Jesus (1 Cor. 6:9-11, 19-20). So there is hope this side of the grave for the worst of sinners to become the best of saints. No one should think he or she cannot be forgiven. God's grace avails to forgive any sin and all sins.

Frequently, a funeral service includes the playing of "Amazing Grace" by a bagpiper. Occasionally, it is sung at funerals. John Newton, the writer of this beloved gospel song, had been a slave trader. One day, however, John faced the ugliness of his sin and turned in faith to Jesus Christ for forgiveness and a brand-new life. "Amazing Grace" expresses his gratitude for the grace God bestowed on him by granting forgiveness and a new life. It begins, "Amazing grace!—how sweet the sound—That saved a wretch like me." That amazing grace is available until death.

At the close of a worship service, a church member commented to her new pastor, "Pastor, I have been of this church for more than forty years but I never knew what sin was until you became our pastor." Hopefully, if she reads this chapter, she will even know what the unpardonable sin is.

7
IF WE DON'T CONFESS OUR SINS, GOD WON'T FORGIVE THEM

IF CONFESSION IS GOOD FOR THE SOUL, WHY WAS A DUSTY confessional offered on eBay to the highest bidder? A church in Vienna, Austria, placed the cherry-wood confessional in auction as a last resort to get rid of it and commented that the congregation planned to give it away if it didn't sell. The church must have had another confessional in use because the one listed on eBay was gathering dust in a storage room. (I'm not sure if the confessional ever sold or not.)

Of course, a Christian doesn't need a confessional to confess his or her sins to the Lord. God is available to hear a confession whenever and wherever a believer offers it. Furthermore, he will respond to sincere confession with forgiveness and cleansing. First John 1:9 promises, "If we confess our sins, he is faithful and just and will forgive us our sins and purify us from all unrighteousness."

Some students of the Bible might argue that 1 John 1:9 applies to unbelievers. They see the verse as an invitation to unbelievers to confess their sins and receive cleansing. However, unbelievers might readily admit they are sinful, confess every sin filed in their memory bank, and still not receive cleansing. Personal salvation cannot be acquired by confessing sin, but by confessing the Lord Jesus and believing in your heart that God has raised Him from the dead (Rom. 10:9-10). God gives salvation by grace through faith, "not by works" (Eph. 2:8-9).

A glance at the context in which the apostle John wrote 1 John 1:9 reveals that this verse applies to Christians. His frequent use of "we" (ten times) and "us" (four times) in verses 6 to 10 indicates that he was addressing members of God's family. Like a caring, elderly father, John arranged his first letter as though he were conducting a family talk. He often addressed his readers as "dear children" (2:1, 12-13, 18, 28; 3:7, 18; 4:4; 5:21) and "dear friends" (2:7; 3:21; 4:1, 7). This is the language of love written to children of the loving heavenly Father.

But even in families guided by a loving father, children push beyond the limits of their father's house rules. I never doubted that my father loved me, although I wasn't always thrilled with some of his rules. When I broke a rule, I did not cease being Dad's son, but I endangered our relationship. I learned that it was better to admit a transgression, "face the music," and receive forgiveness than to cover it up and feel miserable—unable to look Dad in the eye.

When I became a Christian at age sixteen, I quickly discovered that my heavenly Father, too, had family rules: no lying, no stealing, no impure thinking, no selfish behavior, love God, love your neighbor as yourself, be honest, work hard, live above reproach, etc. I learned that he did not disown me when I broke a rule, but I felt miserable when I did. Sin disturbed the fellowship that existed between my heavenly Father and me. Like a wall that had gone up between us, it needed to come down. Fortunately, confession prepared the way for God's forgiveness to crush the wall and build renewed fellowship in its place.

It is this fellowship between a believer and the Father in heaven that the apostle John wrote about. He explained that we cannot enjoy fellowship with God while we "walk in the darkness" (1 John 1:6). Fellowship with God is conditional. We must "walk in the light, as he is in the light" (v. 7). As long as we walk in the light, "we have fellowship with one another" (v. 7); that is, we have fellowship with our Father, and he has fellowship with us. When we sin, we lose that fellowship until we confess the sin.

In my college days, I met many sincere Christian students who believed that God would cast them into hell if they failed to confess their sins. They equated unconfessed sins with loss of salvation. So they tried at day's end to recall every sin they had committed and then confess it before nodding off to sleep.

One day, three students and I were driving from New York State to Virginia and singing hymns as we motored down Highway 15. (Yes, we sang hymns!) I was the only student in the car who believed that every believer possesses irrevocable eternal life. The others believed they would lose eternal life if they failed to stay 'fessed up.

After singing a rousing couple of stanzas of "Blessed Assurance," I asked my friends how blessed or assuring their salvation was if they failed to confess all their sins. "What would happen if you lost your lives in a car crash on this trip and missed your nightly routine of confessing your sins?"

Only the purr of new tires invaded the ensuing silence.

Frankly, I don't think any Christian can maintain an accurate mental or written daily record of his or her sins. Even a Christian addicted to a Palm Pilot would fail to note some sins. (And isn't it a sin to be addicted to an electronic device?) Our sins fall into two broad categories: sins of commission (we do what we should not do) and sins of omission (we fail to do what we should do). The apostle Paul admitted: "I do not understand what I do. For what I want to do I do not do, but what I hate I do" (Rom. 7:15). Expanding on this enigma, he wrote, "For I have the desire to do what is good, but I cannot carry it out. For what I do is not the good I want to do; no, the evil I do not want to do—this I keep on doing" (v. 18-19).

You and I have stood in Paul's sandals, haven't we?

If staying saved depended upon confessing every sin, we would never stay saved. Even if we could account for every wrong we did and confess it, we could not possibly keep track of everything we should have done but failed to do. And lest we think the latter offenses are not sins, James 4:17 charges: "Anyone, then, who knows the good he ought to do and doesn't do it, sins."

In Old Testament times, God required sacrifices for sins of omission. Obviously, he did not dismiss such matters as inconsequential. Leviticus 5:17-18 states: "If a person sins and does what is forbidden in any of the Lord's commands, even though he does not know it, he is guilty and will be held responsible. He is to bring to the priest as a guilt offering a ram from the flock, one without defect and of the proper value. In this way the priest will make atonement for him for the wrong he has committed unintentionally, and he will be forgiven."

What a relief to find that the context for 1 John 1:9 involves fellowship between a believer and the heavenly Father and not instructions for receiving or retaining salvation. But why does a child of God need the forgiveness and cleansing identified in 1 John 1:9? Didn't every child of God receive forgiveness in Christ when he or she became a believer? The answer is yes.

Ephesians 1:7 assures us that in Christ "we have redemption through his blood, the forgiveness of sins, in accordance with the riches of God's grace." But this perspective relates to the justification we each have because we are seated with Christ in the heavenlies (2:6). We are also glorified in Christ (Rom. 8:30), but we don't always live in a Christlike manner. Our standing in Christ never changes. In him, we are fully forgiven, completely justified, entirely sanctified, and thoroughly glorified. Our state, however, may vary like a swirling wind. One moment, we honor our heavenly Father by doing his will. The next moment, we dishonor him by sinning.

As we have seen, we do not lose salvation when we sin but we disrupt our fellowship with our heavenly Father. In order to restore that fellowship, we must confess our sins.

In his model prayer, Jesus taught us to pray to our Father in heaven and, among other things, beseech him to "forgive us our sins" (Luke 11:4). Obviously, then, born-again men and women need daily forgiveness.

But what did the apostle John mean by "confess" in 1 John 1:9? The word "confess" in this verse is homologomen, meaning "acknowledge, agree, say the same thing." We ought to acknowledge our sins, agree with our Father that our sins are offensive, and assume his attitude toward sin. He sees sin as ugly, unholy, vile, and villainous. His Son Jesus bore the weight of our sins on the cross, became sin for us, and paid the utmost penalty for our sins. Our sins, therefore, are not simply minor infractions but heinous crimes against God. They are characteristic of "darkness" (1 John 1:6), and by acknowledging this fact and adopting God's perspective about sin, we escape the darkness and flee to the "light." Our Father forgives us and purifies (cleanses) us from all unrighteousness (v. 9).

Can you recall how comforting it was to receive forgiveness from your earthly father after admitting that you had done wrong? When he forgave you and wrapped his arms around you, you felt secure in his love and at peace with him. Similarly, confession of sin brings a sense of well-being to the soul. We sense God's arms of love enfolding us while his peace settles upon our soul. Fellowship is sweet once again!

Perhaps an incident from Jesus' fellowship with his disciples will help us grasp the difference between the cleansing from sin that occurs at salvation and the cleansing that occurs when we confess our sins.

Jesus and his disciples assembled in an upper room where he would instruct his men about his imminent death and its implications for them. Normally, a household slave would refresh houseguests by washing their feet but no slave was present. Jesus, therefore, assumed the role. He "got up from the meal, took off his outer clothing, and wrapped a towel around his waist. After that, he poured water into a basin and began to wash his disciples' feet, drying them with the towel that was wrapped around him" (John 13:4—5). When Peter saw that Jesus was about to wash his feet, he remonstrated. "No," he said, "you shall never wash my feet" (v. 8).

"Unless I wash you, you have no part with me," Jesus replied.

Peter got the message. He responded, "Then, Lord, ... not just my feet but my hands and my head as well!" (v. 9).

Jesus turned down this request, saying, "A person who has had a bath needs only to wash his feet; his whole body is clean" (v. 10).

What was going on? By faith in Jesus, Peter had already received a "bath"—a complete washing from sin. Having had that "bath," he did not need to be cleansed from sin all over again. However, as he walked through an unclean world, he became defiled by sins and needed partial cleansing.

The foot-washing imagery comes from first-century Roman culture. The Romans frequented public baths, where they washed thoroughly. But as they walked home, dirt from the dusty roads adhered to their feet. Upon seeing dust on their feet, they would not return to the public bath for another full washing; they would simply wash their feet or have a servant perform the washing. Similarly, once a person has been cleansed from all sin and has been justified in God's sight, he doesn't have to be fully cleansed again. He has received complete forgiveness. But as he walks through life, he picks up some of the dust (defilement) of a sinful world and needs to have only "his feet washed." Confession obtains the partial cleansing.

As a boy living only four miles from Lake Ontario, I

often frequented the Port Dalhousie beach and swam in the lake. The hot, slightly tan sand felt great, and the lake water was refreshing. However, after walking from the water to my towel and belongings, I was keenly aware of sand scrunched between my toes and sticking to my feet. What was I to do to get rid of it? I had two options. The first was totally unacceptable. I could swim in the lake again. A swim would definitely wash the sand from my feet. But how could I return to my towel and belongings again with clean feet? The other option made sense. I could fill a small bucket with water and pour it over my sandy feet. Yes, a partial washing would work just fine!

I have often thought of the lake-sand experience as illustrative of the full cleansing received at conversion and the partial cleansing received through confession. Titus 3:5 refers to the "washing of rebirth," and 1 John 1:9 refers to the cleansing of confession.

Failure to confess our sins does lead to unhappy consequences that the Holy Spirit wants to help us avoid. For this reason, Ephesians 4:30 counsels, "And do not grieve the Holy Spirit of God, with whom you were sealed for the day of redemption."

Unconfessed sin injures our prayers. The psalmist who penned Psalm 66 admitted, "If I had cherished sin in my heart, the Lord would not have listened" (v. 18). Just as logs might jam a river and have to be removed before the water can flow freely, so sins can jam the prayer line to God until he removes them when we confess them.

Occasionally, the efforts of concerned fellow believers are required to restore a sinning Christian. Galatians 6:1 urges "spiritual" believers to "restore" a brother who "is caught in a sin." The Greek word for "restore" was commonly used to mean the setting of bones. A dislocated arm, for example, would need to be restored. Left alone, it would cause pain and be useless.

Learning to ride a bicycle seemed to be a painfully slow process when I was a boy. My impatience spurred me to find a shortcut to acquiring the skill. Convinced that it was easier to balance my bike at a fast speed than at a slow speed, I took it to the top of a hill, climbed on, and pushed off. Almost instantly, I was speeding downhill, hands on the handlebars but feet off the pedals. About halfway down the hill I lost control and crashed into a curb. I flew over the handlebars and stretched out my left arm to brace my fall. It was not a good plan but it was my only plan. Sprawled face first on the ground, I saw my left arm jackknife at the elbow. I had dislocated my arm.

I picked up my bicycle with my right arm and walked it home. I wondered how my parents would respond when I explained what had happened. They can't afford a doctor's bill or a hospital bill, I told myself. But I knew something had to be done. A dislocated arm would render me useless in my favorite sports—hockey and golf—and keep me from doing many everyday tasks. Besides, I wanted the pain to stop as soon as possible.

My parents didn't lecture me. Instead, they rushed me to the hospital, where a doctor reset the bones and placed my arm in a sling. Gradually, the pain subsided, and I was able to play hockey and golf again.

A sinning Christian who fails to confess his sin is like a dislocated arm. He hurts, and he is unable to serve the Lord effectively. He may need caring fellow believers to come alongside him, counsel him, and persuade him to confess the error of his way. Then, when he is restored, he can enjoy the peace and productivity that accompany renewed fellowship with the Father.

Colorado is a health-conscious state, and its sunny, dry climate seems to contribute to the jogging's popularity. On almost any given day, joggers take to the streets, trails, paths, and roads for a good workout. I am not one of them, although I walk every day. I have noticed, though, that joggers wear very light clothes. Running shoes, athletic socks, shorts, T-shirts, and a cap make up their attire. I have never seen a jogger with combat boots, heavy pants, an overcoat, a thick scarf, and a fur hat. Jogging while wearing heavy clothes makes about as much sense as fighting a five-alarm fire with a toy water pistol. Yet, some believers try to run the Christian race with a heavy weight of sin in their lives.

Hebrews 12:1 encourages us to "throw off everything that hinders and the sin that so easily entangles, and let us run with perseverance the race marked out for us." Confession is a good way to get rid of excess baggage, so we can run well.

On your mark! Ready! Set! Go!

8
GRACE MEANS "I'M OKAY, YOU'RE OKAY"

SOLID ROCK CHURCH BOASTS THAT IT HAS THE BEST church constitution and bylaws in Springfield County, and according to its pastor they are almost as binding on the membership as the Bible itself. He especially likes the Church Covenant section that includes such statements as "We, the members of Solid Rock Church, agree to refrain from all worldly habits. We will abstain from the use of alcohol, tobacco, and the recreational use of drugs. We further agree that we will not dance, gamble, or view secular movies. We will dress modestly at all times and conduct ourselves in a manner befitting New Testament Christians."

Grace House, just five blocks from Solid Rock, organized as a church two years ago, but already its attendance has skyrocketed to eight hundred. Although it offers three Sunday morning services and a Saturday night service, it has become obvious that the congregation needs a much bigger building.

If you were to ask almost anyone who attends Grace

House what he or she finds so attractive, you would most likely hear, "I have found the grace teaching so liberating. No one on the staff tells me it's wrong to do this or that." Unlike Solid Rock Church, Grace House doesn't have a church covenant. Nor does it have a membership. The pastoral staff and a board of elders map the church's direction and oversee a ministry of small care groups.

These contrasting philosophies of Christian living are fairly typical of two categories of churches, although some churches don't belong in either one. The Solid Rock category would call churches in the Grace House category worldly. The Grace House category would call churches in the Solid Rock category legalistic. Solid Rock-type churches allege that Grace House churches teach cheap grace and insist that grace doesn't give any Christian a license to live like a pagan. Grace House-type churches argue that legalism enslaves its adherents and burdens them with heavy baggage and a guilty conscience. According to Grace House and other churches like it, if the Bible doesn't specifically mention a behavior, believers are free to pursue it. A Christian should not judge his fellow Christian. Rather his attitude should be "I'm okay, you're okay."

This issue of legalism versus the I'm-okay-you're-okay philosophy stretches all the way back to the first century and comes under scrutiny in several of the apostle Paul's New Testament letters. But before we see how Paul addressed this issue, let's understand that, in the strictest sense of the word, legalism is a system of religion that depends on the keeping of rules or laws for salvation. However, in the popular sense, it identifies a rigid Christian lifestyle in which a person's spirituality is judged by what he or she does or does not do. We must also understand that teaching grace is a biblical mandate. We must teach salvation by grace and encourage one another to rely on God's grace for victory over temptation, trials, and sin. But we must not cheapen grace by teaching that grace allows us to live without regard for our personal testimony. After all, God summons all his children to live righteously and godly.

In the days of Moses, God instructed the Israelites: "Consecrate yourselves and be holy, because I am the Lord your God" (Lev. 20:7). Centuries later, the apostle Peter delivered a similar divine summons—this time to Christians: "But just as he who called you is holy, so be holy in all you do; for it is written: 'Be ye holy, because I am holy'" (1 Peter 1:15-16).

It is noteworthy that Paul linked grace and righteous living together in his letter to Titus. He explained: "For the grace of God that brings salvation has appeared to all men. It teaches us to say 'No' to ungodliness and worldly passions, and to live self-controlled, upright and godly lives in this present age" (2:11-12).

Indeed, God gave us the Bible to teach us not only how to be saved but also how to live in a manner befitting saved people. Paul explained to Timothy: 'You have known the holy Scriptures, which are able to make you wise for salvation through faith in Christ Jesus. All Scripture is God-breathed and is useful for teaching, rebuking, correcting and training in righteousness" (2 Tim. 3:15-16).

Who can deny, then, that believers ought to lead righteous lives? But does the legalism produce righteous lives? Does righteous living spring from the belief that Christians are free to live independent of rules?

In Romans, chapter 14, Paul described the legalistic brother as one whose faith is weak (v. 1). Most likely, he was a Jew who believed in Jesus as the Messiah, but he had carried into the Christian life a number of dietary restrictions and the observance of the Sabbath and other special days. Feeling obligated to keep the Mosaic law, the weak brother differed with his brothers and sisters in Christ in matters of conscience. Fie had not yet perceived that Jesus Christ had fulfilled the law and freed believers from its curse. Earlier, in his letter to the Romans, Paul had written: "Therefore, there is now no condemnation for those who are in Christ Jesus, because through Christ Jesus the law of the Spirit of life set me free from the law of sin and death" (8:1-2). He called upon the church at Rome to accept the weak believer.

Ironically, legalistic Christians generally think they are strong in the faith and others are weak. When I was a young pastor, I served a church that had a rule for almost everything. Although many of its members possessed tons of Bible facts, some were intolerant of Christians whom they considered "unspiritual." The judgmental church members refused to take a Sunday newspaper, take a leisurely Sunday drive, eat out on Sunday, or work on Sunday. They seemed to calculate their spirituality by the number of prohibitions they observed. Their legalistic attitude kept me on my toes and on my knees. I had to spend a great amount of time putting out fires ignited by caustic attitudes and scorching remarks.

One day, I led a mother, a father, and their teenage

daughter to Christ. The family had never heard the good news of salvation and expressed great joy upon learning that forgiveness is a gift. They started attending our church and seemed pleased to discover that I preached, as they remarked, "straight from the Bible."

To show that he appreciated his new Christian family, Tad, the father, mowed the church's lawn one Sunday afternoon. But his act of appreciation caught the eye of a gnarly and snarly deacon. Alarmed by this "violation" of the Lord's Day, the deacon called the church's board together that evening and suggested I pay Tad a visit. My instructions were: "Tell Tad he dishonored the Lord's Day and weakened the testimony of our church."

I replied, "Tad mowed the lawn as an act of appreciation and love. How can we censure an act like that?"

Later, I thanked Tad for mowing the lawn. If I had read the law of the Medes and the Deacons to him, I believe he would have been confused and reluctant to do anything else for the church. Fortunately, the incident passed, and Tad and his wife and their daughter became active church members whose vibrant, young faith infused uncommon joy into our congregation.

Paul's letter to the Galatian churches sounds an alarm about legalism. The Galatian believers had stepped out of paganism to embrace new life in Christ. But along came religious teachers who told them they could not be acceptable to God unless they received the Jewish rite of circumcision and agreed to keep the Mosaic law. Like so many religious teachers before and after them, these "Judaizers" believed God rewards religious deeds by saving those who perform them. Paul exposed the error of this belief by telling the Galatians they were not obligated to keep the law. The law's purpose, he explained, was to reveal sin and the need of a Savior. He pointed out that Jesus fulfilled the law, paid our penalty by dying on the cross, and justified all who believe in him (see Gal. 2:15-16; 3:10-13, 19-23).

Legalistic attitudes destroy congregational unity. The legalists establish false standards of righteousness and criticize those who choose not to adopt those standards. They backbite and condemn others while showcasing their loyalty to rules. Like the Pharisees branded as hypocrites, they find little faults in others but ignore their own faults. The question Jesus asked the Pharisees is appropriate to ask legalists today: "Why do you look at the speck of sawdust in your brother's eye and pay no attention to the plank in your own eye?" (Matt. 7:3).

Both in Galatians and in Philippians, the apostle Paul alluded to the divisive, destructive nature of legalism. Having urged the Galatians to stand firm in Christian liberty and reject legalism (5:1-12), he warned: "If you keep on biting and devouring each other, watch out or you will be destroyed by each other" (v. 15). In Philippians 3:2, he counseled: "Watch out for those dogs, those men who do evil, those mutilators of the flesh." Then he renounced all the legalistic trappings of the pre-conversion life he led as a strict Pharisee. Every religious credential and code of conduct he thought earned him favor with God, he had cast aside when he trusted in Christ alone to save him (v. 4-9).

Although the Philippian church had maintained a strong partnership with Paul in spreading the gospel (1:3-5), it faced a crisis. Two female workers in the church, Euodia and Syntyche, had squared off in a bitter dispute (4:2). They needed to reconcile and get back on track (v. 3); otherwise, their personal feud might split the congregation into warring factions.

Perhaps these women favored opposite viewpoints, one favoring legalism and the other the free-to-do-as-I-please view. The latter view received Paul's indictment in 3:18-19: "Many live as enemies of the cross of Christ. Their destiny is destruction, their god is their stomach, and their glory is in their shame. Their mind is on earthly things."

I subscribe to the theory that a legalist may be guilty of the very things he condemns. For example, the person who carps constantly against the evil of pornography may secretly entertain sexual lusts.

Summer camp ought to provide fun and opportunity for spiritual growth for kids, but a legalistic pastor almost drained both from a camp for nine-to eleven-year-old kids. As a fellow pastor and camp teacher, I was appalled by the legalistic pastor's comments. "Some of the girls are wearing pants," he began. "We need to call their parents and advise them to bring dresses for their daughters to change into. We cannot permit girls to wear pants. It is immodest apparel."

Several months later, the front page of our local newspaper carried the shocking story that the legalistic pastor had been arrested for placing obscene phone calls to women in the community, including some in his congregation.

Legalism didn't work for a youth pastor either. He insisted that the teenage boys in his church maintain short haircuts. Hair below the ears was a no-no. So were blue jeans which he insisted were a sign of rebellion. However, green jeans were okay. The teenage girls were prohibited from wearing pants, and their skirts and dresses had to reach below their knees. He lectured on the evils of movies and railed against rock music. His "ministry" ended when someone recognized him in a XXX-rated movie theater and reported him to the senior pastor.

My wife encountered legalism up close and personal when a female neighbor visited her on our front porch. My wife was wearing pants and the neighbor accused her of indecency. "How come you're a pastor's wife and you're wearing pants?" she asked in a caustic tone.

My wife took the criticism graciously but she could have asked the critic: "How come you profess to be a Christian but lock your young children out of the house all day? How come you stick your head outdoors occasionally and swear at your children to be quiet?"

As Jesus indicated, legalists seem more concerned about the speck of sawdust in another person's eye than the plank in their own eye.

But I'm-okay-you're-okay Christians don't find anything in anyone's eye, including their own. Unless the Bible specifically calls an activity sin, they are free to do whatever they want and extend the same license to their Christian brothers and sisters. "Isn't that what grace is all about?" they ask. Who can say a Christian shouldn't down a cocktail or two at the office party or play poker or participate in a football pool or invest a few dollars in the lottery or play the ponies or the puppies or smoke pot occasionally or attend R-or X-rated movies or party the night away?

If we had to produce specific verses of Scripture mentioning and prohibiting those activities, we would face a hopeless task. Not even an exhaustive concordance uncovers the word "cocktail" in the Bible. Nor does the Bible mention poker, the lottery, pot smoking, football pools, R-rated movies (or any movies), partying, or many other activities legalists label unholy.

But grace does not issue believers a license to sin. We are free from sin but we are not free to sin. Romans 6:1-2 reasons: "What shall we say, then? Shall we go on sinning so that grace may increase? By no means! We died to sin; how can we live in it any longer?" Grace has made us free to "live a new life" (v. 4). We have been saved by grace (Eph. 2:8-9) in order to "do good works, which God prepared in advance for us to do" (v. 10).

Legalists ought to make an attitude adjustment and recognize that righteous living is not the product of the flesh. No matter how hard a Christian tries to produce righteous characteristics, he will fail, because righteous character is produced by the Holy Spirit, not manufactured by the human will. "The fruit of the Spirit is love, joy, peace, patience kindness, goodness, faithfulness, gentleness and self-control. Against such things there is no law" (Gal. 5:22-23).

Those who think grace allows them to live as they please need to adjust their attitude and recognize that the fruitful Christian life includes the quality "self-control." Self-indulgence, on the other hand, militates against the Spirit's efforts to produce godly character.

So how can a Christian decide whether an activity is right or wrong if the Bible doesn't mention it? Here are a few guidelines.

Decide Whether Participating In The Activity Will Advance Or Retard Your Spiritual Growth

THE MAIN GOAL of the Christian life is to do the will of God (see Rom. 12:1-2). We ought to consider harmful any activity that keeps us from fulfilling God's plan for us. The activity may consume too much time that belongs to God. It may become an obsession. It may lead to a similar but clearly immoral activity. For example, a believer may feel that he can view R-rated movies without being affected negatively by the foul language and vile images. He may say, "I can chew what's good and spit out the rest," but eventually he may spit out practically nothing. Having become affected by wrong thinking, he may engage in wrong living. Garbage in, garbage out is a biblical principle. No wonder Philippians 4:8 admonishes us to think noble and pure thoughts.

The apostle John urged his readers to cast off harmful cravings and lusts, knowing that "the world and its desires pass away, but the man who does the will of God lives forever" (1 John 2:17).

A billionaire who had advertised for a chauffeur gave each applicant a road test in the rugged mountains near his mansion. He instructed each applicant to drive up the steepest road to dizzying heights. After reaching an extremely high point where there were no guardrails, he asked each applicant to drive as close to the edge of a steep cliff as possible.

One applicant drove within a foot of the drop-off. Another drove within six inches. The third drove within an inch of the cliff's edge. The fourth stayed on course; he did not even try to drive close to the edge.

The billionaire hired the fourth chauffeur,

explaining that he had simply tested the applicants to see which one would resist the urge to see how close to the edge he could get without going over it. He felt safe with the one who showed no interest in seeing how close he could get to the edge without falling off.

The world offers thrills as it beckons Christians to live on the edge, but wise Christians refuse to risk the danger that lies in heeding its call.

Decide Whether Participating In The Activity
Will Enhance Or Hurt God's Reputation

To A GREAT EXTENT, your non-Christian friends, associates, and neighbors build their concept of God on the basis of what they see you do. If you refrain from evil conversation and evil conduct, they will most likely perceive God as righteous. If you display a careless attitude toward sin, they will most likely perceive God as unrighteous or amoral.

Jesus instructed his followers to "let your light shine before men, that they may see your good deeds and praise your Father in heaven" (Matt. 5:16).

Paul counseled, "So whether you eat or drink or whatever you do, do it all for the glory of God" (1 Cor. 10:31), and he challenged the Christians at Philippi to "shine like stars in the universe" (Phil. 2:15).

Who hasn't walked in the open on a clear night, gazed at the stars, marveled at their brilliance, and reflected on the glory of the Creator? When clouds cover the night sky, though, they hide the stars from our view, and we are less likely to think about the Creator's glory. Like a dense cloud cover, activities that fall into a gray area may dim our light and veil God's glory.

Decide Whether Participating In The Activity Will Cause A Weaker Believer To Stumble

AS WE HAVE SEEN, in his letter to the Romans. Paul identified the Christian with legalistic attitudes as "him whose faith is weak" (14:1). But a Christian whose faith is strong must consider how participating in a questionable activity might affect his weak brother or sister. Paul advised, "It is better not to eat meat or drink wine or to do anything else that will cause your brother to fall" (v. 21).

The Christian life is the liberated life. Christ has set us free (John 8:36), but our liberty must be balanced by love. If we love God, we will keep his commandments and refuse to do anything that dishonors him. If we love our fellow Christian, we will try to build him up in the faith and refuse to do anything that might offend his conscience. Our attitude should reflect such love that we can truly say, "If what I eat or do causes my brother to fall into sin, I will never eat meat or participate in that activity again, so that I will not cause him to fall" (1 Cor. 8:13, words in italics added).

On the surface, the I'm-okay-you're-okay philosophy seems charitable. But does that attitude lock us into a false comfort zone and keep us from becoming all that God wants us to be? If we appear to share the same likes, interests, and desires as our pagan neighbors, why should they believe we have been saved from our sins and vested with a power to live above temptation?

The biggest question of all is this: Is our lifestyle okay with God?

9
GOD WILL GIVE YOU THE DESIRES OF YOUR HEART

WHEN I WAS A KID, THE STORY OF ALADDIN AND HIS LAMP fascinated me. You remember how the lamp worked, don't you? Aladdin would simply rub the lamp and make a wish, and then, presto, a genie appeared to grant it. I knew the story was make-believe but I kept my eye peeled for lamps just in case. Several years later, I became a Christian and learned that having the best things in life had nothing to do with a magic lamp but everything to do with trusting the Lord and honoring him. This understanding came about partly because I read Psalm 37:3-4: Trust in the Lord and do good; dwell in the land and enjoy safe pasture. Delight yourself in the Lord and he will give you the desires of your heart.

These two verses include three clear commands and a magnificent promise.

- Command 1: "Trust in the Lord" (v. 3).
- Command 2: "and do good" (v. 3).
- Command 3: "Delight yourself in the Lord" (v. 4).

- Promise: "and he will give you the desires of your heart" (v. 4).

Think of Psalm 37:3-4 as a contractual agreement. When a buyer signs a financial agreement to purchase a car, he agrees with the seller to provide the seller with a stated down payment and pay a fixed number of monthly payments. In return, the seller agrees to provide the car the buyer has chosen.

What chance of success would you predict for a customer who selected a car from the dealer's showroom, told a salesperson that it was his heart's desire to own the car he selected and requested it as a freebie? Nil to zilch chance of getting it? Why then would anyone think God would respond like the genie of Aladdin's lamp to grant whatever the petitioner desired?

Let's bring this issue down to a few more plausible situations.

Tavia has her heart set on owning a brand-new Victorian-style house that she can furnish with antique furniture and accents. She visualizes herself in the home of her dreams and with great pride entertaining guests. She can almost hear the guests' "oohs" and "aahs" as she guides them through the house and points out this and that authentic Victorian feature. Having read Psalm 37:4, Tavia is convinced that God will give her the dream house fully furnished. It is, after all, one of the desires of her heart.

Monte, a sales rep, strongly desires the position of vice president of sales for Domestic Robots, Inc. He, too, believes God has promised to give him the desires of his heart. Often, he fantasizes about the prestige, power, and wealth the position would give him. He would handle a $60 million annual budget, build an efficient sales team, formulate significant policies, travel internationally, and make key decisions binding on the company's 139 sales reps. He pictures the shiny brass nameplate on the door of his spacious office and sighs at the prospect of leaving a dinky cubicle to the sales rep who succeeds him.

Bryant, a fifteen-year-old, was flipping through his Bible last month when he came across Psalm 37:4. Wow! he thought. My super big desire is to be a rock star. How cool to arrive at a concert in a limo, sign a zillion autographs, and have everybody go crazy for my music! Whoa! I'm going to ask God to make it all happen.

What do Tavia, Monty, and Bryant have in common? A misunderstanding of the promise that God gives the desires of the heart carte blanche. They failed to see that this promise comes wrapped in a contract. The conditions God imposes are not stringent, but they are uncompromising.

"Trust in the Lord" (Ps. 37:3) is the first condition.

To trust means "to have faith in" or "to rely on." David, who wrote this psalm in his old age (v. 25), had learned to trust in the Lord and rely on him. Whether felling the giant Goliath or fleeing from King Saul or fending off the Philistines, David trusted in the Lord and learned that he rewards those who trust in him. David, therefore, encouraged the Israelites not to fret "because of evil men or be envious of those who do wrong" (v. 1). He assured them that "evil men will be cut off, but those who hope in the Lord will inherit the land" (v. 9).

The Lord had promised his people an earthly kingdom over which the Messiah would reign in righteousness. At times the prospect of inheriting the promised kingdom seemed bleak, but the Israelites should not worry or abandon hope. The Lord would keep His word.

Sometimes, we twenty-first-century Christians neglect to trust the Lord. In our sophisticated thinking, we map out a plan that we believe will achieve happiness and fulfillment. And we lead such a fast-paced life that we want what we want when we want it. In our worldly wisdom and haste, we present our desires to the Lord for his endorsement. However, his thoughts are not our thoughts, neither are our ways his ways (Isa. 55:8). The Lord states, "As the heavens are higher than the earth, so are my ways higher than your ways and my thoughts than your thoughts" (v. 9).

What a staggering revelation that God's ways and thoughts are so much higher than ours! Recently our concept of the distance between other planets and ours expanded. The Cassini probe satellite entered Saturn's ring plane June 30, 2004, after a seven-year voyage and sent remarkable photos back to Earth. Think of it, seven years were required for a fast-traveling space vehicle to reach this planet located 742.8 million miles from Earth. Yet, the vast expanse of the heavens reaches far beyond Saturn! So, if God's thoughts and ways are higher than ours as the heavens are higher than the earth, how can we possibly imagine that we know better than he what is best for us?

We may desire something we think will improve our life but the Lord may not grant it because he knows it would harm our relationship with him. So for our good and his glory, he overrules our misguided wants.

Vera was in her fifties when I was her pastor. From

childhood, arthritis had stiffened her body and racked it with pain. No one would have faulted her if she had desired a pain-free, flexible body; yet she would say, "Pastor, I'm glad the Lord allowed me to have arthritis. If I had been healthy as a young person, I might have partied and gotten into all kinds of trouble. The arthritis has kept me close to the Lord. I have to depend upon him just to move from one place in the house to another."

Of course, in heaven, Vera will experience neither pain nor disappointment. The Lord will reward her trust in him.

Abraham trusted in the Lord. The desire of his heart initially might have been to stay in beautiful, cultured Ur of the Chaldeans, where the livin' was easy. But, when God called him to leave Ur without announcing a destination, Abram trusted and departed.

Eventually, Abram became a nomad in Canaan. God had promised him the whole land and a son but he spent most of his life without a son and he never owned a stick of property except a burial cave. However, he did have an opportunity once to receive a huge reward from a king. The king of wicked Sodom offered it to him for his daring rescue of hostages and recovery of booty taken from Sodom by the armies of several powerful kings.

"Give me the people [the hostages] and keep the goods for yourself," the king of Sodom offered (Gen. 14:21).

This was Abram's big chance to pluck a fortune from the king's hands. But he trusted in the Lord and preferred to commit his future to him. Boldly he announced: "I have raised my hand to the Lord, God

Most High, Creator of heaven and earth, and have taken an oath that I will accept nothing belonging to you, not even a thread or the thong of a sandal, so that you will never be able to say, 'I made Abram rich'" (v. 22-23).

Talk about trust! But later, Abram seems to have had second thoughts about answering the king of Sodom so boldly. The Lord appeared to him and said, "Do not be afraid, Abram. I am your shield, your very great reward" (15:1). He would not only protect Abram but also reward him. In other words, his desire for Abram was perfect! It surely exceeded anything Abram could have desired.

Abram asked what the Lord would give him, adding "since I remain childless" (v. 2).

The Lord promised to give him a son and innumerable descendants (v. 4—5).

Abram believed the Lord (v. 6), but it would be years before he would see the fulfillment of the promise. Abram's wife was barren and, eventually, Abram would be unable to father a child. But he trusted, waited, trusted, and waited until the Lord did the impossible. Abram and his wife became parents of a baby boy, whom they named Isaac.

Abram had trusted the Lord, and the Lord gave him the desire of his heart. However, the son of promise was also the Lord's desire because the Savior would be born centuries later through Isaac's lineage. The Lord's desire and Abram's desire fused into one.

A second condition to realizing the desires of your heart is to "do good" (Ps. 37:3)

Psalm 84:11 affirms this truth: "For the Lord God is a sun and shield; the Lord bestows favor and honor; no good thing does he withhold from those whose walk is blameless."

Good things are not necessarily material things. In the Sermon on the Mount, "blessings" are identified as citizenship in Jesus' kingdom, comfort, inheritance in the kingdom, spiritual satisfaction, mercy, the prospect of seeing God, being called God's sons, and having reward in heaven (Matt. 5:3-12). Indeed, as a noteworthy plaque suggests, "The best things in life are not things."

The apostle Paul and Demas were both missionaries but Paul's unswerving goal was to do good—to fulfill God's will for his life. At the end of his life, he shivered in a Roman dungeon, where he awaited execution. He asked Mark to bring him the coat that he had left at Troas (2 Tim. 4:13). Obviously, he had few or no possessions but neither did he have any complaints. He had served the Lord faithfully and therefore anticipated receiving a heavenly reward, "the crown of righteousness" (4:8). Demas, on the other hand, swerved from doing good—from doing God's will. Having "loved this world" (v. 10), he tossed aside the opportunity to receive a heavenly crown.

Like Paul and Demas, every Christian must choose whether to invest his or her life in doing good or spend his or her life in getting goods. The desires of the body may be met temporarily by getting goods, but the desires of the heart can be met only by doing good.

Of course, a wealthy Christian may do an enormous amount of good but only if he values God's will more than wealth. Church history has had its share of wealthy believers who supported the Lord's work generously and used their money to open doors of opportunity to missions and evangelism. Actually, a Christian of meager means may be far more materialistic than a wealthy Christian. He may crave money and live to acquire it and end up losing the best things in life. Paul informed Timothy, "People who want to get rich fall into temptation and a trap and into many foolish and harmful desires that plunge men into ruin and destruction" (1 Tim. 6:9).

The third condition we must meet before the Lord gives us the desires of our hearts is, "delight yourself in the Lord" (Ps. 37:4).

Legitimately, we may find delight in any number of pursuits and pleasures. For example, we may delight in listening to a fine symphony orchestra or watching a fast-paced basketball game or reading a son or daughter's outstanding report card or standing atop a mountain and gazing at majestic scenery or reading a captivating novel. But our chief delight ought to be in the Lord.

When we delight in the Lord, we revel in his character and mighty works. We rejoice in who he is and what he does. Just as a person in love delights to spend time with the one he or she loves, so we cherish time spent with the Lord. Like Peter, who accompanied the Lord to the Mount of Transfiguration and beheld his radiant glory, we exclaim, "Lord, it is good for us to be here."

We cannot see the Lord today, but we can enjoy his presence and get well acquainted with him by reading His Word. Notice how the following excerpts from the book of Psalms link delight in the Lord with love for His Word:

Blessed is the man who does not walk in the counsel of the wicked. . . . But his delight is in the law of the Lord. (Ps. 1:1-2)

Your statutes are my delight. (Ps. 119:24)

Your law is my delight. (Ps. 119:77, 174)

As we meditate on God's Word, the Holy Spirit uses it to teach us to disdain sin and desire to do what pleases God. We learn, for example, that God wants us to love him preeminently, to love others as ourselves, to hunger and thirst for righteousness, to pray, to put others' interests ahead of our own, to assume a servant's role, to evangelize, to worship "in spirit and in truth," to keep ourselves pure, to give thanks in everything, and to long for Jesus' return. We find ourselves praying, "I desire to do your will, O my God; your law is within my heart" (Ps. 40:8). Indeed, we find that our desires are precisely God's desires for us.

God's promise to give us the desires of our hearts (Ps. 37:4) fully agrees with his will for us. He is too wise to give us what violates his will and too loving and kind to withhold from us what complements it.

In the days of the judges, Hannah had a rough life. For one thing, she was barren. For another, her husband, Elkanah, had a second wife, Peninnah, who had given birth to sons and daughters. Elkanah loved Hannah, but society judged a woman's worth by the number of children, especially sons, she presented to her husband. So Hannah's self-esteem must have been lower than the Dead Sea. To make matters worse, Peninnah hassled Hannah year after year about her inability to bear a child. As a matter of fact, she drove Hannah to tears.

One day, during a trip to the tabernacle at Shiloh, Hannah wept bitterly and prayed earnestly in the presence of Eli, the priest. She prayed in her heart that the Lord would give her a son, and as she prayed, her lips pursed the words without making a sound.

Observing this, Eli thought she was drunk. "How long will you keep on getting drunk?" he asked her. "Get rid of your wine" (1 Sam. 1:14).

Quickly, Hannah explained that she had not been drinking but was pouring out her heart to the Lord.

"Go in peace, and may the God of Israel grant you what you have asked of him," Eli replied (v. 17).

Hannah strongly desired a son and she believed in pouring out her heart to the Lord. Further, she was dedicated to the Lord. She had promised to give her son to the Lord "for all the days of his life" as a Nazarite (v. 11). The Lord was her delight and her Master. Would he give her the desire of her heart?

He would. His will called for a new judge for his people and the son Hannah would bear would become that judge. At his birth, Hannah named her baby boy Samuel. He grew up at Shiloh under Eli's mentoring and later became Eli's successor. He served Israel as an outstanding judge and even anointed Israel's greatest king, David.

Hannah's desire and the Lord's will were fused together.

Another case of the human desire and the divine will fusing together involved David's son Solomon. When he became Israel's king, he received an opportunity from the Lord to request anything he desired. First Kings 3:5 reports that the Lord appeared to him during the night in a dream and said, "Ask for whatever you want me to give you."

This may seem like a genie-of-the-lamp story but it was a real-time event early in Solomon's royal career and he didn't squander the opportunity on selfish whims.

Recognizing that the Lord's will was paramount, he identified himself as the Lord's servant and asked for wisdom. Verses 8 and 9 record a portion of Solomon's request: Your servant is here among the people you have chosen, a great people, too numerous to count or number. So give your servant a discerning heart to govern your people and to distinguish between right and wrong. For who is able to govern this great people of yours?

Is it any wonder that "the Lord was pleased that Solomon had asked for this" and granted the request (v. 10, 12)? The desires of Solomon's heart aligned perfectly with the desires of God's heart.

The word "desires" in Psalm 37:4 carries the meaning "petitions" and therefore brings to mind prayer requests. God grants the prayer requests of our hearts if they agree with his will. James 4:3 exposes the sin and futility of praying selfishly: "When you ask, you do not receive, because you ask with wrong motives, that you may spend what you get on your pleasures." Following the counsel of Psalm 37:3-4 to trust in the Lord, do good, and delight in the Lord is the sure way to keep selfish prayer requests at bay and to pray according to God's will. It is also the way to receive the desires of our hearts. First John 5:14—15 states, "This is the confidence we have in approaching God: that if we ask anything according to his will, he hears us. And if we know that he hears us—whatever we ask—we know that we have what we asked of him."

The father of a strong-willed ten-year-old boy reminded him often, "Buster, you must not always want your own way."

Buster dropped his head and seemed to be deep in

thought. After a few moments, he answered, "Dad, if I choose to do the Lord's will because I want to, don't I still have my own way?"

Apparently, Buster had learned an important truth about Christian living.

10

REAL FAITH MEANS NEVER HAVING TO SAY LIFE IS TOUGH

Feeling too sick to attend church, I slumped in my La-Z-Boy recliner and set the TV remote to a religious network. What I heard made me wonder if the publisher of my Bible had omitted a hundred pages. I certainly hadn't read in my copy of the Bible what that Sunday morning's TV preachers claimed.

"Jesus doesn't want you to be sick," one preacher consoled. "He died to free you from illness and disease. Today, he wants to heal you—take away the back pain or the diabetes or the migraines or the cancer or whatever else you may be suffering."

Hmmm, I reflected, a perfectly healthy life would certainly say no to death and dying. And a couple of dollars a day donated to this preacher would work as well as an apple a day to keep the doctor away.

Another TV preacher urged his audience to turn their finances around by planting a faith seed in his ministry. Or was it in his pocket?

"Aren't you tired of having unpaid bills stack up?" he asked. "Do you feel defeated because you cannot enjoy an affluent lifestyle? The apostle James hit the nail on the head. He said, 'You have not because you ask not.' And Jesus promised 'all these things' to those who seek the kingdom of God first. So I challenge you to believe and show your interest in God's kingdom by planting a faith seed of fifty or a hundred dollars in this ministry. God will return the fifty or hundred dollars to you many fold, but you have to take the first step by planting a faith seed."

Strange—the more of those TV programs I watched, the sicker I felt. But I watched one more before reaching for the Alka-Seltzer.

"I get letters from viewers who complain that their prayers aren't working," the well-dressed preacher announced. "They heard me say that God answers prayer. If you ask him specifically for a new car, a new house, or a new job, he will give it to you. These complainers forget that I said specifically. Let me explain.

"When I wanted the Lord to give me a Cadillac, I visited a dealer, selected a specific model, wrote down the options I wanted, and picked up a brochure with photos of the car. Then I posted the photos around the house so that I could focus on the car when I shaved, got dressed, and ate a meal. I had that car on my mind all day long, and when I prayed, I asked the Lord specifically for that car. I told him not only the color I wanted but also the options. I was specific.

"That's how you need to pray. You haven't received what you asked for because you haven't given the Lord enough specific details!"

"Tell it to starring Christian refugees in Sudan," I found myself saying to the TV preacher. "And while you're at it, explain that the Christian life is supposed to be a bed of roses."

Most Christians realize that faith doesn't eliminate trials and open the floodgates for a deluge of years of flawless health and material prosperity. They have learned from Scripture and personal experience that faith gets us through each trial not out of it.

If you think faith is never having to say life is tough, why not review the lives of some believers in Bible times whose faith was strong? You may be surprised to learn that they suffered enormous trials.

The Bible describes Job as "blameless and upright," a man who "feared God and shunned evil" (Job 1:1). He was such a good family man that early every morning he sacrificed a burnt offering for each of his adult children (v. 5). We would have to nod our heads and affirm that Job was a man of faith. But trials began to burst like cluster bombs in Job's life.

What happened? Had Job lost his faith? Not at all. Job made two resolute declarations of faith while enduring horrendous trials. The first affirms Job's intention to keep trusting God for the rest of his life: "Though he slay me, yet will I hope in him" (13:15). The second affirms the confidence that he would see God in the afterlife: "I know that my Redeemer lives, and that in the end he will stand upon the earth. And after my skin has been destroyed, yet in my flesh I will see God; I myself will see him with my own eyes—I, and not another" (19:25-27).

Trials took away Job's livestock, his servants, his sons and daughters, and his health, but they could not take away his faith. Even when he was sitting on an ash pile and scraping pus from his sores, he trusted in the Lord as the sovereign, all-wise Creator. His wife advised Job to "curse God and die" (2:9), but Job replied, 'You are talking like a foolish woman. Shall we accept good from God, and not trouble?" (v. 10).

Would you dare to suggest that Job's trials resulted from a lack of faith? I wouldn't!

Another man of faith, perhaps a contemporary of Job, learned that faith in God didn't exempt him from trials. His name was Abraham, and he had received sweeping promises from God about innumerable descendants and a vast amount of land. However, the only property Abraham ever owned was a burial plot; and he lived to light one hundred candles on his birthday cake before he and his wife, Sarah, had their first child.

Talk about trials! Abraham wandered as a stranger in a land God had promised to give him. He waited and waited and waited for the son God had promised to him. When the son, Isaac, was born, Abraham rejoiced, but joy must have dissipated when Isaac was a young teenager. God commanded Abraham to sacrifice Isaac as a burnt offering on Mount Moriah (Gen. 22:1-2). Not one to drag his feet when God issued a command, Abraham left for the designated mountain "early the next morning" (v. 3), taking Isaac with him.

This was Abraham's harshest trial. How could he realize the fulfillment of God's promise of innumerable descendants if Isaac were dead? The answer is that he exercised faith. Hebrews 11:17-19 fills in the picture: "By faith Abraham, when God tested him, offered Isaac as a sacrifice. He who had received the promises was about to sacrifice his one and only son, even though God had said to him, 'It is through Isaac that your offspring will be reckoned.' Abraham reasoned that God could raise the dead and, figuratively speaking, he did receive Isaac back from death."

What rock-solid faith Abraham had! He trusted so resolutely in God that he expected him to raise Isaac from the dead in order to fulfill his promise. But also, what an unspeakably tough trial Abraham faced! He expected to have to slay his only son on Mount Moriah. Surely, not even the prospect of seeing God raise Isaac from the dead could have removed the trauma he would have experienced. The tension between Abraham's faith in God and his love for the son of his old age was almost enough to make the mountain tremble.

A boulder-size lump formed in my throat and a mammoth ache struck my heart when I dropped our only son off at college two states away, knowing I wouldn't see him again for at least three months. Because a father loves his children, separation from any of them seems hard to bear. I cried when I left our daughters at their respective distant colleges, and tears welled up in my eyes when I performed our son's and daughters' weddings.

Beyond a doubt, the toughest trial of separation from our adult children occurred in January 1990 when my wife and I told them goodbye and left our home in Denver for a new ministry in Chicago. As Gloria and I drove away, we both felt the pain of separation. But the pain struck with vicious force when we were traveling on Interstate 76 about sixty miles from home. We were listening to KWBI, a Christian radio station in Denver, where our daughter Heather hosted a music-by-request morning program. We heard her say, "I would like to dedicate this next song to my parents, who are traveling to Chicago today." She had picked "I Thank God for My Family." Tears blocked my vision. "Do you want to turn around and go back to Denver?" I asked.

I knew she wanted to, and so did I, but we drove on. We were committed to God's will.

I can only imagine how Abraham felt when God tested his faith on Mount Moriah. He understood that faith and hard times are not mutually exclusive. But he endured the trial, believing that obedience to God's will must take precedence over everything else, including love for one's only son.

Genesis also profiles Joseph, a man of faith. In spite of dreadful treatment at the hands of his envious, vengeful brothers, the shock of being falsely accused of a crime, and the burden of a long jail sentence, he never lost his faith in God. When Joseph was finally reunited with his brothers, he reflected on the hardship they had inflicted on him and observed, "You intended to harm me, but God intended it for good to accomplish what is now being done, the saving of many lives" (Gen. 50:20).

Some who believe that faith is never having to say life is tough might have written Joseph's story differently. They would have plotted a straight, smooth line from Joseph's comfortable life as a teenager in Canaan to a throne in Egypt. But without the trials, Joseph would not have reached a throne with proven faith and a deep love for all his family members.

Genuine faith always makes us better, not bitter!

Let's leap nearly about 2,500 years ahead to the period called the Babylonian captivity. Judah and its capital, Jerusalem, had fallen to the Babylonians, and the king of Babylon, Nebuchadnezzar, had taken many of Jerusalem's citizens into captivity. Daniel, a young man at the time, was one of those citizens. He suddenly found himself in Babylon and in training to serve in the king's court. Would his faith in Yahweh exempt him from trials in pagan Babylon?

The answer is a resounding no. Early in his Babylonian experience, Daniel encountered brainwashing and all attempts to erase his loyalty to Yahweh. The Babylonians even renamed him Belteshazzar in honor of one of their deities. But Daniel's faith triumphed over this trial of psychological and religious pressure.

Later, during Darius's reign, the king was persuaded by counselors, who were "gunning" for Daniel, to make a highly restrictive law. It forbade everyone from praying to any god or man except Darius for thirty days. Anyone who violated this law would be hurled into a lions' den. Of course, the counselors' plot was designed to rid them of Daniel. They knew he was a man of faith who prayed daily to the God of Israel.

The evil scheme tried Daniel's faith but it did not destroy or even weaken it. Daniel entered his home, went to his upstairs prayer room, and with windows opened toward Jerusalem, prayed as he always had (Dan. 6:10).

Finding Daniel on his knees and praying to Yahweh, his adversaries reported him to the king (v. 11-15). Soon, Daniel was on the lions' menu (v. 16).

But the lions didn't touch their "food," because God had sent His angel to shut their mouths (v. 22). The penalty had been executed, but Daniel had not been executed. Astonished at God's power to rescue Daniel, King Darius decreed that everyone in his kingdom must fear and reverence Daniel's God.

The Bible doesn't disclose the identity of the angel

who delivered Daniel, but it may have been the Lion of the Tribe of Judah, the preincarnate Christ, who is identified in other Old Testament passages as the angel of the Lord.

One thing is certain: God received more glory by bringing Daniel through his severe trial than by exempting him from it. Similarly, God receives more glory by bringing you through trials than by exempting you from them.

Jesus lived a perfect life. He never thought an evil thought or performed an evil deed. He was sinless, and his faith was peerless. But he encountered trials. Immediately after being baptized, he was driven into the wilderness, where he hungered for forty days. Then, in his weakened condition, he came under a battery of assaults from the Devil. Nevertheless, he declined every temptation the Devil hurled at him.

In his earthly ministry, Jesus experienced intense persecution at the hands of self-righteous, unbelieving religious leaders. At times, he had to dodge their attempts to stone him. He had no place to lay his head, owned no real estate, and claimed no personal belongings. At the end of his brief ministry, he saw his disciples desert him. Peter denied him three times and Judas betrayed him. Jesus was arrested, tried in a kangaroo court, sentenced to die, mocked, beaten, spat upon, nailed to a cross prepared for a felon, ridiculed and insulted by onlookers, and left to die.

No one has ever suffered to the extent Jesus suffered. Our trials cannot begin to compare with the trials he endured. Yet, our trials should not take us by surprise. Jesus predicted, "In this world you will have trouble. But take heart! I have overcome the world" (John 16:33).

The apostles were men of great faith after Pentecost. They proclaimed Christ boldly but they suffered brutal treatment at the hands of those who despised the name of Jesus. The book of Acts records that they were beaten and thrown into prison for giving evidence of their faith in Christ. Acts 12 reports that Herod beheaded the apostle James and apprehended the apostle Peter, intending to sever Peter's head from his body after Passover (v. 1-4). But the angel of the Lord rescued Peter from prison.

Perhaps you wonder why God didn't rescue James. Why did James die, yet Peter lived? You might apply that question to contemporary life. Why does one cancer-stricken believer die, whereas another survives? Or you may ask why a particularly dedicated Christian teenager nearly dies in an auto accident and must experience long months filled with surgeries and rehabilitation, whereas less dedicated teenagers enjoy an almost carefree youth.

We may never receive satisfactory answers to such questions, but we can accept what Scripture teaches about the purpose of trials.

An Illinois pastor and his wife must have asked why after literally experiencing a fiery trial of their faith. They and their five children were driving home to Chicago after visiting their son at a college in Wisconsin. Without warning, part of the rear end of a truck broke off, struck their van, and ruptured its gas tank. Instantly their van became an inferno. The parents suffered severe burns but managed to exit their vehicle but all five children perished in the flames. Later, in a television interview, the pastor and his wife testified to God's grace and love. They shared with viewers the comfort they drew from knowing they would see their children in heaven.

The manner in which this couple coped with the horrendous loss of their five children spoke volumes about the hope of heaven and the reality of God's eternal love. Like the apostle Paul, they cherished God's promise that his grace is sufficient (2 Cor. 12:9).

Jesus told a story about a sower and seed. Some seed fell on rocky ground and did not develop roots. He compared this seed to those who hear God's Word but fail to accept it with true faith. When trouble or persecution strikes, these mere professors of faith quickly fall away (Mark 4:16-17). Trials, then, separate real faith from phony faith.

The apostle Peter wrote his first letter to believers scattered by persecution throughout the Mediterranean world. The Romans had confiscated their homes, uprooted them, and forced them to become refugees. Their lives had become extremely harsh but they had not lost their faith. Peter recalled that they "may have had to suffer grief in all kinds of trials" (1:6), but the trials proved the genuineness of their faith, even as fire refines gold and proves its genuineness (v. 7).

Having ministered for more than fifty years, I have seen how the school of suffering graduates outstanding students of faith. A deacon paralyzed below the neck always praised the Lord for his goodness and never complained. His life of true faith touched all who knew him. A husband whose son was killed in a tragic gun accident and whose wife succumbed to liver cancer speaks of God's grace and love. A missionary wife sees her husband shot and killed by terrorists in the Philippines and writes her story affirming God's wisdom and grace. A young woman loses her mother to cancer and her father to a heart attack a few months later but testifies that she wants to serve the Lord all the days of her life. A father learns that a car accident has taken the life of one teenage son and left the other son critically injured. He expresses his desire that the Lord will restore to him "a crescent of joy." Trials strengthen our faith by prodding us to pray. How much praying would we do if life were all sunshine and no rain? As a wise Christian observed, when we are on our backs we are looking up.

Read some of the psalms David wrote when King Saul scoured the wilderness, hoping to find him and kill him. You will see how David exercised his faith by praying. Hear, for example, his words of prayer in Psalm 63:1: "O God, you are my God, earnestly I seek you; my soul thirsts for you, my body longs for you, in a dry and weary land where there is no water."

Another psalmist, Asaph, wrestled with the issue of God's fairness. Feeling alone and baffled by the prosperity of the wicked, he turned to God for answers. He wrote in Psalm 73:28, "But as for me, it is good to be near God. I have made the Sovereign Lord my refuge; I will tell of all your deeds."

Perform a brief honesty check! When have you prayed most earnestly and intently—when everything was sunny or when everything was stormy? Don't you agree that trouble drew you dose to God and strengthened your faith?

I encountered far more trials shortly after becoming a Christian than I had encountered in my entire pre-Christian life. "Why am I having so much trouble?" I asked my Christian friends. Unanimously, they responded by quoting Romans 8:28 (Kjv): "All things work together for good to them that love God." What good can possibly come from the rotten things that are happening to me? I asked myself.

Only later did I realize my friends had not quoted Romans 8:28 in its entirety. The rest of the verse says, "to them who are the called according to his purpose." I learned that God's "purpose" was to conform me "to the image [likeness] of his Son" (v. 29 Kjv). Eureka! God uses even "sufferings" (trials), mentioned in verse 18, to develop Christlike character in his people.

An observer examined exquisite hand-carved horses and watched the craftsman whittle away at another carving. "Sir," he asked, "how can you create such beautiful horses out of wood?"

"Easy," the craftsman responded. "I take a block of wood and whittle away everything that isn't horse."

Similarly, our heavenly Father, the Master Craftsman, chips away from our lives everything that isn't Christ. But he doesn't use a blade; he uses trials.

Genuine faith uses trials as motivational devices whereby we long for heaven. They teach us that a better day awaits us and point our eyes toward heaven. The apostle Paul assured us that "we do not lose heart. Though outwardly we are wasting away, yet inwardly we are being renewed day by day. For our light and momentary troubles are achieving for us an eternal glory that far outweighs them all. So we fix our eyes not on what is seen but on what is unseen. For what is seen is temporary, but what is unseen is eternal" (2 Cor. 4:16-18).

Peter affirmed this truth when he urged his readers to look by faith beyond their troubles to the return of

Christ. He wrote: "These [trials] have come so that your faith—of greater worth than gold, which perishes even though refined by fire—may be proved genuine and may result in praise, glory and honor when Jesus Christ is revealed" (1 Peter 1:7).

A hymn writer captures the optimism of Peter's words. He wrote:

It will be worth it all when we see Jesus.
It will be worth it all when we see Christ.
One glimpse of His dear face All trials will erase.
So bravely run the race, 'til we see Christ.

A young boy floated a toy sailboat on a pond. Suddenly, after the little boat had reached the center of the pond, the afternoon breeze stopped. All was calm and the boy's sailboat was motionless.

Seeing the youngster's despair, an older boy began to throw stones toward the sailboat. The youngster cringed, thinking the older boy was adding insult to injury. As he watched, though, he noticed that each stone landed on the far side of the sailboat and caused a ripple to form and push the sailboat in his direction.

Eventually, the last stone had done its work and the sailboat was within the youngster's grasp.

Trials are not evil. We may think God is throwing stones at us when trials come our way but our loving heavenly Father is simply using the trials to draw us closer to heaven's shore.

Some may think that faith is never having to say life is tough, but faith is really never having to say God's love and grace are inadequate.

President Bill Clinton's sexual escapades with a young intern initially shocked the nation and the world, yet over time many adults developed a laissez-faire attitude about it. They responded to the sullying of the presidency by asking nonchalantly, "Who are we to judge?"

Their response wasn't surprising, given the fact that we live in a post-Christian, postmodern era of no or very few moral absolutes. Sin is often perceived as the exercising of a value judgment on an immoral act rather than the act itself. For example, a congregation that dismisses a pastor because he had an affair may come under harsh criticism. Other congregations may describe the dismissal as a harsh, unloving, and judgmental action. The reasoning goes like this: "Who do those people think they are? They should have forgiven the pastor and allowed him to continue his ministry. After all, we are all sinners. Who are we to judge?"

The question usually spins off an interpretation of Matthew 7:1, "Do not judge, or you too will be judged." This command issued by Jesus in the Sermon on the Mount deserves our careful attention. Does it forbid all judging? Must we shrug our shoulders meekly and blink twice at wrongdoing? Or was Jesus referring only to a specific kind of judging? To find the correct answer we must examine the context.

Matthew 7:1 lies in the context of Jesus' teachings about true righteousness, the righteousness that characterizes his kingdom and its citizens. True righteousness exceeds "that of the Pharisees and the teachers of the law" (5:20). It fulfills the spirit of the law, whereas the righteousness of the Pharisees and the teachers of the law was simply a facade. They pretended to be righteous by appearing to keep the Mosaic law and hundreds of man-made additions to the law. They performed religious acts to be seen and applauded (6:1). When they gave to the needy, trumpets sounded to announce their giving (v. 2). When they prayed, they chose to pray in prominent public places (v. 5). When they fasted, they "disfigure[d] their faces to show men they [were] fasting" (v. 16). Jesus called them "hypocrites" (v. 2, 5, 16).

One segment of Pharisees was known as "Bruised Pharisees," because they received bruises from walking into trees. Why did they do such a stupid, clumsy thing? Because they wanted to appear righteous! When a woman approached, they seized the opportunity to pretend they were too holy even to glance at a woman. So they would close their eyes and intentionally walk into a tree. Hence the bruises.

The Pharisees and scribes (teachers of the law) opposed Jesus and his teachings. Their false sense of righteousness contrasted sharply with the righteousness Jesus associated with the Father's kingdom and innate righteousness (v. 33).

Jesus described hypocrites as judging, that is, distinguishing or deciding by a faulty standard of righteousness. Religious hypocrites, like the scribes and Pharisees, find no fault in themselves but see miniscule faults in others. They look down their noses at others but never examine their own imperfections. Jesus asked, "Why do you look at the speck of sawdust in your brother's eye and pay no attention to the plank in your own eye? How can you say to your brother, 'Let me take the speck out of your eye,' when all the time there is a plank in your own eye?" (7:3-4). He instructed, "You hypocrite, first take the plank out of your own eye, and then you will see clearly to remove the speck from your brother's eye" (v. 5).

Luke 18:9-14 discloses a clear example of a Pharisee's

hypocritical judgment. He and a tax collector entered the temple to pray. The Pharisee took great pride in his self-righteousness. The tax collector claimed no righteousness. When he prayed, the Pharisee thanked God that he was "not like other men—robbers, evildoers, adulterers—or even like this tax collector" (v. 11). He flashed his religious credentials, reminding God that he fasted twice a week and tithed "all I get." Apparently, he had gone to the temple for praise and worship: He worshipped himself and praised himself. The tax collector had gone to the temple to confess that he was a sinner and to cast himself on God's mercy. Verse 13 reveals, "He would not even look up to heaven, but beat his breast and said, 'God, have mercy on me a sinner.'"

God, who peers through hypocrisy and examines the heart, rejected the Pharisee's "worship" but responded to the tax collector's contrition. Jesus said the tax collector "went home justified before God. For everyone who exalts himself will be humbled, and he who humbles himself will be exalted" (v. 14).

A self-appointed judge of her neighbors' children, lifestyle, and care of their property (doesn't every neighborhood have a self-appointed judge?) looked out her kitchen window and was appalled to see splotches of dirt on the laundry hanging on her next-door neighbor's clothesline. Promptly, she marched next door and read the riot act to her neighbor. But when the two women entered the backyard and examined the laundry, they couldn't find even a speck of dirt. The splotches were actually on the outside of the busybody's kitchen window.

Jesus assured his Sermon on the Mount audience that "in the same way you judge others, you will be judged" (Matt. 7:2). Some Bible commentators suggest this statement indicates that God will judge us on the basis of how we judge others. But this interpretation can't be right. If we judge others falsely, will God judge us falsely? Of course not! He is just, and his judgment is always according to truth (see Ps. 75:2; Isa. 11: 3-4; Acts 17:31; 2 Tim. 4:8; Rev. 19:11). A better interpretation seems to be that others will judge us the way we judge them. If we are critical and rush to judgment without weighing the facts, others will be critical of us.

Mr. Stovelli, a street person, received a gospel tract, read it, and believed in Christ as his Savior. The following Sunday, he entered an evangelical church known for its strong support of foreign missions. Somehow, he had obtained a Bible and carried it between the right side of his chest and upper right arm. His clothes were dirty and shabby, but he felt clean inside. As he walked to a seat, he noticed a mural above the platform. It read: "To love God and to share his love with the whole world." Mr. Stovelli noticed something else too—people were casting disapproving looks at him. No one had greeted him, and he wondered if anyone would say hello on his way out. No one did.

The congregation Mr. Stovelli encountered typifies the kind of hypocritical judging Jesus condemned. It advertised its love for the whole world but failed to love a new believer in shabby clothes. It had judged him to be unworthy of its love.

If we follow Jesus' counsel about judging, we will not pass judgment on anyone without first searching our own life for the very thing we condemn in the other person's life. If we find it, we must uproot it and discard it. To do less is to be hypocritical.

According to John 8:3-4, some scribes and Pharisees brought an adulteress to Jesus to see how he would decide her fate. They explained that she had been caught in the act of adultery and that the law of Moses commanded that she be stoned. "Now what do you say?" they asked Jesus (v. 5).

Jesus did not offer a verbal reply. Instead, he bent down and started to write on the ground with his finger. When the scribes and Pharisees kept questioning him, Jesus stood up and said, "If any one of you is without sin, let him be the first to throw a stone at her" (v. 7).

He bent down and wrote on the ground again, and as he wrote, the scribes and Pharisees walked away. Finally, only Jesus and the woman remained (v. 8-9).

"Where are they?" Jesus asked the woman. "Has no one condemned you?" (v. 10).

"No one, sir," she answered (v. 11).

"Then neither do I condemn you," Jesus told her (v. 11).

What? Did Jesus take the who-am-I-to-judge way out of a messy situation? Absolutely not! He did not overlook the woman's sin but offered her forgiveness and the opportunity to live free of her sin. "Go now and leave your life of sin," he commanded her (v. 11).

It is wrong to judge in a self-righteous, hypocritical way, but it is not wrong to judge.

The Bible instructs believers to make judgments. Soon after telling his audience, "Do not judge" (Matt. 7:1), Jesus commanded, "Watch out for false prophets" (v. 15). Obviously, he expected his audience to distinguish between truth and error. But he set the criteria for judging. He explained that false prophets can be identified by their fruit (v. 16). Whereas teachers of truth produce good fruit, teachers of error produce bad fruit (v. 18).

We would not be wrong to judge a religious teacher unworthy of financial support or personal loyalty if he leads an immoral lifestyle or swindles the elderly out of their meager savings or persuades his followers to sell their homes and give the proceeds to his "ministry." A whistle-blower would have been right to judge Jim Jones a teacher of error and try to avert the mass suicide he ordered in Jonestown, Guyana, in 1978. Nine hundred thirteen of his followers might still be alive if they had judged him and his teaching.

Who would have faulted Christians for deciding that Heaven's Gate cult leader, sixty-five-year-old Marshall Herff Applewhite, was a false teacher? Apparently, he taught his followers that the arrival of Hale-Bopp Comet in 1997 signaled their imminent removal to another world. Police found thirty-nine Heaven's Gate followers dead in a mansion in Rancho Santa Fe, California. They had ingested phenobarbital and alcohol, and then plastic bags had been placed over the heads of all but two of the cult members.

And should we not judge the error perpetrated by Jehovah's Witnesses? They deny the deity of Jesus and also claim that he did not rise bodily from the dead.

If we obey Jesus' command "Watch out for false prophets," we will cherish the truth and defend it. The apostle Jude informed his readers: "I felt I had to write and urge you to contend for the faith that was once for all entrusted to the saints. For certain men whose condemnation was written about long ago have secretly slipped in among you" (Jude v. 3-4). Now, note Jude's appropriate judging: "They are godless men, who change the grace of our God into a license for immorality and deny Jesus Christ our only Sovereign and Lord" (v. 4).

Jude's judgment was not based on self-righteousness but on the immoral lifestyle and corrupt teaching of those whom he judged. That kind of judgment is appropriate today as well.

Before Israel entered Canaan, a land inhabited by pagans and dominated by false religion, she received criteria from the Lord for judging between truth and error:

But a prophet who presumes to speak in my name anything I have not commanded him to say, or a prophet who speaks in the name of other gods, must be put to death.

You may say to yourselves, "How can we know when a message has not been spoken by the Lord?" If what a prophet proclaims in the name of the Lord does not take place or come true, that is a message the Lord has not spoken. That prophet has spoken presumptuously. Do not be afraid of him. (Deut. 18:20-22)

In Galatians, Paul chided his readers for deviating from the grace of Christ. Certain religious teachers had infiltrated the Galatian churches and brought along a message of salvation based on works. Instead of judging those teachers as false, the Galatians had accepted them. Paul insisted that there is only one gospel, the gospel of grace that he had preached to them. He implored the Galatians to distinguish between truth and error and reject both the error and the teachers of error. He wrote in 1:8-9: "But even if we or an angel from heaven should preach a gospel other than the one we preached to you, let him be eternally condemned! As we have already said, so now I say again: If anybody is preaching to you a gospel other than what you accepted, let him be eternally condemned!"

Two cultured and attractive young women became temporary residents of a town where I was a pastor. They rented a studio, opened a charm school, and offered high school girls free instruction. However, the charm school was simply a means to an end. The two young women were cult missionaries. Once the high schoolers were a captive audience, they introduced their religious teachings.

A family arranged a meeting in its home between the charming missionaries and me, so we could discuss our beliefs. The meeting became a series of meetings in which I used Scripture to answer the missionaries' avowed beliefs. Although the discussions ended without my persuading the young women to accept biblical beliefs, the family members indicated they had learned the value of using the Bible to judge religious teachings.

The Bible is, after all, the standard of distinguishing truth and error. Jesus declared, 'Your word is truth" (John 17:17). Since the Bible is truth, any teaching that contradicts it or adds to it is error. Therefore, we can make valid judgments about unbiblical religious teachings. Isaiah 8:20 states, "To the law and to the testimony! If they speak not according to this word, they have no light of dawn."

In his old age, the apostle John, who heard Jesus' Sermon on the Mount, summoned believers to make judgments about truth and error. In 1 John 4:1, He challenged: "Dear friends, do not believe every spirit, but test the spirits to see whether they are from God, because many false prophets have gone out into the world." On a similar note, Paul charged the Thessalonian believers to "test everything" (1 Thess. 5:21). Writing to the Corinthians, he warned against false prophets and described Satan as one who "masquerades as an angel of light" (2 Cor. 11:14). Obviously, someone who appears at a Christian's doorstep as a well-mannered, well-groomed religious person may actually be a messenger of Satan. Only sound judgment based on Scripture will safeguard the resident's faith.

In another Scripture, Paul warned against false teachers. "Watch out for those dogs, those men who do evil, those mutilators of the flesh," he advised the Christians at Philippi (Phil. 3:2), obviously referring to the Judaizers.

But not only does the Bible teach us to make judgments about false teachers and errant doctrines, but it also holds us responsible to judge immorality. In 1 Corinthians 5, Paul grieved that the church at Corinth had allowed one of its members to carry on an affair with his stepmother without being confronted (v. 1-2). He ordered the church to discipline the offender (v. 3-5) and reminded its members that he had written in a previous letter that they should not "associate with sexually immoral people" (v. 9), and was writing now to tell them to "not associate with anyone who calls himself a brother but is sexually immoral or greedy, an idolater or a slanderer, a drunkard or a swindler. With such a man do not even eat" (v. 11). "Are you not to judge those inside [the church]?" he asked (v. 12).

What could be clearer? God holds congregations accountable to judge immorality. Just as a police department must conduct an occasional internal investigation to discipline and even weed out bad cops, so a congregation must exercise discipline for the sake of purity and public testimony. If it fails to judge immorality, a congregation loses God's blessing and credibility in the community. And contrary to the belief that a church that judges immorality will surely scare people off, it may actually lose an opportunity to grow dramatically.

The early church at Jerusalem judged sin in its midst. Case in point: the disciplining of Ananias and Sapphira, who had conspired to lie to the Holy Spirit. On behalf of the church, Peter confronted this couple individually and confronted their sin. The result? Ananias fell down dead, and then Sapphira fell down dead (Acts 5:1-10). Great fear—the fear of God—seized the whole church, but "more and more men and women believed in the Lord and were added to their number" (v. 14).

Just as fire purifies gold, so the fire of self-judgment purifies a congregation. The judgment must be exercised in love and with a desire to restore offenders but it must be as thorough as fire. It must not pass over some sinning church members because they give well or are related to a church officer. It must burn the dross wherever it finds it. If a congregation refuses to take disciplinary action while asking, "Who are we to judge?" its love for Christ and His Word will become as a cold as ice. Who would want to worship in a freezer?

Late one night, a small church was engulfed in flames, and a crowd had gathered to witness the tragedy. Among those who had gathered were a deacon and an agnostic.

"Wally," the deacon called to the agnostic, "I never expected to see you at church!"

"Well," said Wally, "this is the first time I've seen the church on fire."

How many of our fellow citizens might start attending church if they see a holy fire blazing in our hearts? How many will stay away if we fail to judge error and sin?

11

JESUS MIGHT JUST SAY, "I NEVER KNEW YOU!"

A COUPLE OF YEARS AGO, A DISTANT FEMALE RELATIVE IN Canada contacted me for information about my brothers, my children, my grandchildren, my deceased parents, and me. I had never met her but appreciated her interest in compiling a family history of the Dyets. My parents had emigrated from Scotland to Canada twice. My father moved to Hamilton, Ontario, Canada, around 1927, and then summoned my mother to follow him to Canada and get married. (I can't pinpoint the years because my parents didn't tell me much, if anything, about that period of their lives.) Mom took Dad up on the proposal. They married in Hamilton, Ontario, and in 1930, my brother Bill was born there. A couple of years later, Mom and Dad returned to Scotland, where I was born in 1935. Apparently, the call of Canada came rushing over the Atlantic again, because my parents returned to Canada in 1939, this time with my older brother and me in tow. They settled in Ottawa, where my brother Bruce was born in 1940.

Because I was so young when I left Scotland, I did

not get to know my relatives there. However, Dad had relatives in Ottawa, whom I had a chance to know for a short while, but one year later my parents moved almost four hundred miles from Ottawa to St. Catharines. So I grew up knowing little about any Dyets other than my parents and two brothers.

I always regretted this fact, so I was happy to learn that a distant relative had taken on the project of identifying members of the Dyet family tree. However, the project involved only those who had settled and raised families in Canada and the United States. I still have no knowledge of relatives living among the highland heather or in lowland towns. Not knowing them saddens me, but I can live without knowing them.

What is not only sad but also tragic is the fact that so many people around the world do not know Jesus Christ. They may know something about him from singing Christmas carols or hearing a Christian broadcast or from some other experience, but they do not know him. If they die without knowing him, they will have lost the opportunity to enjoy a beautiful life on earth and an even better one in heaven.

Will Jesus say to every unbeliever, "I never knew you"? Might he say that to you? For the answer, we need to examine the context in which he spoke those fateful words. It is Matthew 7:15-23, near the end of Jesus' Sermon on the Mount. In his sermon, Jesus exposed the hypocrisy of Israel's religious leaders. They put on an elaborate show of religious fervor and ceremonial observance but their hearts were not right with God. Instead of repenting and trusting in him for righteousness, they felt no need to repent or rely on anything but their self-proclaimed religious credentials. Jesus had warned his audience not to "do your 'acts of righteousness' before men, to be seen of by them" (Matt. 6:1).

He cited hypocritical giving, praying, and fasting as the kinds of worthless displays of religion that mark false religious leaders. Hypocrites in Jesus' day enjoyed having trumpets announce their giving to the needy. They basked in the public attention (v. 2). They also chose to pray on busy street corners because they wanted to be seen by as many people as possible (v. 5). When they fasted, they disfigured their faces.

God cannot tolerate hypocrisy. In his prayer of confession, King David rightly observed, "Surely you desire truth in the inner parts" (Ps. 51:6). Jesus identified false prophets as ferocious wolves wearing sheep's clothing (Matt. 7:15). He also compared them to bad trees bearing bad fruit and deserving to be "cut down and thrown into the fire" (v. 19).

In the end-time, there will come the defining moment of God's judgment, and Jesus will encounter many "applicants" for kingdom citizenship. They will cite reasons they believe qualify them for citizenship. They will not point to what Jesus did for them by dying on the cross but to what they felt they had done for Jesus. They will say, "Lord, Lord, did we not prophesy in your name, and in your name drive out demons and perform many miracles?" (v. 22).

Years ago I worked in a small building while a bigger building was under construction. The Human Resources Department occupied three cubicles near mine. One was directly across from my cubicle; the other two were on my left and right. During a vigorous employee-hiring campaign, the HR cubicles were bustling with interviews. A parade of job applicants filed in and out, and I could not help hearing them describe the skills they proposed to contribute for the good of the company. Many left no self-compliment at the entrance. They were strong leaders, creative, team players, resourceful, cooperative, diligent, productive, loyal, can-do men and women whose work would far exceed expectations. They had instituted cost-saving programs at their previous workplace. They had accomplished incredible tasks and left the competition in the dust. Each applicant firmly believed the company would benefit enormously if it hired him or her. Upon hearing all the braggadocio, I wondered why the applicants did not run for the presidency of the United States.

When Jesus "interviews" applicants for his kingdom, he will encounter many applicants like those I overheard.

They will boast about their personal greatness and outstanding "tract" record but the boasting will not fool Jesus. He will turn them down with a resolute "I never knew you. Away from me, you evildoers!" (Matt. 7:23).

A couple of plausible explanations may help us understand the claims about prophesying, casting out demons, and performing many miracles—all in Jesus' name (v. 22).

First, these supernatural wonders may be attributed to satanic power. The Bible's prophesies assure us the end-times will introduce numerous false prophets and deceivers who will try to pass themselves off as Israel's Messiah. Jesus predicted: "At that time if anyone says to you, 'Look, here is the Christ!' or, 'There he is!' do not believe it. For false Christs and false prophets will appear and perform great signs and miracles to deceive even the elect—if that were possible" (Matt. 24:23-24). We know the false prophet described in Revelation 13 will cast himself in a messianic role by performing amazing feats by satanic power. Revelation 13:13 reports, "And he performed great and miraculous signs, even causing fire to come down from heaven to earth in full view of men." Verse 15 says, "He was given power to give breath to the image of the first beast, so that it could speak." All the world loves a show and Satan will empower end-time deceivers to put on a really big show to attract followers, just as he did with Pharaoh's wicked magicians (Ex. 7:10-13).

Second, the claims about prophesying, casting out demons, and performing miracles may be simply empty claims. The history of religion includes charlatans who duped their followers by making grandiose, but unfounded, claims of religious power. Of course, religious fakes cannot fool Jesus. He knows the human heart and judges as "the faithful and true witness" (Rev. 3:14).

Matthew 25:1-12 offers further insight into the timing of Jesus' words, "I never knew you." He commented in this passage that "at that time [the time of his return to earth; see Matt. 24:44] the kingdom of heaven will be like ten virgins who took their lamps and went out to meet the bridegroom" (25:1). According to Jesus' parable of the ten virgins, five were foolish and five were wise. When the ten virgins went to meet the bridegroom, the five foolish ones did not take any extra oil for their lamps, whereas the five wise ones did (v. 3-4).

All ten grew tired as they waited for the bridegroom to arrive for the wedding banquet. Overcome by drowsiness, they fell asleep (v. 5). At midnight, shouts jolted them from sleep. People were yelling, "Here's the bridegroom! Come out to meet him!" (v. 6).

The ten virgins trimmed their lamps but only the five wise ones had enough oil to fire up their lamps. The others had to go searching for oil they could purchase. And while they searched, the bridegroom arrived and, accompanied by the five wise virgins, entered the banquet hall. Once they had entered, the entry door closed (v. 7-10).

Later, the five foolish virgins returned and called, "Sir! Sir! ... Open the door for us!" (v. 11).

"I tell you the truth," the bridegroom responded, "I don't know you" (v. 12).

Those who heard Jesus' parable would have understood the wedding customs of the day. Traditionally, a wedding took place in the bride's house, after which the bridegroom and bride would lead a procession to the bridegroom's house, where a marriage supper would take place. Jesus, the Bridegroom, will come in the air someday for his bride, the church. Like the five wise virgins, she will be seated at the wedding banquet, the marriage supper of the Lamb, but the unbelieving pretenders, like the five foolish virgins, are shut out.

The biblical writers Matthew, Luke, and John allude to this celebration:

I [Jesus] say to you that many will come from the east and the west, and will take their places at the feast with Abraham, Isaac and Jacob in the kingdom of heaven.

(Matt. 8:11)

He will reply, "I don't know you or where you come from. Away from me, all of you evildoers!" There will be weeping there, and gnashing of teeth, when you see

Abraham, Isaac and Jacob and all the prophets in the kingdom of God, but you yourselves thrown out.

People will come from east and west and north and south, and will take their places at the feast in the kingdom of God. (Luke 13:27-29)

Then I heard what sounded like a great multitude, like the roar of rushing waters and like loud peals of thunder, shouting: "Hallelujah! For our Lord God Almighty reigns.

Let us rejoice and be glad and give him glory! For the wedding of the Lamb has come, and his bride has made herself ready. Fine linen, bright and clean, was given her to wear."

(Fine linen stands for the righteous acts of the saints.) Then the angel said to me, "Write: 'Blessed are those who are invited to the wedding supper of the Lamb!'" And he added, "These are the true words of God." (Rev. 19:6-9)

Clearly, at his return to establish his earthly kingdom, Jesus will make a decisive distinction between those who truly know him and those who merely profess to know him. Those who know him are "sheep" who entered the fold through Jesus, the one and only gate (John 10:7, 9). Jesus declared, "I am the good shepherd; I know my sheep and my sheep know me" (v. 14).

We can conclude from passages related to Matthew 7:21-23 that Jesus will not allow into his kingdom those who merely pretend to be his followers. He "will tell them plainly, 'I never knew you. Away from me, you evildoers!'" (v. 23).

Based on what Jesus taught following this statement of rejection, we must raise a warning flag for all who know Jesus' teachings but not Jesus. He related a story of two builders and compared them to two different kinds of hearers of His words. One builder was wise. He built his house on "the rock" (v. 24). When rains pummeled his house and floods swept over it and wind struck it violently, it stood secure on its firm foundation. Jesus said everyone who hears His words and "puts them into practice" is like this wise builder (v. 24). Another builder built his house on sand (v. 26). Pelting rain, rising floods, and relentless wind demolished this builder's house (v. 27). Jesus compared everyone who hears His words but fails to put them into practice to this foolish builder (v. 26).

Jesus must have been addressing the scribes and Pharisees directly but also indirectly all who hear His words and ignore them. The warning applies today to all who hear Jesus' words but ignore or reject them. Someday, everything they have built, whether it be a materialistic life, a life of pleasure, a life of popularity or fame, or one of academic pursuit, will come crashing down. Even a life of empty profession of faith—a hypocritical life— will crash under the weight of Jesus' incontrovertible judgment.

According to a humorous, but applicable, anecdote, several teenage pranksters decided to play a practical joke on a country church known for its emotionally charged worship. They outfitted one of their buddies in a devil's costume: red suit, black tail, pointed ears, horns, and a pitchfork. Silently, they crept up to the church and eavesdropped on the worship.

The worship grew louder and louder as the congregation shook, clapped, and shouted. When the worship reached a fever pitch, the pranksters opened the church's front door and shoved the devil into the building.

Down the center aisle slinked the devil, extending his pitchfork menacingly. Swoosh went the churchgoers as they rushed out the exit doors and bolted through the windows. Everybody catapulted from the church. Well, everybody but one very portly deacon in his mid-sixties. Just as he was about to enter the aisle, his belly got wedged between two pews.

Seeing the devil with pitchfork pointed at him, the deacon screamed, 'Just a minute, Mr. Devil. Stop right where you are. I want you to know I have been a member of this church for forty-two years but I've been on your side the whole time."

Not humorous at all is the fact that many churchgoers today resemble the deacon. For years they have attended church regularly, listened to Jesus' words, participated in the weekly offering, taken Communion, and perhaps taught Sunday school or served on the church board or sung in the choir; but they have been on the Devil's side the whole time. They have never trusted in Jesus as their Savior. If they die without knowing Jesus, they will hear Jesus say to them in effect, "Depart from me. I never knew you."

In the final analysis, religious works and good deeds cannot save even one person. The apostle Paul informed the Ephesians that God saves by grace through faith and added that salvation is "the gift of God—not by works, so that no one can boast" (Eph. 2:8-9).

Named after Israel's first king, Saul, Paul (formerly Saul of Tarsus) knew firsthand the truth he expressed in writing. Before being saved by grace through faith in

Jesus Christ, Paul had buried himself in religion and taken great personal pride in his religious credentials (Phil. 3:4—6). In accordance with Mosaic law, he had been circumcised when he was eight days old. He was an Israelite (a member of God's chosen race). He belonged to the tribe of Benjamin, famous for its fighting ability and loyalty to King David. Unlike Jews who observed Gentile customs and spoke a Gentile language, Paul was a Hebrew of the Hebrews (v. 5). He had been a Pharisee, fully devoted to the law. No one's zeal for the Jewish religion had exceeded his. He had demonstrated white-hot zeal by persecuting the church. Further, he had faultlessly adhered to legalistic religion.

But Paul had learned on the Damascus road that all his religious credentials and deeds failed to make him righteous in God's sight. He discarded all his religious baggage, believed in Christ for salvation, and testified, "I consider everything a loss compared to the surpassing greatness of knowing Christ Jesus my Lord" (v. 8).

Personal knowledge of Christ as Savior assured Paul that Jesus would never say to him, "Depart from me." To the contrary, Paul testified in 2 Timothy 1:12: "I know whom I have believed and am convinced that he is able to guard what I have entrusted to him for that day."

I have had the privilege of preaching not only in churches but also in rescue missions and prisons. Often, the response to the gospel has been better among convicts and derelicts than among churchgoers. The reason is simple. Convicts and derelicts readily admit their shortcomings and need of salvation, whereas few unbelieving churchgoers admit their guilt and need. Churchgoing hypocrites try to hide their true condition behind a facade of religiosity. But they cannot hide from God.

Near the end of Revelation, the last book of the Bible, the final drama of history unfolds. God pulls the curtain back to give us a glimpse of the drama. The apostle John narrates the scene. He identifies "a great white throne and him who was seated on it. Earth and sky fled from his presence, and there was no place for them" (20:11).

This is the final judgment of all unbelievers, including hypocrites who merely pretended to know Jesus. These arraigned lost souls try to flee from the judgment. They learn, however, as Jonah did a long time ago, that you can run from God but you cannot hide. They find no hiding place and must appear before the righteous Judge, who judges them according to their works (v. 12).

The open record of their works shows they are unfit for heaven. Then, all who stand before the throne of judgment are sentenced to the lake of fire because their names do not appear in the Book of Life (v. 15).

Could the Lord say to you someday, "Depart from me. I never knew you"? You alone can answer this question. If you know him as your Savior, you will hear him welcome you to heaven. If you pass from this life without knowing him as your Savior, he will banish you from his presence forever.

The apostle John explained the entire issue of eternal life in a simple formula: "He who has the Son has life; he who does not have the Son of God does not have life" (1 John 5:12).

12

THE BODY OF CHRIST WORSHIPS HERE EVERY SUNDAY

PASTOR MIKE GREETED THE CONGREGATION WARMLY. "We are so glad you chose to worship at Good News Church. We welcome you and pray that the worship will lift you spiritually and emotionally and be the highlight of your week. If you are visiting for the first time, please plan on making today the beginning of a long and happy relationship with Good News Church. The body of Christ worships here every Sunday morning at ten o'clock, and we hope to see you often."

We cannot fault Pastor Mike's sincerity and friendliness, but was he correct to say, "The body of Christ worships here every Sunday"? Just what is "the body of Christ"?

The term is used two ways in the New Testament. The first and more obvious meaning is the physical body of our Lord. The apostle Paul wrote in Romans 7:4, "So, my brothers, you also died to the law through the body of Christ, that you might belong to another, to him who was raised from the dead, in order that we might bear fruit to God." Paul looked back to the crucifixion and understood what Jesus accomplished for believers by sacrificing his body to free us from the penalty of sin imposed by the law. The apostle Peter affirmed this truth in 1 Peter 2:24: "He [Jesus] himself bore our sins in his body on the tree, so that we might die to sins and live for righteousness; by his wounds you have been healed."

The second use of the term, the body of Christ, applies to the church, the organism composed of all Christians. Christ is the head of the church; he dwells in the church and fills it. The Ephesian letter presents significant truths about the church, the body of Christ. According to Ephesians 1:22-23, God appointed Christ as the church's head, the church is Christ's body, and he fills it. Ephesians 2:11-22 declares that saved Jews and saved Gentiles share a union with Christ and a spiritual unity in the church. Ephesians 3:21 identifies the purpose of the church, the body of Christ. It is to bring glory to Christ. Ephesians 4:4 proclaims that the church is one body, and subsequent verses teach that Christ has gifted individuals to edify (build) the body, the church, so that she may achieve "unity in the faith and in the knowledge of the Son of God and become mature, attaining to the whole measure of the fullness of Christ" (v. 13). Ephesians 5:25-27 focuses on the church as the object of Christ's love. He died for the church "to make her holy" and to "present her to himself as a radiant church, without stain or wrinkle or any other blemish, but holy and blameless."

In 1 Corinthians 12:12-13, Paul explained how believers, regardless of their diversity, become members of the body of Christ. He wrote: "The body is a unit, though it is made up of many parts; and though all its parts are many, they form one body. So it is with Christ. For we were all baptized by one Spirit into one body—whether Jews or Greeks, slave or free—and we were all given the one Spirit to drink."

Galatians 3:27-28 affirms this truth. These verses teach: "For all of you who were baptized into Christ have clothed yourselves with Christ. There is neither Jew nor Greek, slave nor free, male nor female, for you are all one in Christ Jesus."

When a person believes in Jesus as Savior, the Holy Spirit baptizes him or her into Christ. At that moment, that person becomes a member of the church, the body of Christ. It is appropriate, however, to join a local church and to fellowship with other believers.

When the Holy Spirit descended at Pentecost and united the believers into the spiritual organism called the body of Christ, those who believed joined together as a local body of believers at Jerusalem. They functioned as a local church, devoting themselves "to the apostles' teaching and to the fellowship, to the breaking of bread and to prayer" (Acts 2:42).

No doubt, the vast majority of Christians who refer to the local church as the body of Christ do so as a slip of the tongue. They do not actually believe that their church is the body of Christ. However, others do honestly believe this. This belief is a tenet of their theology. They reject the belief that the body of Christ is a spiritual organism usually called "the universal church" or "the invisible church." They interpret 1 Corinthians 12:13—"baptized by one Spirit into one body"—like this: "baptized": immersed in water "by one Spirit": in one spirit (lowercase), suggesting agreement, unity "into one body": membership in the local church Those who reject the concept of the universal church generally charge that the doctrine is a Scofieldian error. Here's a sample of what Dr. C. I. Scofield wrote concerning the nature of the church:

The Church, composed of the whole number of regenerate persons from Pentecost to the first resurrection (1 Cor.15:52), united together and to Christ by the baptism of the Holy Spirit (1 Cor. 12:12, 13). Is the body of Christ of which He is the Head (Eph. 1:22, 23). As such, it is a holy temple for the habitation of Cod through the Spirit (Eph.2:21, 22); is 'one flesh' with Christ (Eph. 5:30, 31); and espoused to Him as a chaste virgin to one husband (2 Cor.11:2-4); and will be translated to heaven at the return of the Lord to the air (1 Thess. 4:13-17)

In all fairness to those who believe the local church is the body of Christ, we ought to examine a Scripture verse that seems to support their view. Addressing the members of the Corinthian church, Paul stated: "Now you are the body of Christ, and each one of you is a part of it" (1 Cor. 12:27). Doesn't this verse seem to suggest that the church at Corinth was the body of Christ?

It does until we read it in the Greek New Testament and find that the word "the" does not appear in the verse. The Greek indicates: "Now you are Christ's body and members each in his part." Although this translation is similar to what many English Bibles state, we must understand that things may be similar without being the same. The absence of the definite article "the" does not point to the church at Corinth as a body of Christ because there is only one body of Christ, not many. The quality of the noun, "body," is stressed by the absence of the definite article. The Corinthian believers shared in the character or essence of Christ's body, the church.

A similar Greek construction occurs in John 1:1. The definite article the does not precede "God" in the statement "and the Word was God." Jehovah's Witnesses wrongly conclude that the translation should be "and the Word was a god." But, as we have seen, the absence of the definite article emphasizes the quality of the noun. Therefore the "Word," meaning Jesus, was God in his essential nature.

Returning to the status of the Corinthian believers, we recognize they were not the members of Christ's body but members each in his part. They could claim membership but they could not claim exclusive membership. Other believers in many parts of the Roman world were also members of Christ's body, the church. Indeed, all believers, whether dead or alive, from Pentecost until Christ's return, are members of the church.

To believe that every local church is the body of Christ is to believe in a plurality of bodies of Christ. To believe that only our own local church is the body of Christ is to deny the equal spiritual standing that all believers have in Christ. We are like the congregation that called themselves the Jesus only people and hung a sign outside their church building that read JESUS ONLY. One day, a severe windstorm rattled the church building and blew away the sign's first three letters, leaving US ONLY.

But further issues confront the belief that the local church is the body of Christ.

JESUS SAID HE WOULD BUILD HIS CHURCH

"And I tell you that you are Peter, and on this rock I will build my church" (Matt. 16:18). If there is no universal church body, which local church did Jesus promise to build?

JESUS SAID, "THE GATES OF HADES WILL NOT OVER-COME [HIS CHURCH]" (MATT. 16:18)

Sadly, more than one local church has fallen to the attacks of Satan. Churches that used to boldly and clearly proclaim the gospel are vacant, padlocked, and in disrepair. If the local church were exclusively Christ's church, how would we explain Jesus' promise of victory over the gates of hades?

His promise must apply to the universal church, the organism called his body. Satan has been attacking this church from its inception until the present. He has hurled malicious charges against the church, unleashed vicious enemies against her, pitted destructive philosophies against her, employed godless political systems to censure or silence her, and tripped up her leaders but the church keeps marching onward.

Confidence in the indestructibility of Jesus' church led John Newton to write the following stanza of "Glorious Things of Thee Are Spoken":

Glorious things of thee are spoken, Zion, city of our God;

He whose word cannot be broken, Formed thee for His own abode.

On the Rock of Ages founded, What can shake thy sure repose?

With salvation's walls surrounded, Thou mayest smile at all thy foes.

EPHESIANS 4:4 AFFIRMS THERE IS "ONE BODY"

There is one Spirit, one hope, one Lord, one faith, one baptism, and one God and Father. If the local church were the body of Christ, which local church would that be? If every local church were the body of Christ, there would be thousands of bodies of Christ. The only reasonable conclusion is to recognize the body of Christ as an organism composed of all believers from Pentecost to the return of Christ.

First Corinthians 12:12 also refers to Christ's body, the church, calling it "a unit." The unit "is made up of many parts and though all its parts are many, they form one body." Succeeding verses emphasize the giftedness of all who belong to the body. Like the smooth-working parts of the human body, the gifted parts of Christ's body, the church, contribute to the church's spiritual health and effectiveness.

JESUS NOT ONLY FOUNDED HIS CHURCH BUT ALSO

DIRECTS AND FILLS HIS CHURCH

Ephesians 1:22-23 declares that Jesus Christ is "head over everything for the church, which is his body, the fullness of him who fills everything in every way." To limit Jesus' domain to the local church is to diminish his headship. His lordship and fullness must surely extend beyond the local church.

JESUS GAVE HIMSELF AT CALVARY FOR THE CHURCH

Ephesians 5:25 states, "Christ loved the church and gave himself up for her." Further, verses 29 and 30 allude to the church as Christ's body: "After all, no one ever hated his own body, but he feeds and cares for it, just as Christ does the church—for we are members of his body." If the local church were the body of Christ, which local church did he love and die for? Which local church does he feed and care for? Where would such restricted love, redemption, feeding, and caring leave the rest of us?

Although I disagree with those who identify the local church or the sum of local churches as the body of Christ, I applaud their esteem for the local church. Every Christian ought to identify with a local church and employ his or her gifts to edify other believers and to assist in making disciples. Clearly, Jesus authorized his followers to proclaim the gospel worldwide, to disciple all nations, to organize local churches, and to teach believers to obey him. Matthew 28:18-20 is a key passage in this regard.

Then Jesus came to them [the disciples] and said, "All authority in heaven and on earth has been given to me. Therefore go and make disciples of all nations, baptizing them in the name of the Father and of the Son and of the Holy Spirit, and teaching them to obey everything I have commanded you. And surely I am with you always, to the very end of the age."

Every church, indeed, every Christian, ought to take this challenge to heart. The Greek word for "church" is ekklesia, meaning called-out ones but our Lord did not call us out of the world to sit on the sidelines and watch everyone else stumble blindly until they fall into eternal perdition. He called us out of the world's evil pattern of thinking and behaving but he commissioned us to take the message of life into the world. In his High Priestly prayer, Jesus talked with his Father in heaven about the role of his called-out ones. Lie said: "My prayer is not that you take them out of the world but that you protect them from the evil one. They are not of the world, even as I am not of it. . . . As you sent me into the world, I have sent them into the world" (John 17:15-18). Jesus does not want us to be isolated from the world but he does want us to be insulated from its evil.

Members of Christ's body, the church, serve as ambassadors for Christ. God has placed us in strategic places around the world so that we might help to establish peaceful relations between him and those who are estranged from him. As the apostle Paul shared with the Corinthians, God "gave us the ministry of reconciliation" (2 Cor. 5:18).

How well we represent our Lord as his ambassadors depends on a number of factors. (1) Does our lifestyle reflect his righteousness? (2) Do we display the fruit of the Spirit ("love, joy, peace, patience, kindness, goodness, faithfulness, gentleness and self-control" [Gal. 5:22-23])? (3) Does the way we live give unbelievers a solid reason to want to become like us by believing in Christ? (4) Do we present a solid front to unbelievers, or do they see us as a divided, bickering segment of society? How do church splits and denominational rivalries affect our message of Christ's love and our claims that Christians are one in the bonds of love?

A story about three neighboring churches in a small town may help us rethink the oneness we profess. On a hot July Sunday, all three churches had opened their windows so worshippers could catch an occasional cool breeze. Unchurched people seated on park benches nearby could hear the hymn singing. The first congregation sang "Will There Be Any Stars in My Crown?" The second congregation sang "No, Not One." The third lifted their voices and sang lustily "Oh, That Will Be Glory for Me."

Churches should not discard their doctrinal distinctiveness for the sake of feigned unity, but true believers should show the world that they love one another. Jesus said, "By this all men will know that you are my disciples, if you love one another" (John 13:35). A Pentecostal employee and a Baptist employee working for the same company will have different opinions about certain doctrines but they can demonstrate to their unbelieving associates that they share a love for Christ and for each other. Congregations of various denominations can reach out lovingly to a community by contributing their time and resources to evangelistic efforts. Men and women who love the Lord can launch a neighborhood Bible study and agree to disagree agreeably about peripheral doctrines while majoring on sharing the good news.

In 1925, the possibility of an epidemic of diphtheria confronted the people of Nome, Alaska. In January of that year, Dr. Curtis Welch discovered seven cases of diphtheria in the area, but the town had no diphtheria antitoxin. The good doctor immediately organized a volunteer effort to fetch 300,000 units of antitoxin from Nenana to Nome by dogsled relay teams. The Nome Nugget of January 31, 1925, reported twenty-two cases and five deaths. The situation was looking very grim. However, on February 2, 1925, Gunnar Kaasen arrived with the antitoxin, and his lead dog, Balto, became famous.

The relay dog mushers, who were trappers and prospectors, had traversed 658 miles in snow, strong winds, and subzero temperatures to rush the life-saving serum to Nome. The quarantine that had been imposed on Nome on January 21 was lifted on February 21.

The church today would do well to rush the lifesaving message of divine grace to the many thousands who face eternal death. In these perilous times, we should be far more concerned about rescuing the perishing than resting in the pews.

13

LORD, DON'T TAKE YOUR HOLY SPIRIT FROM ME!

I WAS THE GUEST SPEAKER AT A CHURCH KNOWN FOR ITS commitment to sound doctrine and I was happy to learn that its children's choir was scheduled to sing before I preached.

Upon hearing the children sing, I understood why the church was proud of the kids. They sang enthusiastically and their voices blended smoothly. Their words were distinct, and their smiles captivated the congregation. But what they sang contradicted the church's doctrinal position and sent the wrong message not only to the congregation but also to the children themselves. The words "Cast me not away from thy presence; and take not thy Holy Spirit from me" were completely out of tune with New Testament teaching.

But aren't those words scriptural? What could possibly be wrong with singing scriptural words?

King David framed those words in his well-known prayer of confession. Psalm 51 includes the whole prayer and verse 11 gives the words the children's choir sang so well but so inappropriately.

David had committed adultery with Bathsheba, and the guilt blighted his soul, stabbed his conscience, troubled his mind, and drained his energy. He feared that God might abandon him if he failed to repent and confess his sin. Perhaps he recalled that the Spirit of the Lord had departed from his predecessor, King Saul. First Samuel 16:14 states: "Now the Spirit of the Lord had departed from Saul, and an evil spirit from the Lord tormented him."

Unlike Saul, David presented a broken and contrite heart to the Lord, confronted the ugliness of his sin, acknowledged his guilt, and cried out for renewed fellowship with the Lord. He believed that God would not despise a broken and contrite heart (Ps. 51:17), and he was right. We know from Psalm 32 that God did not abandon David, nor did he withdraw his Spirit from him. Joyfully, David reported: "I acknowledged my sin to you and did not cover up my iniquity. I said, 'I will confess my transgressions to the Lord'—and you forgave the guilt of my sin" (v. 5).

Occasionally, in Old Testament times, the Holy Spirit came upon individuals and later left them, although he did dwell in a few. At Pentecost, he came upon all who believed in Jesus and since then has dwelled in every believer. In the Old Testament, the Holy Spirit filled select individuals and equipped them for specific tasks. Since Pentecost, the Holy Spirit has been giving spiritual gifts to individual believers instead of to only a select group of believers.

In Exodus 31:2-5 the Lord informed Moses, "See, I have chosen Bezalel, son of Uri, the son of Hur, of the tribe of Judah, and I have filled him with the Spirit of God, with skill, ability and knowledge in all kinds of crafts—to make artistic designs for work in gold, silver and bronze, to cut and set stones, to work in wood, and to engage in all kinds of craftsmanship." Thus filled and equipped by the Spirit, Bezalel would superintend the constructing and furnishing of the tabernacle.

Since Pentecost, the Lord has been building a tabernacle or temple of believers. We call it the church. The apostle Paul asked the Corinthian believers, "Don't you know that you yourselves are God's temple and that God's Spirit lives in you?" (1 Cor. 3:16). In 1 Peter 2:5, the apostle Peter wrote: "You also, like living stones, are being built into a spiritual house." However, all believers serve a "Bezalel" role, because the Spirit has gifted all of us for the task of building God's spiritual house (see Rom. 12:3-8 and Eph. 4:7-13).

Here are a few Old Testament reports of the Spirit's coming upon individuals: Judges 6:34 reports that "the Spirit of the Lord came upon Gideon." Judges 14:6 says, "The Spirit ... came upon [Samson] in power." First Samuel 10:10 announces, "The Spirit of God came upon him [Saul] in power." First Samuel 16:13 reports that "the Spirit of the Lord came upon David in power." First Chronicles 12:18 declares: "Then the Spirit came upon Amasai, chief of the Thirty." And 2 Chronicles 24:20 says: "Then the Spirit of God came upon Zechariah son of Jehoiada the priest."

With the formation of the church on the day of Pentecost, there came an end to the phenomenon of the Holy Spirit's coming upon select individuals. However, the book of Acts records several events in which the Spirit came upon groups.

First, he came upon all the believers who had gathered together in Jerusalem in anticipation of the Spirit's arrival (1:4-5). According to Acts 2, the Spirit descended on these believers, filled them, and endowed them with the ability to declare God's wonders in languages they had never learned. Peter, the spokesman for the believers, explained to the Jews gathered for the Feast of Pentecost that God had poured out his Spirit in fulfillment of prophecy.

Later, a group of Samaritan believers received the Holy Spirit when the apostles Peter and John—both Jews—prayed for them and placed their hands on them (Acts 8:14-17). This event signified that God had accepted the Samaritan believers into the church just as he had accepted Jewish believers.

Acts 10:44-47 records another occasion when a group of believers received the Spirit. It happened in the home of Cornelius, a Gentile. The Spirit came upon all who heard Peter's message about forgiveness through faith in Jesus. All the recipients of the Spirit were Gentiles, and the event convinced Peter that God had accepted Gentiles into the church.

We read in Acts 19:1-7 about another instance of the Spirit's coming upon a group. In this case, the recipients of the Spirit were Jewish disciples of John the Baptist. As soon as they learned from Paul that Jesus was the Messiah John had predicted, they believed in Jesus and were baptized. When Paul then placed his hands on them, they received the Spirit, spoke in tongues, and prophesied. These two phenomena validated Paul's message and linked this Jewish group to the church founded at Pentecost.

Now that God had given evidence that Samaritan and Gentile believers were united together in one body, the church, there would be no further descending of the Spirit on believers.

Jesus had foretold a brand-new relationship between the Spirit and every believer. The Spirit, he said in John 14:15-17, would not only be with believers forever but also in them.

The promised Spirit would be "another Counselor," Jesus assured his own. "Another" and "Counselor" are significant words. Two words in the Greek New Testament are translated "another." Alios (another) means another of the same kind. Heteros (another) means another of a different kind. Perhaps we can distinguish the meanings by thinking about a backyard cookout. Joe prefers rib-eye steak, whereas Jerry prefers T-bone, but both choices are the same in the sense that they are the same kind of meat—steak. Jim, however, prefers hot dogs. Although hot dogs are another (heteros) meat, they are not another {alios) of the same kind as rib eye and T-bone.

Jesus said the coming Holy Spirit would be the same kind {alios) of Counselor as he had been. The disciples should not expect anything different!

The Greek word for "Counselor" combines two words, one meaning "alongside" and the other meaning "called." So the Holy Spirit would be called alongside believers just as Jesus had been alongside them. He would be their helper, their teacher, their strength, their comfort.

It is unthinkable that Jesus would have abandoned his disciples when they disappointed him. He did not forsake them when they experienced lapses of faith or showed disloyalty or lost their temper or tried to keep others from him or exhibited shameless self-ambition or rebuke him because he said he would suffer and die. Why, then, would anyone think the Holy Spirit might leave a believer? After all, the Holy Spirit is another Counselor of the same kind as Jesus.

As the Counselor, the Holy Spirit has been called alongside every believer. He comforts us in our sorrow, teaches us God's will, challenges us to obey God's will, strengthens and equips us to do God's will, convicts us when we violate God's will. When we are unfaithful, he is still faithful. He will never leave our side.

Didn't Jesus promise that the Holy Spirit would be with us forever? His promise carried no conditional clauses. There are no riders to Jesus' promises, nor can we interpret "forever" to mean less than forever.

During my college years, I met many students who believed the Holy Spirit belonged only to Christians who had "prayed through" to receive him. They also believed his stay might be temporary. A sinning Christian, they said, could lose the Holy Spirit. I believed such thinking was strangely out of tune with Jesus' promise that the Spirit would be with believers forever (John 14:16).

Furthermore, Jesus told his disciples the Spirit "will be in you" (v. 17). This indwelling is not a reward for asking for the Spirit or for staying in a faith relationship with Christ; it is a gift to every believer listed in the will Jesus outlined in John 14.

The apostle Paul taught this Unth. In Romans 8:9 he wrote, "And if anyone does not have the Spirit of Christ, he does not belong to Christ." We may safely say, therefore, that only unbelievers do not have the Holy Spirit, and by contrast, all believers (those who belong to Christ) have the Spirit.

But how long will you and I, as believers, belong to Christ? Forever! Jesus promised that we will never perish and that he will not let us slip from his hand. To borrow an advertising slogan, we are in safe hands with Jesus.

It may also help us to understand that the Spirit will never leave a believer under any circumstances if we know why the Spirit lives in each believer. He has taken residence in us so that he may perform a great work in us, namely, the work of transforming us into the image of Christ. Because that gracious work is a lifelong one, the Holy Spirit will live in us for the rest of our days.

Paul attributed this transforming work to the Spirit when he wrote, "And we, who with unveiled faces all reflect the Lord's glory, are being transformed into his likeness with ever-increasing glory, which comes from the Lord, who is the Spirit" (2 Cor. 3:18). In a similar vein, he credited the Spirit with interceding for us according to the will of God, which he defined as God's marking us out to be "conformed to the likeness of his Son" (Rom. 8:26-29).

Have you known any quitters? A golfer may set the goal of breaking one hundred but gives up golf after trying for years to reach his goal. A dieter may choose to shed eighty pounds but, after eating low-carb food for a couple of months, return to a diet rich in French fries, big-bun burgers, and pecan pie. A would-be author may plan to write a three-hundred-page novel but abandon the plan when she runs out of ideas on page five. However, the Holy Spirit cannot and will not fail to finish the work he came to do in us.

Writing to the believers at Rome, Paul described the Spirit's work of conforming Christians into the image of

Christ as an accomplished fact. Sharing God's perspective, he explained, "And those he predestined, he also called; those he called, he also justified; those he justified, he also glorified" (8:30). We may be confident, therefore, that the Holy Spirit will never leave us. His work is far too important to abandon.

God did not design the Christian life to be one of worry. He gave each of us the Holy Spirit to assure us, to keep us on the path of righteousness, and to escort us to heaven. Instead of doubting that he is with us for the entire pilgrimage, we ought to cooperate with him and rely on him to make the pilgrimage satisfying and successful.

MINISTRY HAS ITS MOMENTS

A HUMOROUS JOURNEY THROUGH 60 YEARS OF MINISTRY

This book is dedicated to the Lord,
and
to my wife Gloria who shared the journey with me,
and
to my children, Sherrie, Heather, and Brian, who adjusted to
new places, new homes, new schools, and new friends as
their dad answered the call to serve various churches,
and
to all who called me Pastor.

AUTHOR'S NOTE

The names of individuals mentioned in this book have been changed to protect their identity.

PREFACE

My ministry has taken me on a long journey, but it seems like only yesterday that I answered the call to preach. I began preaching in 1955, when I was a student at Moody Bible Institute. The Office of Practical Christian Work at the Institute instructed me to preach every Sunday morning at Pacific Garden Mission. The assignment lasted until I graduated two years later. The following year, while I was a student at Houghton College, I preached on street corners in Wellsville and Olean, New York. I also opened a closed church near Rushford that I served as pastor until I graduated, married, and returned to my hometown, St. Catharines, Ontario. Now retired, I look back on 60 years of pastoral ministry and guest preaching in the Province of Ontario and 26 states.

Although it is a high calling and a privilege to preach and shepherd some of God's people, it can also be taxing and challenging. A pastor can succumb to discouragement, doubts, and defeat unless he keeps his eyes on the Chief Shepherd and maintains a sense of humor.

I have looked back on some of the lighter moments in my ministry and shared them in this book. It is my prayer that reading about those moments will encourage pastors to view their lighter moments of ministry as comic relief.

—*Jim*

"A merry heart does good. like medicine"
—Proverbs 17:22, NKJV

1
ON THE HUNT

My wife Gloria and I had been married for four months when a church in Northern Ontario invited me to preach. Because the church needed a pastor and I was available, we were excited about the possibility of my becoming the pastor. However, the excitement dwindled.

Fall was in the air in the heavily wooded area about two hours north of Toronto, and moose hunting season was under way. Saturday night, the church had booked us into a rustic motel surrounded by ice-covered rocks. Our room was warm enough, but we shared the bathroom with the hunters who occupied the room next to ours.

The next morning, we eagerly entered the church but, to our disappointment, the attendance was all-female with the exception of one elderly man. The rest of the men were hunting moose. Because the congregation was almost exclusively female, I avoided saying, "Dearly Beloved."

After church, a hospitable lady invited us to her

home for Sunday dinner but she explained apologetically that we would not be able to drink water. "A rat fell into our well," she sighed. She added, "And my oven hasn't been working right, so the meal may not be perfect." We soon learned the truth of her words. The meat was undercooked and, to our dismay, it was pork.

On our return home, I reflected on the weekend. The moose were loose and so were we.

2

POOR, SICK GRANDPA!

My first invitation to be a church's pastor came when I was a bread salesman, delivering bread and baked goods to homes and restaurants in Niagara Falls, Ontario. Mammy's Bread was the company I worked for and kids often approached my parked truck and sang:

*"Mammy's Bread is full of lead.
If you eat it, you'll soon be dead."*
I would answer:
*"Mammy's Bread is light as a feather.
If you eat it, you'll live forever."*

I know, the theology was bad, but the bread really was good.

My salary as a bread salesman—straight commission—averaged $100 a week. The salary I accepted from my first church was $50 per week. It was clear that delivering the bread of life would not be as lucrative as delivering regular bread. Nevertheless, I knew what my calling was and that eternal rewards accompanied ministry. Therefore, at the ripe old age of 23, I moved with my 22-year-old bride to a small town in Southern Ontario, where we met our small flock.

Most of the men of the church were dairy farmers but they faced an issue. The area lay a few miles north of Lake Erie and had become a key target for tobacco companies. Consequently, many dairy farmers were selling their land to tobacco growers for smokin'-hot deals. The church's farmers questioned what their response should be, whether to sell or continue to work as dairy farmers.

The parsonage was a two-story frame house that was heated by two space heaters. A hole in the ceiling allowed only a paltry amount of warm air to rise to the upstairs. Gloria and I chose to live downstairs.

The church building was a renovated three-story armory. The auditorium occupied the first floor. The second floor housed a gymnasium. The third floor? I never learned what was there, but I was glad it wasn't the pastor's living quarters.

Two canons pointing away from the church flanked the sidewalk that led to the church's entrance. I thought about putting a sign at the entrance that would read: ENTER IF YOU DARE!

Shortly after our arrival in town, Gloria became pregnant and very sick. The mere smell of food triggered a throw-up reaction. For a few weeks, she was too sick to attend church. This prompted people to ask what was wrong. I was too embarrassed to say she was pregnant, so I simply described the symptoms. "I know what she has," one woman responded. "My grandfather has had the same thing for weeks."

Poor, sick Grandpa. He regained his health in a couple of weeks but Gloria had to wait months to regain hers.

3

OH, WHERE, OH, WHERE HAS OUR MOVING VAN GONE? OH, WHERE, OH, WHERE CAN IT BE?

IN THE SPRING OF 1960, I RECEIVED A CALL TO BE THE first full-time pastor of a church in New York State. Gloria and I were both excited to move back to the United States. Gloria had grown up in Alexandria, Virginia, and I had graduated from Moody Bible Institute in Chicago and Houghton College in Houghton, New York. Nevertheless, there were legal hoops I had to jump through to enter the States. I was born in Scotland and was a Canadian citizen. In 1960, the U.S. Department of Immigration considered requests for permanent residence in the United States on the basis of a person's place of birth. A quota was assigned to each country and the quota for Scotland was lower than the quota for Canada. Therefore, it took three months to get accepted into the United States. For one thing, I had to have clearance from the chief of police in my hometown. Also, I had to prove that I had sponsorship, a job waiting for me in the States.

Finally, all the paperwork was approved and moving day arrived. The moving van parked in front of the parsonage and the crew started packing our earthly goods. "It is only a four-hour drive to your new home," the driver said. "You won't need to load your car. I'll arrive almost as soon as you do." That was encouraging information. Soon, we were on our way.

Our daughter Sherrie was nine months old when we transitioned from Canada to the United States. She was born in Brantford, Ontario the same year and in the same hospital as the Great One, hockey star Wayne Gretzky.

We passed through Customs at Niagara Falls and two hours later arrived at our destination—an empty parsonage. However, we were sure it wouldn't stay empty for long. Very soon, the moving van would arrive and our furniture would be in place.

We were wrong. Three days later we were still waiting for the moving van and for three days we stayed in the home of a church family.

When the van arrived with a driver we hadn't met, we learned the original driver had a bone to pick with the moving company. As a protest, he had parked the van at the side of the road and walked away. In those days, there was no way for the company to contact him.

We finally settled into our new home but, to say the least, our transition from Canada to the States was a very moving experience.

4
OUCH!

The family that graciously hosted us during the three days we waited for the moving van was highly intelligent and strictly regimented. The father was a chemist. The mother was a college grad who was committed to raising a teenage daughter and a teenage son. The teenagers were both overachievers, straight-A high schoolers with a remarkable proficiency in music. Their day started early with music practice that awoke us and our nine-month-old daughter. Breakfast time featured old-fashioned cooking and family devotions.

Exodus 28 was the Bible reading the first morning of our stay. This chapter contains the word, "ouches." Turning to me, the father asked, "Pastor, what's an ouch?" I had no idea. I thought it was what a tabernacle builder yelled when he hit his thumb with a hammer.

My Bible dictionary was on the moving van so I couldn't consult it. My only recourse was to be honest. "I'm sorry," I replied, "I don't know."

The situation was embarrassing, and I am sure the

host family questioned later among themselves whether they had chosen a biblically illiterate pastor.

Ouch!

IN CASE you are wondering what an ouch is, here is *Unger's Bible Dictionary's definition*: "an archaic term referring to the gold work, which not only served to fasten the stones upon the woven fabric of the ephod, but formed at the same time clasps or brooches, by which the two parts of the ephod were fastened together." (*Unger's Bible Dictionary*, Moody Press, 1966, p. 814)

5
ALARMING MOMENTS

I WAS CONCLUDING MY SERMON AT 12 NOON WHEN AN alarm clock rang loudly. The unexpected ringing jolted me but the congregation seemed to welcome it. A ripple of laughter spread through the church. I quickly brought my sermon to a close, wondering who had brought the alarm clock to church.

I learned from a highly embarrassed mother that her eleven-year-old son had sneaked the alarm from his bedroom and carried it to church and kept it hidden like a concealed weapon. She and her mischievous son seemed relieved when I laughed and said, "Well, it worked."

Years later, while I was living in Colorado Springs, I received an invitation to speak at the fiftieth anniversary of that Western New York church. After exchanging warm greetings with the congregation, I opened my Bible to begin my sermon. *Rrrring!* An alarm clock reverberated in the auditorium. No, the perpetrator wasn't the eleven-year-old boy, now 61 years old; it was a 78-year-old retired fifth-grade schoolteacher. She was a charter member of the church with a good sense of humor and a healthy memory. Apparently, the earlier alarming moment had left an indelible impression on her. When the laughter ended, I returned to my sermon.

I suppose every pastor can recall surprising moments in a church service but mine was not only alarming but also productive. From the first *Rrrring* until now, I have managed to conclude each sermon before 12 noon.

6
PITY THE PSYCHIATRIST!

DEPRESSION CAN COVER A PERSON LIKE A DARK, HEAVY blanket but I don't think it always indicates that a depressed person is out of fellowship with the Lord. Furthermore, launching a depressed person on a guilt trip only intensifies the depression. Some cases of depression can be traced to lack of adequate sleep, certain medications, abuse, thyroid disease, smoking, a vitamin deficiency, and even winter weather. In an effort to learn the cause of his depression and a cure for it, Frank made an appointment with a psychiatrist in Rochester. However, Frank, a single, middle-aged person lacked the confidence to drive 35 miles from his home to the psychiatrist's office. Therefore, he turned to me, his pastor, for help, and I agreed to drive him to his appointment.

Without a doubt, Frank was depressed. During the trip to Rochester, he sighed, sighed, and then sighed deeply. But he rarely sighed on the way home. What amazing therapy did the psychiatrist apply to make such a noticeable difference?

Frank clued me in. "That poor guy sure has a lot of problems," he volunteered. "He thinks his wife is seeing another man. He owes back taxes. His dog is aggressive and he may have to put him down." On and on, Frank spewed out a tale of the psychiatrist's woes. It became apparent to me that Frank forgot his own troubles—at least for a little while—because they seemed light in view of the psychiatrist's troubles.

Perhaps the number of personal pity parties would decline if we focused more on the needs of others who are hurting and less on our own troubles.

7

FASTER THAN A SPEEDING BULLET

IN AN EFFORT TO EVANGELIZE THE COUNTY, OUR CHURCH offered every home a free Bible study course. We chose the Good News correspondence course published by Moody Bible Institute. On Saturdays, a deacon and I would drive down country roads to farmhouses and deliver a letter from our church, explaining that we would pay the enrollment fee for the course.

One Saturday, the deacon and I drove down a long lane and I parked beside a large, wood-frame farm house. A wide, grassy field separated the house from a neighbor's house. I hesitated to get out of the car because a fierce-looking German shepherd stood between the car and the entrance to the house. At first, I considered turning the car around and driving to the next house. Then I thought, *I am a pastor. I need to act as an example of faith for this deacon's benefit.* So, I cautiously exited the car and stepped up to the house. To my relief, the dog merely watched as I spoke to the homeowner and returned to the car.

"Friendly dog," the deacon observed."

I smiled, "Sure is."

While driving to the next farmhouse, we spotted the dog bounding across the wide field. When we reached the house, the dog was standing near the entrance and staring at us. Now, it was the deacon's turn to deliver the letter. He slowly approached the entrance. The dog growled. He dropped the letter on the porch and started to return to the car. That's when the dog charged, snapping at his heels. With the speed of Superman, the deacon raced to the car. Fortunately, he was able to climb in and slam the door between him and a set of vicious canine teeth.

Why didn't the dog attack me at the previous house? We concluded that he was just visiting that house, whereas he lived at the second house. He must have known he was fed to guard the second house, not the first.

8
THE REST OF THE STORY

CHARLES BLONDIN WAS A FRENCHMAN WHO THRILLED spectators by tightrope walking over Niagara Falls, 1,300 feet above Niagara's swirling whirlpools. He performed the stunt 300 times on a narrow rope. Occasionally, he performed acrobatic stunts on the rope and once he crossed with his manager on his back.

Speaking at a Junior summer camp in Pennsylvania, I told the kids a popular story about Blondin. Undoubtedly, numerous preachers have told the same story. It illustrates the difference between giving only mental assent to Jesus' ability to save and a heartfelt trust in him. Here's how it goes:

After thousands saw Charles Blondin walk across Niagara Fall on a tightrope, Blondin asked: "How many of you believe I can tightrope walk across Niagara Falls?" The subsequent cheers showed unanimous belief that the daredevil could do it. "Well, then," asked Blondin, "who is willing to climb onto my back and let me carry him across Niagara Falls?" Only one boy in the crowd accepted the challenge. The crowd believed with their minds but the boy believed with his heart and trusted Blondin.

As I was relating this story, I noticed a pig-tailed girl squirming in her seat and jerking a hand up and down. Obviously, she wanted to say something. Fortunately, she said nothing until after I concluded my talk and the other kids had left. "Do you know the rest of your story?" she asked. I smiled, "Tell me it." She shook her head. "The next time he didn't make it!"

The girl's statement prompted me to research the life of Charles Blondin. Talk about fake news! I learned that my story and the little girl's report of Blondin's attempted next crossing were both spurious. Neither one held one ounce of truth. Blondin died in 1897 at age 72 from complications of diabetes.

I have not told the story of Blondin's challenge since I spoke at that Junior summer camp.

9

TEMPORARY TEMPERANCE

I drove into town on a late Saturday afternoon and knocked at the door of the house where a couple planned to host me that night. The husband was a deacon at the church where I was scheduled to preach the next day. The wife met me at the door. She stood about 5'4 and was a rather plump middle-aged woman. Her long, black dress, broad black hat, high heels, white gloves, dangling earrings, pearl necklace, and diamond bracelet exuded wealth. She looked like she was going to the Kentucky Derby. "You must be our guest speaker. I'm Linda," she volunteered. "It's a pleasure to meet you. My husband is closing up one of our businesses. I will give you a quick tour of our town and then pick him up at our furniture store." With that, she pointed to a luxury car in the driveway.

As we drove around town, Linda pointed to one establishment after another and commented after each one, "My husband owns that business." We passed one street like a rocket. "The parsonage is down that street," she said but she failed to point it out.

Finally, we picked up her husband, Archie, a dapper kind of man, who was wearing a dark blue business suit with a red tie. When we reached The Old Chapel Inn, a former church building with stained glass windows, Linda commented, "This is our favorite restaurant." Archie shook his head in agreement. "We eat here at least four times a week."

A petite, blond hostess in a black skirt and white blouse greeted us with a smile. She called Linda and Archie by name and said she was pleased to see them again.

We didn't have to wait more than a minute for a waiter in black pants, white shirt, and black bowtie to approach our table and hand each of us a menu. Linda held hers in front of her face and whispered to the waiter: "No cocktails tonight!"

I thought, *There's no need to abstain from drinking on my account. What matters is having a clear conscience in the Lord's sight.*

10

BOYS WILL BE BOYS

THE CHURCH IN WESTERN NEW YORK HAD AN ABUNDANCE of teenage boys and eventually an abundance of teenage girls. The boys were a bit rowdy but very athletic. In the fall, they loved to play tackle football on the church grounds. They didn't suit up in pads; their style was hit 'em hard and hear 'em groan. Also, they loved to include me in every game. The Defense was almost ecstatic when the quarterback handed me the ball. I can't count the times I was knocked to the ground. Can you guess how hard the ground is in New York State in the fall?

The same teenage boys played a practical joke on me one Sunday. After I shook hands with everyone after the morning service, my wife and I went to the place I had parked our car. Our car wasn't there. Had I parked it in a different spot? Had someone stolen it? The answer to both questions was no. Here's what happened. While I was saying goodbye to the congregation, the boys had physically lifted the car and carried it to a field. Fortunately, for their muscles, the car was a fairly light, compact Renault. And fortunately for my wife and me, they told us what they had done. Soon, they carried the car back to the church's parking lot.

A few years later, I officiated at the weddings of three of the car snatchers and, to my deep satisfaction, two of them entered full time Christian service. One became the principal of a Christian school, the other, a pastor. As far as I know, they did not purchase Renaults.

11

THE TEST OF SMELLY WATER

When I was a guest speaker at a church of 200 in Western New York, I had a noxious experience. After the morning service, the chairman of the pulpit committee took me across the church's parking lot to see the parsonage. When he opened the parsonage's front door, the smell of rotten eggs nearly blew us off the porch.

The chairman explained, "The church building has city water but the parsonage has well water. We could switch the parsonage to city water but we think the smelly well water provides a good test of a preacher's call to be our pastor."

I did not feel called!

12

MAN UNDER THE BED

One dark night, during a Sunday school staff meeting, a teacher asked Beth what she would do if she went home and found a man under her bed.

Beth, a petite, energetic, spunky, single 50-year-old answered immediately. "I would get down on both knees and say, Thank You, Lord."

Telling this story is not meant to reflect negatively on single life. Whether married or single, we experience life's greatest joy by being who God wants us to be and doing what He wants us to do.

13

A DRUNKEN GIVEAWAY

THE FATHER OF THE BRIDE WAS DRUNK BUT HE WALKED HIS daughter down the aisle. Or did she walk him down the aisle? At any rate, when I asked, "Who gives this woman to be married to this man?" he did not reply. After what seemed like an eternity of silence, I repeated the question. Again, he said nothing.

"Just say, 'Her mother and I do,'" I whispered.

No reply.

Once again, I whispered, "Just say, 'Her mother and I do, '" and I added. "And be seated."

"I'm not sure I wanna give her to this guy," he blurted but finally said, "Her mother and I do."

Next, he shook hands with all the wedding guests and sat down at the back of the church.

The bride was clearly embarrassed, and I was flabbergasted, but the rest of the ceremony went smoothly.

14

RAIN, RAIN, GO AWAY!

I STARTED PLAYING GOLF WHEN I WAS A CADDY IN Ontario. One day, I caddied for Joe Louis, the World Heavyweight Boxing Champion. He was a perfect gentleman with a powerful golf swing but he tended to punch the ball. At any rate, I developed a love for golf and, in the ensuing years, I played in all kinds of weather: sunshine, rain, hail, thunder and lightning, and even snow. If I could have controlled the weather, I would have made every golf day a pleasant, sunny day.

Of course, only the Lord can control the weather. The story of his calming the wind and the waves in the middle of the Sea of Galilee illustrates his power to control the weather.

I was playing golf in Indiana one day with three other men when it started to pour. Most courses give golfers a raincheck to play another day if they have completed only a few holes when rain stops play. Unfortunately, we were on the 12th hole, when the skies opened up and the rain soaked us. "Reverend," one of the men called to me, "can't you do something to make this rain stop?" I replied, "Sorry, I can't control the weather. I'm in Advertising, not Production."

As Matthew 5:45 points out, the Lord sends rain on both the just and the unjust.

15

MOUTH-TO-BEAK RESUSCITATION

I DOUBT THAT MANY VISITORS ATTEND A WATCHNIGHT service but one showed up at our church in Pennsylvania. She was a schoolteacher who asked me to visit her early in the new year. When I obliged and visited her, she told me she had attended the watchnight service because she was depressed. She explained that she had lost her pet parakeet, whom she named Jerry III, and hoped to receive some comfort at church.

She explained. "For several years," she said, "I had a wonderful pet parakeet. He was my Jerry and he was free to fly anywhere in the house, but he would never go far from me. Often, he would perch on my shoulder and sing to me. Well, it was a sad day when Jerry died. Apparently, he had a heart attack."

Her story continued. "After a while, I purchased another parakeet, Jerry II. He and I became very close and I let him fly freely around the house. One weekend, I was visiting my sister in Pittsburgh and Jerry was with me. I made the mistake of letting out of his cage and, to my horror, my sister's boxer dog ate him."

But her story didn't end there. Teary-eyed, the schoolteacher continued: "I bought another parakeet, Jerry III, and became very attached to him. I also gave him the freedom to fly around the house. Last Monday, when I was eating breakfast with Jerry III close by. The phone rang in the living room, so I went to answer it. When I returned, I found Jerry III face down in my glass of orange juice. I attempted face to beak resuscitation but I couldn't revive my dear friend. I had hoped to find some comfort at your church."

To this day, after counseling scores of distraught individuals, I still do not know how to comfort a grieving parakeet owner.

16

I WANT TO GIVE YOU A POKE

I LEARNED A NEW DIALECT WHILE I SERVED A CHURCH IN Central Pennsylvania. I learned, for example, that redd up means to clear a table. After having a meal, a mother might say, "It's time to redd up." I learned, too, that the meaning of let and leave was often reversed. Often, paid parking lots posted signs that directed motorists to let their keys in their cars. A person might say, "I will leave you have your wish." One woman in our church shocked me by telling me, "My husband kept saying he wanted to buy a new car, so finally I left him."

Another colloquialism was that of referring to "my one arm" instead saying "my right arm" or "my left arm." It was not unusual to hear a person complain of pain in his or her one leg. Nor was it unusual to hear a person with a few siblings mention "my one sister" or "my one brother."

I also learned that a legislator is a solon, the shoulder of a road is a berm, and instead of saying, "The ushers will receive the offering," a pastor would say, "The ushers will lift the offering."

One day, I answered the telephone—my one telephone—to hear an elderly, homebound member of the church say, "Pastor, you know I haven't been able to attend church for a long time but, if you will come to my house, I will give you a poke."

What was that all about? Here's the answer. A poke in Central Pennsylvania is a bag. The homebound church member had saved his offerings and put them in a bag—a poke—that he would give me if I came to his house.

17

MIDNIGHT SHOCK

While I was a pastor in Central Pennsylvania, I substitute taught German and French in an area high school. One year, I taught French for the last six weeks of the school year because the regular French teacher had fallen off a train and broken her hip and shoulder. Fortunately, the train wasn't moving when she fell. The accident happened when she was disembarking. Sometime during those six weeks of teaching French, I taped a brief devotional to be viewed at the TV station's midnight sign-off. Area pastors volunteered to take turns at giving the sign-off devotional.

The morning after my midnight sign-off devotional aired, I began a French class but noticed a student with his hand raised, "Yes, what is it?" I asked.

The student explained, "I was shocked last night. I fell asleep while the TV was on and when I woke up, I saw you. I thought it was a nightmare. Are you a preacher?"

"*Oui*," I responded.

The student seemed to be greatly surprised that a pastor knew something in addition to the Bible.

18

A GRATE WEDDING

Everything was perfectly in place for Becky's wedding. Flowers and candles graced the platform. The family members, other relatives, and guests had been seated. The guest soloist sat near the platform. The maid of honor and the bridesmaids stood, bouquets in hand, to my right. The groom and I stood at the center of the formation and the best man and groomsmen were at our left. The organist began playing, "Here Comes the Bride," and Becky entered on her father's left arm. Everyone stood and gazed at the bride. It promised to be a beautiful wedding.

But suddenly there was a hitch. A cold air return covered by a metal grate lay in the aisle about halfway between the entrance and the platform. To Becky's horror, her left heel caught in the grate and she stepped forward, dragging it. Fortunately, Becky's father came to the rescue by stepping on the grate and liberating his daughter. Unhitched from the grate, she would soon be hitched to the man she loved.

I have learned through the years that wedding plans sometimes go awry.

19

A MEMORABLE ANNUAL BUSINESS MEETING

A CHURCH'S ANNUAL BUSINESS MEETING IS AN IMPORTANT part of the church calendar. Committees report on their activities of the past year, the clerk or secretary reads the minutes of the previous business meeting, new business is conducted, and officers are elected for the coming year or beyond. Occasionally, items of new business can raise blood pressure, trigger emotions, and divide the membership, but there should always be an agreement to disagree agreeably.

The reports at the annual business meeting can bring joy to the church members if they show the church has experienced progress and blessing. I heard about one church's report that announced the following:

Conversions last year: None
Baptisms: None
Membership Additions: None.

Praise God, we are holding our own.

My most memorable annual business meeting occurred the night our white toy poodle gave birth to puppies. She started delivering puppies shortly before the business meeting was to begin. She must have sensed that my wife was nervous because she would not deliver a puppy for her. I took over. Quickly, two puppies arrived just in time for me to walk past two houses, arrive at the church, and begin the annual business meeting.

The meeting was well under way when our five-year-old daughter Sherrie, wearing a pink nightgown, walked down the side aisle. She whispered in my ear, "Daddy, Fluffy is having a hard time. She needs you!"

I asked the chairman of the deacons to take my place as moderator, excused myself from the meeting, and hurried home with Sherrie. Almost as soon as I entered the house, Fluffy gave birth to another puppy. Soon, I was back at the business meeting and delivered the birth announcement.

The following year, at the annual business meeting, the church clerk read the minutes of the preceding annual business meeting. Sure enough, entered into the minutes was a report of Sherrie's visit and Fluffy's delivery of her third puppy.

20

COUNTING BY PORXY

WHEN I WAS A PASTOR IN ALTOONA, PENNSYLVANIA, the local newspaper, the *Altoona Mirror*, was extremely cordial to churches. Every summer, a two-week Bible conference took place in a city park. Churches throughout the city and in nearby towns participated and throngs of Christians attended the sessions. Well-known Bible teachers spoke at the conference and the *Altoona Mirror* printed every word of their messages.

The *Altoona Mirror* also published, every Saturday, the local pastors' sermon titles and the times of the services. I appreciated the opportunity to announce my sermon titles and never failed to send them to the newspaper. One Saturday, however, I was surprised to read in the paper that the following morning I would be preaching on "Counting by Porxy." The sermon title was supposed to be "Courting by Proxy."

The sermon title, "Counting by Proxy," was based on the beautiful love story found in Genesis 24. The aged patriarch Abraham charged his oldest servant with the task of going to Abraham's homeland to find a bride for his son Isaac. It is hard enough for a man to find a bride for himself without having to find one for another man but the servant faithfully traveled to the city of Nahor, Mesopotamia, where he prayerfully found Rebekah. He presented her with a gold ring and two gold bracelets. The courting by proxy had begun. Later, he revealed his mission to Rebekah's close relatives, gave expensive jewelry to everyone, and received Rebekah' consent and her relatives' blessing to accompany him to Abraham's home. As they drew near to the homestead, Rebekah saw Isaac, Isaac saw her, and the rest is history. The courting by proxy had worked!

I wonder how many readers of the Altoona Mirror thought I was planning to use a Sunday service to present a recently discovered version of new math.

21

PIZZA BY THE SLICE

A Sunday evening church service is rare now but in the 1960s in Altoona, Pennsylvania, every evangelical church held one. Ours ran from 6:30 P.M. to 7:30 P.M. However, without fail, every Sunday evening at precisely 7:25 a pizza truck offering pizza by the slice parked outside the church and rang a loud bell. Of course, the sound of the bell and the smell of pizza wafting through the church got our taste buds dancing. It took a Herculean effort to suppress our desire to rush out of the church and purchase pizza at 15 cents a slice.

One Sunday, before the evening service, I located the pizza truck and asked the driver to arrive at our church ten minutes later than the usual time. "You and I will both do a better business," I assured him.

The driver agreed to change his schedule. Sure enough, as I was greeting the people after the evening service, we heard, *Clang, Clang, Clang,* and caught the smell of hot pizza Within a few minutes, the congregation joined a throng of neighbors at the pizza truck.

Sometimes, ministry and pizza sales benefit from a minor adjustment and cooperation.

22

A PAPER PAYDAY

A COUPLE OF PAPER MILLS WERE LOCATED A FEW MILES from Altoona. One, in Tyrone, emitted an "aroma" that often wafted all the way to Altoona. Creative minds called it Evening in Tyrone. If you have ever lived near a paper mill, you know the aroma. One year, I enjoyed the privilege of preaching each evening, Thursday through Saturday, and twice on Sunday at a paper mill a few miles south of Altoona. Although the church was located directly across the street from the mill, it was odor free.

The pastor told me the church was experiencing financial difficulties so I shouldn't expect more than a small honorarium. That was fine with me; I was glad to be of service to the congregation. At the close of the meetings, I received neither check nor cash. My honorarium was scrap paper from the mill. Apparently, a number of church members worked at the mill and were allowed to take home paper that didn't measure up to quality standards. I received so much paper that it filled the trunk of my car.

Our young daughters were overjoyed with my honorarium. They drew pictures and scribbled on sheets of legal pads and notebook paper for weeks on end.

23

ROCKS FOR SALE

When our daughter Heather was six and we were living in a small Indiana town a mile west of the Wabash River, Heather became a salesgirl. No, she didn't sell Girl Scout cookies; she collected rocks—ordinary rocks—and went door to door in our neighborhood trying to sell them. Surprisingly, sales were good. I think our neighbors couldn't resist the appealing smile of a little girl.

The following year, Heather sold her second-grade teacher on the idea of attending a service at the church where her daddy was the pastor. Her teacher remarked that she had not darkened the door of a church in nearly forty years but she might visit Heather's church.

The teacher was sold on Heather's invitation. She visited our church one Sunday. Further, she responded to my invitation to trust in Christ as Savior. Later, I had the privilege of baptizing her and welcoming her into the church's membership. She became an outstanding member, faithfully attended church, and took on the role of Sunday school teacher.

Heather's rock-selling was quite an accomplishment but her greatest accomplishment was that of introducing her second-grade teacher to the Rock of Ages.

24
A PUPPY TALE

Our toy poodle Fluffy had a second litter of puppies that we advertised for sale at $75 each. Today, of course, the price would be around ten times that amount. In response to our ad in the local newspaper, a young woman holding a baby in her arms knocked on our door. She agreed to purchase one of the puppies, and asked, "Will you accept a check?" "Sure," I answered.

I held the young woman's baby for her while she wrote the check. "Do you need a ride home." I asked. "I don't see a car parked anywhere."

"No thanks," she replied. "I parked around the corner." With that, she lifted the puppy into her free arm and walked away.

Her check bounced and later the chief of police called me. The young woman was at the jail, charged with counterfeit and writing bad checks all over town. "She says she is sorry," the police chief offered. "She said the puppy is in her unlocked trailer and you can retrieve it there. Let me give you the address."

"No thanks," I replied. "I won't enter her trailer without a police escort."

The chief of police agreed to meet me at the trailer.

End of story. I brought the puppy home, after affirming the truth of Psalm 118:8, the middle verse of the Bible. "It is better to trust in the Lord than to put confidence in man." I'm certain "man" in this verse is generic and even includes a young woman carrying a baby.

25

AN EMBARRASSING FACEOFF

When a church in Indianapolis asked me to preach, I agreed to do so on a weeknight. I didn't want to be absent from my own pulpit on a Sunday.

A huge stuffed lion in a cage greeted me as I entered the foyer of the Indianapolis church. After the service, the church's pulpit committee asked me to return as a candidate. However, the stuffed lion and part of the committee's description of the church's ministry convinced me I would not be a good fit for the church. The church seemed to depend on gimmicks to build attendance whereas I believed life-related Bible teaching would get the job done. So, I told the committee I was not interested in becoming the pastor.

The following Sunday, Gloria and I were entertaining our deacons in the parsonage. The occasion was the birthday of one of them. Just as we were about to enjoy cake and ice cream, there was a knock at the door. I opened it to behold the members of the pulpit committee from Indianapolis.

"May we come in?" they asked.

What could I say, except, "Sure, come on in."

The pulpit committee did not divulge its identity but simply told our deacons they were out for a Sunday afternoon drive. (Quite a Sunday afternoon drive! Seventy miles from Indianapolis!) Everyone exchanged names, Gloria served the visitors cake and ice cream and the two groups faced off as each one tried to outwait the other.

Our deacons left first.

The pulpit committee explained to me that it felt led to drive to West Terre Haute and ask me again to candidate. I had not changed my mind, so I emphasized again that I was not the right man to be their pastor.

The whole situation was embarrassing but memorable.

26

NO AUTHOR SIGNING

We moved from Indiana to Denver, Colorado, when I became an editor for a Christian publishing company. My involvement in pastoring continued, though. During my editorial career, I served 14 churches either as a part-time pastor or as an interim pastor.

While our daughters were in college, my wife Gloria worked part time in a Christian bookstore in Lakewood. The store was well stocked and well organized. If a customer asked whether the store carried a certain book and a salesperson wasn't sure it was part of the inventory, she would ask for the author's name and then track the book by name. The system worked well until . . .

One day, the manager of the store greeted a man near the Bible Reference section. He asked her, "Do you carry the Greek New Testament?"

"I don't know," she replied. "Who wrote it?"

Of course, God authored the Greek New Testament. Second Timothy 3:16 proclaims, "All scripture is breathed out by God. . . ." As you might guess, the bookstore did not schedule an author book signing.

27

AN OLD WEST HEIST

I LIKE WYOMING AND ITS PEOPLE. THE STATE IS SPARSELY populated and its topography is diverse. The east side of the state is flat and quite barren but the west side is mountainous. Streams flow unabated from the mountains. Fishing and hunting abound. It gets quite windy in Wyoming but one person in Wyoming assured me people in Wyoming don't worry about the wind unless they see white caps in the commode.

Cheyenne, Wyoming, is famous for its Frontier Days rodeo. It's the granddaddy of all rodeos. If you visit Cheyenne, you may want to purchase a pair of cowboy boots. If you can't find good cowboy boots in Cheyenne, you can't find them anywhere.

Chugwater, a town of about 200, flanks I-25 just north of Cheyenne. The town got its name from the practice of Indians driving buffalo over a nearby cliff and into the creek below. The Indians referred to it as the place where the buffalo chug.

Farther north lies the city of Casper, Wyoming's second-largest city. It is famous for its oil production and cowboy culture. At Casper, you can view the deep ruts made by wagons that rolled along the Oregon Trail.

One Friday night, I spoke at a Wyoming church's spaghetti dinner in a town that I came to regard as somewhat infamous. Arriving early, I placed books I had written on a table near the entrance to the gym in which the dinner was held. I also placed on a table a For Sale sign, a box of money, and a note asking people to make their own change when purchasing a book,

The dinner was outstanding. The spaghetti came with a choice of meatballs or Italian sausage. Slices of bread were crusty and fluffy. Spumoni was the perfect dessert but I had a bad taste in my mouth when I returned to the book table. All the books were gone and so was all the money. I called the incident an Old West Heist. Unfortunately, Wyatt Earp was not available to track down the outlaw.

28

ONE FOR THE GUINNESS WORLD RECORDS

CLARENCE AND LINDA WERE NEWLYWEDS, BUT NOT YOUR typical newlyweds. They were both in their mid-seventies. He was a retired CEO of an engineering company. She was s retired college professor. He was a widower. She had never married. Each of them was a Christian and both were members of different churches and they had agreed to find a church they could start attending together. They selected ours.

They always attended our church in high style. Linda wore an attractive dress, a hat, heels, and a purse that matched her outfit. Clarence wore a pressed suit and tie, and his shoes were so shiny I almost needed sunglasses to look at them. They were friendly and seemed to enjoy getting to know the members of the congregation.

One evening, Linda and Clarence entertained Gloria and me in their home. After dinner, they said how much they appreciated my preaching and the friendliness they had encountered at church. They had decided they wanted to join the church. Gloria and I were delighted to hear this news. At the next business meeting, the membership voted unanimously to welcome Linda and Clarence into membership.

The Sunday arrived when I welcomed them into the membership of our church. I called them to the platform, said something nice about each of them, extended the right hand of fellowship to them, and then they returned to their seats.

Minutes later, I started to preach. To my great surprise, Linda and Clarence stood up and walked out of the church. Every effort to contact them failed. Everyone was mystified. Why had they left, never to return? I doubt that even Sherlock Holmes could solve the mystery.

A couple of years later, I received a phone call from someone who identified herself as Linda's sister. "Reverend Dyet," she began, "I want to tell you why Linda and Clarence left your church. Linda is a very vain person. She told me they left because you said more nice things about Clarence than about her."

The mystery was solved. I didn't feel free to tell the congregation about the phone call but I was more convinced than ever that I couldn't please all the people all the time.

29

A HUMBLING DAY OF GOLF

AFTER MY GOLF BOOK, *OUT OF THE ROUGH*, WAS published, I received invitations from various groups to play and speak at golf outings. I was also invited to speak at the Centennial celebration of the course in St. Catharine, Ontario, where I had caddied as a kid.

One invitation to play golf and speak came from Sunshine Gospel Ministries, an inner-city mission in Chicago. I was especially happy to accept the invitation because, when I was a student at Moody Bible Institute, I had preached every Sunday morning at Pacific Garden Mission and taught Sunday school at Chicago Gospel Mission.

Pheasant Run Resort in St. Charles, Illinois, was the site of the golf outing that was a fundraiser for Sunshine Gospel Ministries. Two Chicago Bears players participated as celebrity players and some inner-city kids were also present. The kids enjoyed riding golf carts around the course during the event. The weather was good and the course was in good shape but my golf game was in bad shape.

Like most courses, Pheasant Run has ample water hazards: narrow streams cutting across fairways and a few ponds. True to my Baptist affiliation, I could not avoid water. Even a tiny stream drew my ball to it like a magnet draws metal. I think I immersed more golf balls on the front and back nines than I had immersed people in five years of ministry.

Golf is a humbling sport, and it certainly humbled me at Pheasant Run.

After such a pitiful performance, I was left with four choices:

1. Quit golf.
2. Practice, practice, practice.
3. Play only desert courses.
4. Become a Methodist.

30

SNAKE IN THE GLASS

ONE SATURDAY IN EARLY MAY I TOOK A PLANE FROM Denver's Stapleton Airport to Philadelphia. The flight was uneventful and it touched down on time at 12:25 P.M. at Philadelphia International Airport. I disembarked at met my contact at the gate. He greeted me with a smile and a warm handshake. Wearing blue shorts, a white T-shirt, sneakers, and a Phillies baseball cap, he seemed to be relaxed and approachable.

"Do you want to get a bite to eat," he asked.

"No thanks," I replied, "I had lunch on the plane." (*Who remembers having lunch on a plane?*)

"Would you like to take a brief tour of Philadelphia," he asked.

"That would be great!"

As we drove down Broad Street, I could see that the grass and trees had turned lush green, the flowers and flowering shrubs were in full bloom, pretzel vendors were doing a brisk business, and the sky was so blue that I felt like singing, "Blue skies smiling at me. Nothing but blue skies do I see."

Our tour took us to the Liberty Bell and to Independence Hall before we drove north beside the Delaware River.

When we arrived at his home, I met his hospitable wife who had dinner under way. "You must be hungry," she said. "We are looking forward to having you preach at our church tomorrow. Our son is staying with a friend for the weekend, so you can sleep in his bedroom tonight."

Sleep? I didn't sleep a wink that night.

The teenage son's bed was comfortable but I wasn't. A few inches from the bed was a glass aquarium that held a big snake that I took to be a boa constrictor. All that separated him from me was a screen cover with a rock on it.

All night, my ever-watchful companion kept slithering up the side of the aquarium and bumping its head on the screen. It was obvious that it wanted to get a close look at the guy who was in its owner's bed. And perhaps it wanted to crawl into the bed for an even closer inspection.

The next morning when I stood up to preach, I wondered if I would fall asleep before the congregation did.

That afternoon I boarded the return flight to Denver and slept almost all the way home.

31

DISMISSED!

WHEN I ANSWERED THE PHONE, THE CALLER IDENTIFIED himself as Kent Millhouse. He said, "Reverend, my girlfriend Becky and I want to get married and my grandparents suggested I call you. They said you might be willing to do the wedding."

I replied that I would like to talk with him and his girlfriend before agreeing to perform the wedding.

We met at a restaurant. I judged the couple to be in their early twenties. We spent almost an hour discussing their spiritual status, their commitment to each other, and what should be included in the ceremony. Satisfied with their answers, I agreed to perform the wedding. After setting a time and place for the wedding, we parted company.

As I was on my way home, a hit-and-run driver struck my car. The left side of my car was badly damaged but a couple of days later my ego was damaged. Kent, the young man who asked me to perform his and Becky's wedding, called again. This time he said, "Reverend, we don't need you to do our wedding. We found a younger pastor who will do it."

"That's fine," I replied. "Thanks for letting me know."

A quick look at my face in the hall mirror confirmed what I already knew. I wasn't as young as the average pastor. Nevertheless, I assured myself, I wasn't too old to tie a wedding knot.

Upon reflecting on what had occurred, I wondered how long the couple would be married before deciding to trade in their spouses for younger ones.

32

CLERGY GOLF

I HAVE PLAYED GOLF WITH MANY PASTORS OF VARIOUS denomination through the years, and I must say from my observation that Southern Baptists are the best clergy golfers. Maybe the reason lies in the fact that many Southern Baptists hail from the South, where longer summers and shorter winters allow golfers to play often.

My curiosity leads me to speculate how golfers might play the grand old game if their golf matched their theology. It might go like this:

Baptists would never miss an opportunity to immerse a golf ball in a pond or stream. Also, they might stay off a green because it is often called "the Dance Floor." Presbyterians would play from sprinkler to sprinkler. Pentecostal preachers would take huge divots so they would feel the ground shake under their feet. They would also make a number of miraculous recovery shots and play best in the wind. Conservative pastors would play only on the right side of each fairway, while liberal pastors would stay on the left side of each fairway. Lutheran preachers would refuse to adjust their stance. Calvinistic pastors might wear golf shirts that say, "Born to play golf," and they might write their score on the scorecard before playing even the first hole. Arminian pastors, on the other hand, might start well but not be sure they will be able to finish. Pastors who preach extensively on grace might give themselves an unlimited number of mulligans and remove the out-of-bounds markers. Legalistic pastors might needlessly give themselves extra penalties and move the out-of-bounds markers into the fairways.

When I have to hit out of a sand trap, my thoughts become evangelistic. I feel like saying, "I want every head bowed, every eye closed, and no one looking around."

33

NOT THAT KIND OF PREACHER!

I don't think I look like a member of the Mafia or a drug dealer although my stereotype image of those individuals may be totally inaccurate. At any rate, I don't understand why a Drug Enforcement officer at Chicago O'Hare International Airport stopped me from boarding my flight to Toronto one Saturday afternoon. It may have been a random check. I was walking on the jetway, very close to entering the plane, when she stopped me. "Sir," she said, "I need to talk to you."

I stepped aside to let other passengers board the plane.

"Where are you going?" the stone-faced officer asked.

"Toronto."

"How long will you be there?"

"Just until Monday."

"Are you a U.S. citizen?"

"Yes, I am."

"I need to see proof of citizenship."

Reaching into my attaché case, I pulled out my

decades-old citizenship document and showed it to her. She glanced at it and handed it back.

"What is the nature of your business in Toronto?"

"I am going to preach there."

The officer asked pointedly, "Are you carrying more than ten thousand dollars with you?"

My answer did not change her stern expression. "I'm not that kind of preacher."

"You may board now," is all she said.

I don't think all Drug Enforcement officers lack a sense of humor but the one who questioned me certainly did.

34

AN AUDIENCE OF ONE

I DON'T THINK ANY PASTOR WELCOMES FUNERAL SERVICES. Even when the deceased is a believer, sadness touches the hearts of family members and friends. Although they know the deceased person is in heaven experiencing face-to-face fellowship with the Lord and endless joy, it is hard to part with a loved one.

One funeral stands out in my memory as sad and highly unusual. Wilbur, the notorious town drunk, had died. He had attended a church when he was young but, in later years, he never attended. The funeral director who asked me to conduct Wilbur's funeral explained that Wilbur's pastor had refused to do so. I accepted the invitation.

I arrived at the funeral home with my Bible in hand and a prepared funeral message. Delivering the message would not be easy but I would do my best to comfort the mourners.

Knowing Wilbur's reputation, I didn't expect many mourners to attend the service. Neither did the funeral director. No one showed up at the appointed time. "Let's wait a while," the funeral director suggested. I agreed. Twenty minutes later, no one had arrived. "Reverend," the funeral director said, "I will have a seat and why don't you say what you planned to say. I will listen."

I appreciated his thoughtfulness and so I delivered my prepared message. A brief committal service followed.

The funeral director gained my respect that day. I was certain he would always serve the community impartially and faithfully. He would always be the last person to let someone down—in more ways than one.

35

A COUNTY ROAD SURPRISE

On her third visit to our church, a woman I judged to be about 70 asked me to pray for her husband. She told me his name was Martin and he had advanced throat cancer. I assured her I would pray for him but I was willing to visit him.

"Thank you," she said, "but Martin doesn't like preachers. I don't think he would let you see him."

"Tell him I'm non-threatening and I promise not to preach at him."

To my surprise, Martin agreed to let me visit. He and his wife lived about 8 miles down a country road. When I was halfway there, I found myself behind a very slow county dump truck. Because a solid line separated my lane from the oncoming one, I couldn't pass. But suddenly, the truck driver stuck his hand out his window and waved for me to pass. I appreciated his signal and passed his truck.

I had no sooner passed the county truck than I saw a state trooper approaching from a distance. He pulled around and pulled me over. I explained why I had crossed the solid line but he reminded me that the truck driver was not the law. In short, he wrote a ticket and gave it to me.

My first visit with Martin was cautiously friendly. He talked with the help of an electrolarynx and occasionally his wife had to poke a long cotton swab into the hole in his throat to clean his throat. He told me he was the Grand Master of his lodge.

Martin seemed to welcome each of my visits and eventually he trusted in Christ as his Savior. Not long after he made his profession of faith, he passed away and I conducted his funeral.

Thinking back on all that had transpired, I was glad I was able to visit Martin in spite of receiving a traffic ticket. It was worth it all. I paid the traffic ticket but Martin received a ticket to heaven that was absolutely free.

36

PRAYER IN A JAPANESE RESTAURANT

MY WIFE AND I CHOSE A JAPANESE RESTAURANT FOR lunch. We had never eaten in a Japanese restaurant so we were hoping for a new experience. We were not disappointed.

We were seated at a table for six but we were alone until a family of four joined us. A silver-haired grandmother, her daughter, and two young grandsons took their places. The table was shaped like a rectangular C with one side open for grilling and serving. Gloria and I were seated at one end of the table, the grandmother and the boys' mother sat at the other end, and the boys sat at the side. A dinner plate, knife and fork, chopsticks, and a glass of ice water lay in front of each of us.

Soon, a Japanese chef with a white chef's hat, white shirt, and black pants placed abundant food on the flat grill, ignited a gas burner, and started to work his magic. As the food swirled and its aroma kindled our appetite, the chef dazzled us. He deftly twirled a knife and metal spatula to cut and mix an assortment of beef, seafood, noodles, vegetables, and bamboo shoots. Then he separated the food into six piles and placed one pile on each plate.

Turning to the younger boy, the mother asked, "Josh, will you say grace?"

An embarrassed Josh shook his head from side to side. "Ask Matthew to pray," he implored. But Matthew said, "Ask Grandma!"

"Not me," Grandma responded.

Clearly the whole family seemed to be too shy to pray in the company of strangers. "Do you want me to pray?" I asked.

Looking relieved, the mother responded, "Please, do."

After I prayed, Gloria explained, "He's a pastor."

The mother answered, "We are Christians, and I'm a graduate of Hope College."

It turned out to be a happy, memorable experience with good food and enjoyable fellowship. If we meet again for Japanese food and I am designated to pray, I may conclude my prayer by substituting *Sayonara* for Amen.

37

FREE AT LAST

Mike was proud of his ability to perform magic tricks. He could surprise a person by finding a coin behind that person's ear. He could place a handkerchief over a tennis ball and, when he removed the handkerchief, the ball would no longer be there. He could make a coin disappear. (His tricks employed illusion and sleight of hand.)

One Sunday, Mike told a Sunday school audience that he wanted to show how Jesus frees us from our bondage to the devil. The trick was supposed to work like this: An assistant would tie a rope tightly several times around Mike's chest and tie a slip knot. Mike would say, "The devil binds us in sin." Then he would say, "When we ask Jesus to save us, he frees us from sin." At that moment he would pull the end of the rope and the rope would loosen and fall to the floor.

On the Sunday Mike wanted to show how Jesus frees us from sin, the assistant failed to use a slip knot. When Mike pulled the end of the rope, the rope got tighter around his chest. The more he pulled, the tighter the rope became until Mike struggled to breathe. We had to use a knife to cut the rope and then Mike was free at last.

Sometimes an object lesson can resemble a three-legged dog. It can't walk on all fours.

38

WWJD?

Sometimes waiting at a Taco Bell counter can be boring but it was not boring one day. While waiting for my order to arrive, I overheard the young man at the counter summon his manager.

"See that woman walking to her car in the parking lot?" he asked his manager.

"I see her," the manager replied. "So what?"

"I overcharged her five cents. What should I do? Should I take the five cents to her or just forget it?"

"Well," said the manager, "what would Jesus do?"

Looking somewhat puzzled, the young man answered, "I don't know. Jesus never worked at Taco Bell, did he?"

Undoubtedly, like the confused young man, many people don't know what Jesus would do at their workplace. However, a study of the Gospels shows us what Jesus did in a number of situations. What he did and what he said provide sufficient guidance for our actions and speech in the office, at home, and everywhere.

39

IS THERE A CODE FOR GOLF?

I THINK DOCTORS HAVE TO ASSIGN A CODE TO THEIR CASES in order to collect from insurance companies. I was lying on a bed and waiting for a technician to begin my echocardiogram when the technician learned my medical insurance would not pay anything for the procedure. He discovered he had not entered the right code. When he entered the proper code, the procedure could begin.

When doctors learn that I play golf, most of them spend more time chatting with me about golf than they do discussing my medical condition. A dermatologist found out that I was a golfer because I blamed the presence of precancer cells on my bald head to too much time under the sun on a golf course. I jokingly said it might be safer to spend more time in my pastoral office and less time playing golf. He asked how I became interested in golf. When I told him I had caddied as a boy, he said that's how he got started. He learned, too, that we both enjoyed playing at the Eisenhower Golf Course at the United States Airforce Academy. Later in the golf conversation, he told me that his son was a member of the golf team at a prestigious university. He was still talking golf as he accompanied me through the patients' waiting room and out the exit.

Another doctor asked me for advice on how to lower his golf score. He said he sliced badly. So there in his office, we discussed how to grip a club and how to swing properly. Several times, he went through the virtual motion of hitting a golf ball properly. He did spend a few moments addressing the reason for my visit.

I wonder if there is a code for a golf conversation that doctors use to charge a medical insurance company.

40

AN INQUISITIVE UROLOGIST

I was diagnosed in 2008 with prostate cancer. From that date until he retired, my urologist and I discussed my medical condition but our conversations touched on a variety of topics ranging from politics to ministry. The urologist enjoyed golf, although he confessed he was a duffer. Further, he never failed to ask where I had preached the previous Sunday. During one office visit, he asked, "What did you preach about last Sunday?"

"Turn Out the Lights. The Party's Over," I replied.

He looked puzzled. I added, "It was about Belshazzar's feast."

The urologist leaned forward. "I never heard of him. Tell me about him."

"He was a Babylonian king who was proud, profane, and promiscuous. He hosted a feast for a thousand of his lords and drank wine from vessels that had been consecrated in the temple at Jerusalem to God. While everyone was drinking, the fingers of a man's hand wrote something on the wall. Seeing just the fingers of a hand writing on the wall terrified Belshazzar. His knees knocked and his loins loosened. No one could interpret the writing until the prophet Daniel was summoned. He interpreted the writing to mean Belshazzar had been weighed in the balances and found wanting. His kingdom was divided and given to the Medes and Persians. That night, Belshazzar was killed and his kingdom fell to Darius the Mede."

"Interesting," the urologist replied. "It sounds like our country." Then he put on a surgical glove.

I had discussed the fingers writing on Belshazzar's wall but I am far too reserved to describe how the urologist used his finger.

41
POCKET KNIFE, PLEASE!

Dan was a Christian college grad with a pioneering spirit. He built a concrete block basement far out in the country and that's where he, his wife, and five children lived. It was also each of the children's birthplace. Dan delivered all five of them.

He had also built a sailboat. One Sunday evening, he and his family arrived late for the evening service. He explained they were sailing on a nearby lake but had to be rescued when rough weather capsized their boat.

Another Sunday they were late for morning worship. He said they were late because one of the children had fallen and split his forehead open. Dan cleaned the wound and stitched it up.

I shudder to think what might have happened if I had an attack of appendicitis while preaching and Dan had a pocket knife handy.

42

WHO'S ON FIRST?

My wife and three adult children are big fans of baseball but I am not. I prefer football, hockey, and golf. One Sunday, though, I had to listen to a baseball game in church. The church I served for almost seven years was located within a mile of a radio station.

During my sermon, the voice of a sports announcer overrode the church's PA system and gave the congregation a play-by-play description of the game. Our PA system and the radio station must have been on the same frequency.

I don't remember the teams' names or who was on first base but I know I didn't get to first base with the congregation that Sunday. I definitely struck out!

43

STAMP OUT DRIPPY PIOUS SAYINGS

I CONFESS. I DETEST DRIPPY PIOUS SAYINGS. HERE ARE some I would like to stamp out:

"He is a real blessing!" (*Is there such a thing as an unreal blessing?*)

"Bless your heart!"

"Praise the Lord" (*Repeated ad nauseam.*)

"The Lord spoke to me during my morning devotions." (*Direct revelation?*)

"It was a God thing."

"It was such a miracle!"

A young pastor conducted a funeral for a 92-year-old woman who could no longer drive the considerable distance to the church I served as an interim pastor. She had chosen the young man's church because it was close to her home. After the service, I introduced myself to the young pastor and asked in a cordial tone, "How is your church doing?"

He looked offended. "It's not my church. It's God's," he snapped.

I took his words to be drippy pious. "That's good," I said. "If it fails, you will know whom to blame."

My response may not have been very courteous but it was a small effort to stamp out drippy pious words.

44

SCOTTISH SYNAGOGUES IN TEXAS?

SHORTLY AFTER THE DENVER BRONCOS LOST THE SUPER Bowl to the Dallas Cowboys, I spoke at First Baptist Church, Dallas, Texas. Dr. Criswell was the pastor then and he was a gracious host.

I introduced my message by referring to the Broncos' loss to the Cowboys. I explained I was born in Scotland, and I had some advice for the Broncos that would guarantee a win in every game. I would advise the Broncos to hire big, burly Scotsmen to play Defense and give them the motto, "Get that quarter back!"

After the service, a gentleman approached me, identified himself as a fellow Scotsman, and gave me his business card. The card announced that he was available to play the bagpipes at weddings, funerals, graduation parties, barn raisings, anniversaries, and bar mitzvahs. I am sure Texas has plenty of weddings, funerals, graduation parties, barn raisings, and anniversaries, but how many Jewish synagogues does it have?

I suspect bagpipes are absent from synagogues but if

my friend blew his pipes in a synagogue, he might substitute "If I Were a Rich Man" for "Scotland the Brave."

45

A RIGGED CONTEST

FALCON, COLORADO, LIES ABOUT TEN MILES EAST OF Colorado Springs. It used to be a quiet small town surrounded by ranches and prairies. Many people moved there to get away from the city but recently the city has moved to Falcon. The ranches and farms morphed into housing developments and traffic in and around Falcon has become congested. About 20 years ago, when Falcon was still small, I had the privilege of serving a church there as interim pastor.

During my two years as interim pastor, I thoroughly enjoyed ministering to the congregation. The people were friendly and attentive to every sermon. The music was uplifting, the youth and children were engaging, and the deacons were caring and cooperative. A nine-year-old girl took notes when I preached and was always eager to show them to me. A teenage boy timed each sermon and reported the time to me. The teenagers took turns reading the Scripture selection at the morning services, and after the "timekeeper" took his turn, I told how many minutes it lasted.

The congregation had a good sense of humor, including Fred, a deacon, who challenged me publicly to a putting contest. I accepted the challenge and we agreed the contest would take place after a potluck dinner. When the set time arrived, the fellowship hall was full of eager spectators. A tin cup turned on its side served as the hole. Fred had his putter ready and I had mine.

Fred went first. His first and second shots failed to find the cup but his third shot hit the mark.

Fred handed me a golf ball which I placed on the floor. I gripped my putter, placed it behind the ball, and thought, *This is going to be easy. I am sure to get in the cup in two strokes, and perhaps one.*

I was wrong. When I hit the ball, it wobbled to the left and wobbled to the right, to the left, back to the right and stopped about three feet from where I hit it. The spectators roared in laughter, and Fred could not contain his glee.

I had been tricked. Fred had given me a goofy ball. It looked like a real golf ball but another ball was inside it. The contest had been rigged.

I laughed along with everyone else. Perhaps my response to a practical joke was one of the best sermons I delivered in Falcon.

46

GROWING OLD IS NO JOKE

Likely, every pastor has a library of jokes. Unless a pastor can laugh, he may not last. One of my favorite jokes that I no longer tell featured three elderly brothers who lived together.

One brother was in the upstairs bathroom. He was standing with one leg in the bathtub and the other leg out of the tub. He shouted to his brother who was on the stairs: "Was I getting in the tub or out of the tub?"

"You were getting in the tub," the brother replied. Then he called to his brother in the kitchen. "Was I going upstairs or downstairs?"

"Upstairs," the brother in the kitchen called. So, the brother on the stairs continued to go up the stairs.

"Whew," sighed the brother in the kitchen, "I hope I will never be like those two. Touch on wood. Let's see, was that the front door or the back door?"

Now that I am elderly, I do not tell the three brothers joke. I realize firsthand that memory loss among us older people is no laughing matter. It can be a very serious medical problem such as dementia.

Senior citizens often remark that growing old isn't for sissies. I agree and that's no joke.

47

EXCUSES, EXCUSES!

My high school French teacher assigned homework. When she asked a student, "Did you do your homework?" she might hear the student say no and offer an excuse. Her response was always the same, "*Qui excuse s'accuse*," meaning, "*Whoever excuses himself accuses himself.*"

Perhaps her response fits many excuses people offer for not attending church. Here are a few of those excuses:

"We had company."

"We were attending a family reunion."

"My parents made me go to Sunday school when I was a kid."

"I thought I was going to be sick."

"I had a headache."

"We attended the County Fair. We never miss it."

"It's too hot in church."

"It's too cold in church."

"My needs aren't met there."

"No one at church likes me."

"I prefer to worship God in nature."
"Hymns are so boring."
"I can't stand choruses."
"Shaking hands spreads germs."
"The music is too loud."
"I can't hear what's said at church."
"The church is only interested in money."
"My football team was playing at 11:00 a.m."
"The crying babies bother me."
"The service lasts too long."
"The preaching is too shallow."
"The preaching is way over my head."

Although some excuses are more creative than others, they are still just excuses and *qui s'excuse s'accuse*.

48

THE SECURE BACK PEW

ANNA STARTED ATTENDING A CHURCH DURING MY FIFTH year as the interim pastor. I judged her to be 70 something, about 5' 2", and weighing around 150 pounds. Her hair was white. She wore glasses, pearl earrings, a pearl necklace, a dark blue dress, and black shoes, and her smile was delightful. There was nothing unusual about the way she looked but there was something unusual about her. She always sat in the last pew at the back of the auditorium.

When I was a young pastor, I roped off the back pews of a church but as I grew older I reasoned that people have a right to sit wherever they chose. After all, they don't have to attend church; they choose to do so. In return, I choose to welcome them and let them select their seating. Therefore, I let Anna sit in the last pew at the back of the auditorium. I wondered, though, why she preferred to sit there when several empty pews separated her from the rest of the attendees. One day, she volunteered an answer to that question.

Just before morning worship began, Anna beckoned

to me. "Pastor," she said, "You must be wondering why I always sit in the back pew."

I kept silent.

Whispering, she continued, "It's because I have back door gas."

I agreed to keep her secret confidential.

Frankly, under the circumstances, I was glad Anna had chosen the back pew. The only sound I wanted to hear during my preaching was an occasional Amen.

MOMENTS OF GRACE

ENCOURAGEMENT FOR THE SENIOR YEARS

1

A FAITHFUL WALK

"...his compassions, they fail not. They are new every morning: great is thy faithfulness"
(Lamentations 3:22b-23).

AT THE STRONG URGING OF MY PHYSICIAN, I (JOE) recently began a regular exercise program. Nothing too extensive, just a half an hour each morning of walking briskly at the local track. I've grown to love this special time as it gives me an opportunity to enjoy many of the aspects of God's natural creation. I listen to the birds, take in the scenery, and even take note of some of my fellow walkers.

One gentleman who I've come to admire is Burt. Burt usually gets to the track long before I do and has finished many laps before I've even started. In his eighties, he presents quite a sight. He's a tall man and very lean with the longest arms I've ever seen. His gait is somewhere between a fast walk and a trot, a kind of shuffle. He doesn't go very fast but that doesn't seem to bother him. With his arms dangling at his sides and his huge hands pushing backwards, he just plods along lap after lap, piling up the yardage. When someone walks or jogs by him, he always greets them with a pleasant, "Good morning! What a beautiful day!"

One day, I didn't see Burt at the track and wondered what might have happened. Frankly, I was even somewhat worried. Later, at the local MacDonald's, where many seniors find their way each morning, I was relieved to see Burt having his breakfast. I greeted him and said, "I missed seeing you this morning." He looked up and with just a hint of impertinence replied, "Whadd'ya mean? I was there. Put in eight and a half miles." Oops, I should have known. Burt never misses.

Burt's commitment and faithfulness to his exercise regimen reminds me so much of the faithfulness of the Lord Jesus, the One who has promised to never leave us or forsake us and continually proves it by His presence and care. Even when we tend to feel lonely, we are never alone, because He is always there with us, guiding and comforting through every step we take. . .even on a walking track.

"LORD, *thank you that I can depend on your constant presence. Amen.*"

2

A FIRST TIME FOR ALMOST EVERYTHING

"I HAVE BEEN REMINDED OF YOUR SINCERE FAITH, WHICH first lived in your grandmother Lois and in your mother Eunice and, I am persuaded, now lives in you also" (2 Timothy 1:5).

The word "first" carries significance. Our nation's "first lady" is the President's wife. Nancy Reagan was called "the first lady" when Ronald Reagan occupied the White House." She was neither Mr. Reagan's first wife nor the first woman to live at the White House but the title of respect and endearment fit her well. She served Ronnie and us well and stayed by her husband to his final breath.

Coming in first in the World Series is significant too. The champs don their World Series Championship caps almost as soon as the final out ends the last game. The fans go wild, the President invites the champions to the White House, and the hometown throws a victory parade. Don't be surprised to see the Chicago Cubs win the World Series soon. When they do; their fans will go crazy. The celebration in Chicago will make Times Square on New Year's Eve seem like a wake.

You have had some memorable firsts, haven't you? You may not remember your first steps to Momma but you remember your first steps into the Division of Motor Vehicles when you applied for a driver's license. And how about the first steps down the wedding aisle?

No one has to remind you how great you felt when you received the keys to your first car or first house. Even now, you smile when you think about it.

Taking first place in a music or vocal contest is a big deal too. Consider the excitement generated by the TV show, American Idol. Approximately 45 million Americans each week vote for the vocalist they believe deserves the title, "American Idol." You may never become an American idol but weren't you elated when you took place in piano, violin, trumpet, or vocal?

How did you feel the first time you fell in love?

What were you thinking when you sat in a dentist's chair for the first time or received your first flu shot? How did you feel when you first tried a hula hoop?

How excited and sleepless were you during your first night away from home?

How nervous were you when you first met your future spouse's parents?

Granted some memories of first times can be traumatic but our first introduction to Jesus as Savior stands out forever as the best "first" anyone can experience. The apostle Paul referred to this greatest "first" as having marked the lives of three generations of family members: Timothy's grandmother Lois, his mother Eunice, and Timothy himself (2 Timothy 1:5).

If you are a believer, thank God for the time you first

believed on Jesus and help others—family members, friends, and neighbors—to believe on Him. The day they do so will set off a celebration in heaven that will exceed even what follows the World Series' declaration, "Cubs win! Cubs win!"

"I THANK YOU, Lord, for the day I first believed in You have always been a faithful Friend and Guide. Help me to persuade others to believe on You."

3
HOMELAND SECURITY

"And I give them eternal life, and they shall never perish..." (John 10: 28).

AFTER THE HORRIFIC EVENTS OF SEPTEMBER 11, 2001, OUR government determined that we had to establish many new safeguards to protect our country. Hourly briefings kept the nation updated on the steps being taken to counter future acts of terrorism. Our military mounted a devastating reprisal on the parties responsible for these shocking attacks.

A new government agency was established to deal with any and all subversive activity planned within our borders. This new office, called The Office of Homeland Security, has already paid huge dividends.

Numerous planned acts of terrorism have been thwarted, with many prospective terrorists arrested.

But homeland security is nothing new to America. Remember the weekly air-raid drills during World War 2? Our family lived in a small apartment on the north side of Chicago and at a specified time, everyone had to turn off their lights and close their drapes or curtains so that everything was completely dark. The streets were deserted, except for Air-Raid Wardens who were responsible for a designated section, such as a city block. Wearing yellow helmets and carrying whistles and flashlights, these people patrolled the streets, making sure all lights were off. If anyone had not darkened their home, the wardens would blow their whistle and call out for immediate compliance. I can still remember sitting in the dark with my parents waiting for the all-clear to sound. Pretty scary stuff for a four-year-old!

In the First Century, Jerusalem, as well as all of Palestine, was invaded and controlled by the Romans. This sacred city was now under the rule of pagan Rome, and, for the Jews, there was continued chaos as their homeland was in political and social upheaval. Although the Jews were free to worship, they knew it was only a matter of time before even that privilege would end. Sure enough, in 70 AD, Rome destroyed Jerusalem, killing thousands of Jews and causing thousands more to relocate and hide in temporary shelters.

When Jesus spoke about homeland security, He had something much better in mind. In the tenth chapter of John He said, "My sheep hear my voice and they follow Me, and I give unto them eternal life and they shall never perish. Neither shall any man pluck them out of My hand." In this precious promise, Jesus referred to the homeland as Heaven and the security as being eternal.

Even though we live in perilous and uncertain

times, we who follow Christ can have the assurance that we are eternally secure in Him.

"LORD, help me remember that however dangerous my life's journey may be, my ultimate destination has been secured by you forever."

4
SAL'S BIGGEST CHALLENGE

"...whose god is their belly..." (Philippians 3:19).

SAL BONSIGNORE WAS A GREGARIOUS MAN.

He loved his family, He loved his job, He loved people in general. Most of

all, Sal loved food, especially the foods that befitted his heritage: pizza, pasta, pastries, cheese, and especially bread. Oh, how Sal loved warm bread!

Unfortunately, Sal's size reflected his love of food. He had always been chubby but, as a child, aside from being made fun of at times, it really didn't matter. Now, in his senior years, his overeating was causing some serious problems. It seems Sal's health can be described best by the adjective "high." He has high blood pressure, high cholesterol, high blood sugar and, of course, high weight. Concerned, Sal's doctor developed a diet for Sal that introduced a new word, "low"—low carbs, low fat, low portions, and no sugar.

What a dramatic change for Sal! All the foods he

had enjoyed throughout his life, he now had to do without. Let's face it, Sal lived to eat. Now, with all these restrictions he has become depressed, a condition that makes him crave food even more.

Faced with this monumental challenge, Sal did the only thing that seemed appropriate to him. He changed doctors!

Although humorous, this story points out a serious problem in the Western World: obesity. We've all heard about the problems with youngsters being obese but did you know that obesity is also a serious problem among seniors? Actually, it is even more serious when we consider how few of the elderly exercise.

It's interesting that when the apostle Paul condemned self-indulgence in

Philippians 3:19, he used the belly as his primary example. Then, as now, people had a problem controlling their cravings for food. Yet, the solution was the same then as it is now. We need to treat obesity as a sin and deal with it as such. Once we understand that God can forgive us and also give us the self-control we need to overcome the nagging temptation to overeat, we can begin to enjoy food for what it was meant to be.

Eventually, Sal's serious health difficulties brought him to his senses. Now, he will tell you it was when he realized he loved life more than he loved food that he began to lose a significant amount of weight, He is now involved in a regular exercise program and his whole lifestyle has changed. He still eats some of his favorite foods from time to time but he has controlled his diet with a new-found discipline.

Here are some tips that helped Sal:

- Get in the habit of preparing and eating smaller portions. It may seem difficult at first, but your body will adjust, usually within a week.
- Don't eat in the room you cook in. It's too easy to go back for seconds since food is so accessible
- Never eat in front of the TV. The fast food industry spends millions of dollars each year to make their products alluring.
- Don't eat after seven o'clock at night
- Eat slowly, putting down your fork after every bite, and chew each mouthful at least twenty times. It takes the stomach twelve minutes to signal the brain that it has had enough. We need to let the brain get the message.
- Drink plenty of water and avoid alcoholic beverages.
- When eating out, try to get an advanced copy of the menu (perhaps on the internet) so you can make good choices before arriving.
- Don't feel pressured when you are the only one in the group who avoids dessert. Remember, your goals are more important than a few moments of tasty pleasure.
- Begin a regular exercise program of walking briskly at least twenty minutes a day, three or four times a week.

Beyond a doubt, the greatest way to find help with our eating problems is through prayer. God will give us the discipline and direction as we deal with this difficult problem. That's what Sal learned!

"LORD, help us to see food as what You meant it to be—enjoyed but not worshiped."

5

STAMP OUT THE GRUMPY STEREOTYPE

"Consider it pure joy, my brothers, whenever you face trials of many kinds" (James 1:2).

HOW DOES THE YOUNGER GENERATION VIEW THE 60-PLUS generation? The answer depends in large part on whether it sees us smile or frown and whether it hears us grumble or rejoice. The fact is, too many of us "mature" citizens do not smile and rejoice enough. Consequently, we are often perceived as grumpy old codgers.

Hollywood produced a movie called "Grumpy Old Men," but it has yet to produce a "Grumpy Young Men" movie. Not long ago, the Colorado Springs Gazette printed a story about the only two retirees on the City Council. It referred to the two as "grumpy old men." Although the piece was lighthearted, it jabbed at the tendency of the two councilmen to answer citizens' questions sharply and to rebuff each other coarsely. It did point out, though, that the grumpy twosome gets along royally after each council session.

Grumpiness dogged the Israelites' steps in the wilderness. The Israelites griped from Egypt's border to Canaan's. They wearied Moses with their constant grumbling and they tested God's patience. Wilderness travel is hard enough without having to listen to more than a million chronic grumblers!

Sure, if we want to find something to be grumpy about, we don't have to look far. Arthritis is no picnic. A shoestring budget is anything but fun. Rising health care costs are more inflammatory than a pinched nerve. And taxes, taxes, taxes hardly motivate us to do cartwheels. But even the dull side of life can be brighter if we polish it with faith.

Faith enables us to claim God's promises. We grip them, pull them close to our hearts, and hold on to them tightly. We believe God brings into our lives only what is for our good and His glory. We focus on the pearls that irritating trials produce. We find that heavy loads are easier to bear when we place them on Jesus' broad shoulders. And we see roses where those without faith see only thorns.

So, there's no reason to be grumpy. Let's stamp out the stereotype and give the younger generation good reason to ask, "What do you have to be so happy about?"

"Lord, as I get older, may my joy increase. May I be gracious, not grumpy. Thank you for Your promises that encourage me daily."

6
THE PERFECT HOUSE

"Now we know that if the earthly tent we live in is destroyed, we have a building from God, an eternal house in heaven, not built by human hands" (2 Corinthians 5:1).

WE'VE ALL HEARD HORROR STORIES ABOUT THE ONGOING problem of people living in squalor. Often these conditions have gone on for years, in some of the most established neighborhoods, with no one ever suspecting. It presents a troubling question with no clear-cut answers. Experts in the field of sociology say that this situation is much more common than we realize. Unfortunately, most of those discovered living in these dreadful conditions are seniors. You have to wonder how things can deteriorate to such a level of degradation. What about the person's family? Do they even know what has happened? Do they care?

Often, because they don't live in the same area, they are not aware of their family member's situation.

Take the case of Charley.

Charley lived alone in middle-class suburban home, amidst a cross section of young and middle-aged families. The atmosphere was typical with the sounds of children playing, dogs barking and the aroma of outdoor cooking heavy in the air. But it was another smell, one coming from Charley's house that alerted neighbors. They eventually called the police. When the authorities arrived, they found Charley sitting on the floor of his living room covered with fleas and surrounded by at least a dozen cats. "They really don't bother me," he said of the insects crawling all over him. At eighty-two, Charley had simply given up. His house was the most valuable asset he had and he didn't want to lose it but the upkeep had become more than he could handle.

Some of Charley's neighbors decided to pitch in and provide some help. While he was staying in a local Senior Services facility, they cleaned, painted, recarpeted, and rewired Charley's house. They even installed new furniture and appliances and convinced their local officials to waive the heavy fine they had threatened to give Charley. When Charley returned home, he was totally overwhelmed. He said it was like finding the perfect house.

Not long before Jesus died, He told his disciples that He was going to prepare a place for them and all who believe in Him. He said, "In My Father's house are many rooms . . .I am going there to prepare a place for you." Now, that will be the perfect house. Not because of furniture or carpeting or appliances but because the loving hands of Christ are preparing it.

. . .

> "LORD, thank You for not only dying for me, but also for preparing a place for me where I can worship You forever."

7

GRANDKIDS SAY THE FUNNIEST THINGS

"A good man leaves an inheritance for his children's children" (Proverbs 13:22a).

A TEACHER ASKED HER YOUNG PUPILS HOW THEY SPENT their vacation. One child wrote the following:

"We always spend our vacation with Grandma and Grandpa. They used to live here in a big, brick house, but Grandpa got retarded and they moved to Florida and now they live in a place with a lot of other retarded people.

"They live in a tin box and have rocks painted green to look like grass. They ride around on big tricycles and wear nametags because they don't know who they are anymore.

"They go to a building called a wrecked center, but they must have got it fixed because it is all right now. They play games and do exercises there, but they don't do them very well."

Let's face it, sometimes grandparents can be as puzzling to their grandkids as grandkids are to their grandparents. And occasionally what the grandkids say about us can be downright humbling:

"Have you always been fat, Grandma?"

"How come you married Grandpa? He doesn't have any hair. And when I ask him for a dollar, he says he doesn't have any money."

"Grandpa, how come you sleep so much?"

But grandkids can also say things that make us feel ten feet tall. Recently our six-year-old granddaughter told my wife, Gloria, "Grandma, next to Jesus, you are the nicest person I know."

Timothy was an outstanding pastor in the first century but his training for a commendable life and ministry didn't begin in a seminary. It began at home. As was typical of first-century families, Grandma Lois, Mom Eunice, Timothy's dad, and Timothy all lived together when Timothy was growing up. Grandma Lois must have made a significant impact on the boy's spiritual life. In his second letter to Timothy, the apostle Paul commented: "I have been reminded of your sincere faith, which first lived in your grandmother Lois and in your mother Eunice and, I am persuaded, now lives in you also" (2 Timothy 1:5).

A grandparent may bequeath money and personal items to the grandkids but don't you agree that a godly testimony is a far better inheritance? Memories of the grandparents living in a tin-box house with rocks painted green to look like grass may stick with the grandkids for a while but memories of Grandpa and Grandma's faith will last a lifetime. Timothy would say Amen to that!

8

LIVE WHERE YOU LIVE

"... He blesses the home of the righteous" (Proverbs 3:33).

ABOUT EVERY OTHER YEAR MY WIFE AND I (JIM) SCOPE out the Parade of Homes in our city. It's fun to see what kinds of houses contractors and designers put on the market to entice buyers to invest hundreds of thousands of dollars. But viewing beautiful houses isn't all fun, at least for me. Slipping footies over shoes before entering a model home may be a cakewalk for young lookie-loos but it's a killer for me. I have had the same inflexible back for more than seventy years. It might be simpler for a centipede to give itself a pedicure than for me to get my shoes into footies. You can imagine how my back feels after repeating the procedure at each doorstep of twenty-something houses. Ouch! *Snap, crackle, and pop!*

I must admit some houses in the Parade of Homes seem like palaces compared to our house but I am content to simply shuffle through them, return home, and appreciate what I have. At home, the taxes are lower, the yard is landscaped, my recliner feels so good, and the whole house is footies-free! So, Lord willing, I expect to live right where I live for a long time.

From sea to shining sea, we seniors plant ourselves in a variety of dwellings—from ranches to retirement villages, apartments to adobes, bungalows to boathouses, cabins to condos, and single occupancies to multiplexes. But where we live isn't as important as how we live. Nor is what we spend on a place as important as what we invest in the days we live there. Sure, the grass may look greener elsewhere but life may not be as rosy there.

Take stock of what makes the "good life" really good:

- the presence of the Lord
- contentment
- a clear conscience
- joy and laughter
- faith
- a well-worn Bible
- prayer
- open lines of communication with family and friends
- a reason to keep on keeping on
- a grateful heart

Someday you may choose to move to a different residence and you may have to downsize. Nevertheless, you can take along everything that really matters. Check the above list again and determine that today and every day you will *live* where you live until you take possession of your home in heaven.

. . .

"Lord, bless this house. May the joy of knowing you are present here brighten every corner and extend to my neighbors."

9

LOVE IS WONDERFUL THE TWENTY-FIRST TIME AROUND. OR IS IT?

"Listen to advice and accept instruction, and in the end, you will be wise" (Proverbs 19:20).

VINYL RECORDS HAVE GONE THE WAY OF THE DINOSAUR but you may remember the joke pastors told when vinyl records were still spinning. Two recording stars asked a pastor to marry them but he refused. He reasoned they were incompatible. He was 45 and she was only 33 and 1/3.

Recently, in northern Malaysia, a thirty-three-year-old man married a 104-year-old woman. How compatible is that?

I know what you're thinking—he married her for her money. Think again! She was dirt poor. He explained mutual respect and friendship led to love.

By the way, this marriage was number 21 for the woman so she knew the way down the wedding aisle. No doubt, she walked more slowly this time than the first time but she arrived on time for the ceremony.

Understandably, widows and widowers struggle

with loneliness. If an opportunity for friendship with someone of the opposite gender comes along, unmarried seniors may welcome it. If the friendship develops into a loving relationship, the couple may choose to marry. But before they tie the knot they should face the compatibility issue. Age may not be an issue when both partners are seniors but such matters as faith, family relationships, personality, finances, and values are certainly issues worthy of discussion. Of these, faith is the most important matter. A Christian must not marry a non-Christian at any age. Second Corinthians 6:14 commands: "Do not be yoked together with unbelievers."

It is tempting for a Christian senior to think marriage is the end of all his troubles but it may be the front end if he marries a non-Christian. He should, therefore, commit his way to the Lord and obey Him.

"LORD, I need your instruction in my senior years as much as when I was younger. Grant me the guidance and courage I need to make wise decisions."

10

I DON'T DISCUSS RELIGION!

"For God so loved the world that he gave his one and only Son, that whoever believes in him shall not perish but have eternal life" (John 3:16).

I UNHOOKED THE WIDE FARM GATE AND DROVE DOWN A long dirt driveway to a house where Sally, a terminally ill 80-year-old woman was expecting me. At the request of her daughter, I had visited her several times in the hospital. Now she was resting at home and facing her life's inevitable end.

Sally's daughter and two big, friendly dogs escorted me into the house.

When I entered Sally's room, she smiled at me from a heavily pillowed recliner. She had consented to my visit, telling her daughter that when I visited her in the hospital I was friendly and nice, prayed, and didn't stay long.

We shook hands.

"How are you getting along, Sally?" I asked.

"Fine. Just awfully tired."

"I have been praying that the Lord will give you strength and patience for each day."

"Uh, huh."

"But something is more important than physical health, Sally. Jesus died to give us spiritual health—everlasting life. We are all going to leave this world sometime but if we ask Jesus to be our Savior, we will go to heaven, where there is no more sickness or dying."

Silence.

"Sally, would you like to have everlasting life? Would you like to believe on Jesus as your Savior?"

Turning her face away from me, Sally intoned, "I don't discuss religion."

"That's good," I replied, "neither do I. All the religion in the world can't forgive sins or get anyone into heaven. Jesus didn't come to earth to bring religion. He came to bring eternal life and He died and rose again to make it happen."

"I don't want to talk about it."

"Okay, Sally, but I hope you will think about it. You can believe on Jesus as your Savior whether I am here or not."

Like Sally, many seniors hold the I-don't-discuss-religion attitude. It's the-head-in-the-sand approach to life's greatest issue. This attitude makes as much sense as driving blindfolded down a freeway to avoid having to acknowledge traffic exists and you have to deal with it. Why would anyone want to ignore Jesus, the One who loved us and laid down his life for us?

. . .

"LIFE IS SO FLEETING, Lord, but you made it possible for me to have eternal life. Let me share this good news with at least one person today."

11
ONLY A SHADOW

"Even though I walk through the valley of the shadow of death, I will fear no evil, for you are with me; your rod and your staff, they comfort me" (Psalm 23:4).

ANNETTE HAD DIED, LEAVING A HUSBAND AND TWO YOUNG daughters. Her husband was a pastor; her daughters, Kristen and Kari, were 5 and 7 respectively.

The sorrowful pastor had tried repeatedly to ease his daughters' pain by explaining that their mother had gone to heaven. He wanted them to know that death is not a terrifying experience for a believer. But his words failed to comfort little Kristen and Keri.

Then, stopped at a traffic light on their way to the funeral home, the pastor called his daughters' attention to the shadow of a truck that had pulled alongside their car.

"Girls," Dad, asked, "would you rather get run over by a truck or by its shadow?"

"Daddy," Kristen replied, "a shadow doesn't hurt."

"You're right, Kristen. The Bible says that dying is like walking through a valley called 'the shadow of death.' When Mommy died, she walked through a shadow and Jesus was waiting beyond the shadow to meet her."

When Jesus voluntarily died for our sins, He took the full brunt of God's wrath, being made sin for us (2 Corinthians 5:21). The physical suffering was intense but the spiritual suffering was even more intense—inflicting on Jesus far more agony and anguish than the human mind can comprehend. Isaiah 53:11 mentions "the suffering of his soul." Because He was bearing our sins on the cross, He became the object of divine judgment. The punishment we deserved fell on Him even to the point that God turned away from Him. However, because Jesus experienced God's full wrath, believers experience His full love. Because the Father forsook Jesus, the Father accepts believers. Because Jesus died, believers live. Because He was "run over" by death, only the shadow of death can touch us. Because He arose from the grave and ascended to heaven, He waits beyond death's shadow to welcome us home.

"I THANK YOU, Lord for taking my place on the cross, for conquering death, and for saving me. 'Even though I walk through the valley of the shadow of death, I will fear no evil, for you are with me; your rod and your staff, they comfort me.'"

12

IF THE HAT FITS...

"Every good and perfect gift is from above, coming down from the Father the heavenly lights, who does not change like shifting shadows" (James 1:17).

MY SON AND MY OLDER DAUGHTER BOUGHT ME (JIM) a really nice watch for Christmas five years ago. I especially liked it because it was a golf watch. Limited edition. Brown leather wristband. Recessed etching on the face—of a golfer, caddy, green, and flag—in gold. Elegant black lettering around the design boasts "FOSSIL AUTHENTIC." As the grandkids say, "It's cool!"

I wear that watch proudly on and off the golf course.

But a not-so-cool hat came with the watch. It's a green baseball-style cap and it's hanging on a hook in the garage. I put it there when I carried the torn Christmas giftwrap to the trashcan and it has been hanging there ever since. I just haven't had the heart to toss it out. After all, it was a gift from my son and daughter. What kind of dad would junk a gift from his kids?

So, here's the problem. The hat, like the watch, says FOSSIL. Fossil watches are popular but who wants to wear a hat that says FOSSIL? Can you imagine the stares and not-so-funny comments I'd get if I wore it? "Look at that fossil." "Did you see that fossil with the FOSSIL hat?" "Now there's a guy who likes to advertise his age!" No thanks: I can get along nicely without that kind of attention.

So, the FOSSIL hat will stay right where it is in the garage.

Now, this Christmas, if my kids give me a golf hat that says, "PAR MAN," I'll even wear it to bed!

Strange, isn't it, how we accept some gifts enthusiastically but consider others inappropriate, even unwelcome. I guess that explains why gift exchange lines are so long the day after Christmas. Yet, God's gifts are always appropriate and welcome. You see, He knows exactly what we need, what suits us best, and what we can use. The apostle James wrote: "Every good and perfect gift is from above, coming down from the Father the heavenly lights, who does not change like shifting shadows" (James 1:17).

The apostle Paul commented about the variety of spiritual gifts God gives to believers. He said, "We have different gifts, according to the grace given us" (Romans 12:6). Then he counseled us to use our specific gift faithfully.

Let's not hang our spiritual gifts on a hook somewhere!

. . .

"THANK YOU, Lord, for choosing just the right spiritual gift for me. May I take it wherever I go and use it faithfully in ministry to others."

13

FEELING DEPRESSED?

"Why are you downcast, O my soul? Why so disturbed within me? Put your hope in God, for I will yet praise him, my Savior and my God" (Psalm 42:11).

DEPRESSION IN SENIORS IS NOT UNUSUAL BUT IT CAN BE serious. It affects about 6 million senior Americans, but fewer than one million seek help. Depression leads to suicide among seniors more than among any other age group.

If you recognize common symptoms of depression, you may be able to help a senior friend or spouse—or even yourself. They include the inability to sleep at night, daytime sleepiness, withdrawal, feelings of hopelessness and sadness, lack of interest in life, confusion, self-deprecation, death wishes, neglect of personal care, memory loss, lethargy, irritability, inappropriate guilt, and loss of appetite.

Elijah showed signs of depression when he fled for his life from Israel to the desert south of Judah (1 Kings

19:1–4a). Wicked Queen Jezebel had put a contract on his life because he had exposed the phoniness of her pet religion, Baalism, and had slain 450 of Baal's prophets (1 Kings 18:25–40). Her fury had quickly knocked the props out from under his faith.

Deep in the desert and exhausted, Elijah succumbed to guilt. He felt hopeless, alone, and worthless (1 Kings 19:4b). He even asked God to end his life—a request Jezebel would have gladly honored had Elijah stayed in Israel.

Hard to believe, isn't it, that such a courageous prophet could slide quickly into self-pity and despair? But, as James 5:17 reminds us, there's some Elijah in each of us (James 5:17). We, too, can ride a roller coaster of emotions from the zenith of faith to the depth of despair. One day we can feel high enough to tickle the toes of the angels. The next day we feel so low that we give up on everything and everyone including ourselves.

But there is hope. The Lord pulled Elijah out of depression and gave him a new lease on life. He can do that for us too.

"LORD, I am tired of feeling down. Give me the help I need to feel renewed and to face life courageously and confidently."

14

RECOVERING FROM DEPRESSION

"After the earthquake came a fire, but the LORD was not in the fire. And after the fire came a gentle whisper" (1 Kings 19:12).

THE PROPHET ELIJAH TUMBLED. HE HAD SHOWN tremendous faith by confronting and triumphing over 450 prophets of Baal on Mt. Carmel, but his faith deflated faster than a punctured balloon when Queen Jezebel threatened his life. He fled far into the desert where he asked God to end his life. To put it plainly, Elijah was depressed.

Some forms of depression have medical causes and require medical attention but others, like Elijah's, result from a lapse of faith, worry, weariness, and a sense of overwhelming guilt. Elijah's faith went poof when Jezebel said "Boo!" He worried and ran for his life. Exhausted, he plopped down under a broom tree and asked God to take his life.

So how did God restore Elijah's spiritual and emotional wellbeing?

First, He let Elijah rest (1 Kings 19:5a). A pastor used to say, "Christians on their way to heaven should be in bed by eleven." If we fail to get adequate rest, we may succumb to depression.

Second, God fed Elijah and provided a jar of water too (vv. 5b, 6). Proper sleep and nourishment often help us move out of "the dumps."

Third, God gave Elijah a new revelation of His presence. He showed Elijah He was with him in the stillness as well as in life's exciting times. He was present in the desert just as He had been on Mount Carmel (see vv. 12, 13).

Finally, God gave Elijah new assignments. He commissioned him to anoint a successor and two kings (vv. 15, 16). God doesn't write us off when we write ourselves off. He has specific assignments for each of us. A sense of mission rejuvenates us.

"LORD, when I battle depression, please remind me of your presence and grant me a renewed sense of mission."

15

SERVICE WITH A SMILE

Be kind one to another ... (Eph. 4:32).

FOR OVER 25 YEARS, IT HAS BEEN MY (JOE'S) GREAT privilege to lead a weekly men's Bible study. Each Wednesday morning has come to be a very special time, not only for me but also for the many who have attended. In addition to the spiritual growth we've all experienced, becoming acquainted with this outstanding group of men has been an added bonus. Some have been attending faithfully for more than 20 years.

Len is a prime example.

Len and his wife, Sue, had two fine sons, one of which spent many years on the mission field in Africa. His grandchildren are all involved in full-time Christian work, as well. When Sue died, Len felt the need for the fellowship and support a group like ours offered and began attending. The first thing I noticed about Len was a smile that didn't seem to quit. His radiant face could light up the darkest room. He was often the first one there, which was significant, considering we started at 6:30 A.M. He loved studying the Scriptures and the prayer and fellowship that eventually ended at a local restaurant for breakfast. We all came to love him, too. He told me once that he had never felt comfortable praying out loud. You would have never guessed it from his prayers.

When Len was well into his eighties, physical problems began to limit his leaving the house. Although he didn't venture out much, he still managed to continue to volunteer each Tuesday at the local hospital (a task he loved to perform) and get to the Bible study. His winning smile made him a natural at the hospital as he greeted and directed patients and visitors alike to their various places. He could also be seen wheeling patients around the lobby, always with that smile and a kind and encouraging word.

When Len died, many acquaintances and fellow workers from the hospital came to the funeral and specifically mentioned his gracious manner and kind demeanor. They marveled that at his age and physical condition he could still cheerfully and effectively serve others. It wasn't a mystery to the ones who knew him. Len was faithfully reflecting the love and mercy of the Lord, everywhere he went.

Len used to wonder what he had to contribute. Like many genuinely humble people, he didn't realize to what extent the Lord was using his unselfish willingness to faithfully serve others.

We, seniors, need to realize that, as long as we're here, the Lord has something for us to offer others—even if it's just our smile.

. . .

"LORD, thank you for the example of this wonderful man and what you accomplish through all of us."

16

LIFE IN THE BIG HOUSE

"In my Father's house are many rooms; if it were not so, I would have told you. I am going there to prepare a place for you. And if I go and prepare a place for you, I will come back and take you to be with me that you also may be where I am" (John 14:2, 3).

IN THE OLD DAYS, PEOPLE REFERRED TO INCARCERATION AS doing time in the Big House. We don't hear that term often now but it's an accurate description of most state and federal prisons that are home to thousands of inmates.

Thousands of seniors, too, live in a big house. It's home, sweet home, where they raised their kids, celebrated birthdays, repainted, redecorated, repaired dripping faucets, and replaced countless light bulbs. The living room, dining room, kitchen, and family room or parlor often launched lively conversation with extended family and friends. Occasionally, guest bedrooms afforded out-of-town company a good night's rest. At times, the kids hosted sleepovers in the big house but they resembled stay-awake-overs more than sleepovers.

Now the kids are grown and have their own big houses. You and your spouse survey the homestead and ask, "What are we going to do with all this extra space?" If you retreat to watch TV or read a book in separate rooms, neither of you can hear the other's comments or questions. Strange, isn't it, how our ability to hear decreases as the size of our house increases? "George, come in here and help me find my glasses," sounds like, "Juries creep and so does molasses." And "The Nuggets lost again," sounds like, "No guts, no gain."

You have considered downsizing but that option is about as appealing as downsizing your waist by eight or nine inches. To accomplish the task, you have to give up so much of what you love. Some of your friends have moved into a retirement community but you like the sound of kids at play in the neighborhood. Further, if you had to get rid of your birdhouse collection and woodworking tools, the trauma might kill you. You wouldn't need retirement community living then.

So, for now, you will keep living in the big house. You realize you will have to leave it eventually but, for now, it's a good fit, even if it is too big. The memories feel good and so do the familiar surroundings—the sofa with the crocheted afghan, the recliner, the photos on the mantle, plus lots of other things you enjoy.

If you spend the rest of your life in the big house, you will have no regrets. In the meantime, you will thank the Lord for good memories, present comforts, and His future care.

Jesus gathered His disciples in an upper room and assured them: "In my Father's house are many rooms; if it were not so, I would have told you. I am going there to prepare a place for you. And if I go and prepare a place for you, I will come back and take you to be with me that you also may be where I am" (John 14:2, 3).

Cherish this promise and anticipate your ultimate moving day to your heavenly Father's big house in heaven. Everything will be just right there. Custom designed and furnished to satisfy your personal taste. And you will never be billed for utilities, property taxes, telephone, or water. The roof will never leak. The windows will never stick. The floors will never squeak. Best of all, you will never have to downsize.

"Lord, thank You for the house I call home. It may be a bit big now, but it's still home. And thank You, Lord, for my eternal home in heaven. "

17

MUCH BETTER THAN HIGH TECH

"Evening, morning and noon I cry out in my distress, and he hears my voice" (Psalm 55:17).

DO YOU REMEMBER WHEN A BLACKBERRY WAS A BLACK berry? You ate it; you didn't "play" with it. And you didn't have to use your thumbs. Now we have i-Pods, i-Tunes, i-Photos, i-Chats, IDVDs, and a host of other high-tech gadgets that make our heads swim. If you know your way around computers and other techie toys, you are either a senior with a uniquely wired brain or a teenager who picked up this book by mistake. Most of us wonder how the world got so high tech and what quantum leaps lie ahead. We fear change and we are too old to jump.

Even the purchase of a new telephone can lead us to the edge of a nervous breakdown. How do you set the date, day, and time? How do you adjust the ringer's volume? Voice mail, call forwarding, call waiting, and setting up a frequently-called numbers directory can produce night sweats and even nightmares. You can plop the receiver down almost anywhere in the house. It doesn't have to remain on the base station. But at our age, we tend to forget where we place an object, so who wants to turn a house upside down and inside out in search of a phone?

Think back to "the good old days." A manual typewriter hardly ever broke down. Occasionally, we had to clean the keys and roller and install a new ribbon but we never had to rely on techies to rescue us at $100 per hour.

If we wanted to make a phone call, we simply dialed the number. Either the person we called answered or didn't. If no one answered, we called again later. We could call our doctor's office and talk to a live person. That made scheduling an appointment or getting test results a lot easier than what we endure today. "Please listen to all options before making a selection. If this is a life-threatening emergency, please hang up and call 911. If you are calling from a physician's office or a pharmacy, dial one now. To refill a prescription, contact your pharmacy, and your pharmacist will call you. For a new prescription, press two now. To leave a message for a nurse or to inquire about test results, press three now. To schedule an appointment, press four now. For billing, press five."

It seems high tech has gummed up most communication lines. A customer can't even contact his telephone company without having to negotiate his way through a series of menu options that lead to a long hold followed by a response by someone who is struggling with the English language.

Fortunately, we don't have to go high tech to reach God. Prayer gets us straight through to heaven from anywhere at any time. We never hear, "If this is a life-threatening emergency, hang up and call Michael the Archangel or Gabriel."

God promised, "Call to me and I will answer you" (Jeremiah 33:3). Now that may not be a high-tech system but it is user friendly, voice activated, and reliable. Prayer never crashes, never experiences a power outage, and never puts us on hold.

"How wonderful, Lord, to be able to voice my concerns, praises, and requests to You from anywhere at any time."

18

TITANIC'S LAST AMERICAN SURVIVOR

"Teach us to number our days aright, that we may gain a heart of wisdom" (Psalm 90:12).

LILLIAN GERTRUD ASPLUND, THE LAST AMERICAN survivor of the Titanic, died May 6, 2006, at the age of 99 in Shrewsbury, Massachusetts.

Although two or more survivors are still living, they were less than a year old when the Titanic plunged below the Atlantic April 15, 1912. Lillian Asplund, five at the time, could recall the event. Her father and three brothers perished but her mother and another brother survived with her.

Life is precious but uncertain. Who can explain why so many perished while others survived when an iceberg carved its way into a ship that was supposed to be invulnerable? Who can explain why one human life ends in crib death while another exceeds a century? We may not be able to answer such questions but we can trust the One who holds all the answers to life's mysteries and long for a heaven void of tears, sorrow, and pain.

When I (Jim) read or hear about the Titanic, a couple of personal memories and a humbling question come to mind. My parents, brother Bill, and I crossed the Atlantic in May 1939, leaving our native Scotland behind for a new life in Canada. Although I was not quite four at the time, I remember seeing icebergs and participating in life-jacket drills. World War II had begun and our ship was an easy target. My parents often mentioned later that on its next crossing it was torpedoed by a German U-Boat. So, I ask even now, why was my life spared? After all, my parents could have booked passage for the next crossing.

Surely, our lives are in His hands and He has a purpose for them. We cannot determine how long we will live but, to a great extent, we can determine how well we will live. If we serve the Lord, we will enjoy the truly good life, full of significance, peace, joy, and awareness of His presence.

"LORD, 'teach [me] to number [my] days aright, that [I] may gain a heart of wisdom." (Psalm 90:12).

19

TURNING DESPAIR INTO HOPE

"Many are asking, 'Who can show us any good?' Let the light of your face shine upon us, O LORD" (Psalm 4:5).

A PAINTER STEPPED BACK FROM THE CANVAS AND VIEWED what he had painted. The scene portrayed a dark-gray farmhouse set on a drab landscape. A broken shutter dangled precariously from an upstairs window, and a thin line of smoke wisped upward from a crooked chimney. In the foreground stood a lone, leafless tree. Its barren branches, like long, misshapen bony fingers, pierced a cloudy sky. Near the top of the painting, a full moon veiled by a cloud added an eerie character to the already gloomy painting.

Contemplating what he had painted, the artist decided to title his work "Despair," But a sudden burst of inspiration changed his mind—and his painting. He dabbed a paintbrush into his brightest yellow and dabbed the window with the broken shutter. Instantly, light emanated from the farmhouse, stating in effect that life was inside.

Once more, the painter stood back, viewed his work, and then affixed the title "Hope." Just one touch of light had turned the whole scene from "Despair" to "Hope."

Senior living can get mighty tough, especially when the cost of living soars and our personal income falls. At the same time, our health may deteriorate and our social relationships may dwindle significantly. Aches, pains, and anxieties may become more plentiful than dandelions after a spring rain. Despair may plunge us into a dark and gloomy existence unless we yield to the divine Artist's hand and trust Him to apply light to the window of our soul.

That light may come in the flash of a Bible exhortation and promise. For example, "Cast all your anxiety on him because he cares for you" (1 Peter 5:7) may be just what we need on one of those downcast, gray days. Or a call from a Christian friend to say, "I'm praying for you," may brighten our day. So, take heart; the Master moves His brush across the canvas of our lives in strokes of genius. His hand is always steady and His work is always perfect.

Hang tough. There's hope!

"SOMETIMES, the present seems dark and the future is shrouded in a dense fog. Despair cloaks my mind and heart, Lord. But the light of Your promises and the touch of Your hand can drive away the darkness and lift the fog. Help me to live each day by faith and reach for tomorrow with bright hope."

20

TRUE LOVE STANDS THE TEST OF TIME

"It [love] always protects, always trusts, always hopes, always perseveres" (1 Corinthians 13:7)

HUMORIST AND AUTHOR SAM LEVENSON OPINED, "LOVE at first sight is easy to understand. It's when two people have been looking at each other for years that it becomes a miracle."

Sam was on to something but married partners of 40, 50, or 60 years know lasting love isn't miraculous; it is simply the result of loyalty, respect, determination, and unselfishness. Maybe we should pass a law that no couple under the age of 21 can get married without having a few counseling sessions with a couple that has been married for forty years or so. The older couple can explain what real love is and what it takes to walk through life holding hands instead of grudges. A few stories from the heart about treasuring each other "for better or for worse, for richer or poorer, in sickness and in health" may help a young couple tie a strong marriage knot instead of a slipknot. Sure, a youthful glance over pizza may seem sweet but will it be just as sweet over Shredded Wheat? It can be!

Several years ago, Margaret and Dewey celebrated their sixtieth wedding anniversary. If you were to walk into their church any Sunday morning, Dewey and Margaret would be the first to greet you—Dewey with a firm handshake and Margaret with a big hug, and both with a smile as bright as the sun. They don't look old enough to have been married more than sixty years. Six plus-decades of mutual love must combat aging better than vitamins, supplements, and "miracle" skin care products.

When asked the secret of their enduring love, Dewey and Margaret observed...

- Christ has to be the Head of the home.
- You need to read God's Word daily and pray together.
- Don't fail to say, "I'm sorry" and "Please, forgive me."
- Unexpected hugs and kids are always special.
- Compliment each other.
- Communicate with each other.

These priceless tips for a long and successful marriage are worth their weight in gold. Put into practice, they will make any marriage golden.

"FATHER, I thank you for my spouse. May I honor you by maintaining a partnership of three—You, my spouse, and I in perfect harmony."

21
THE PUMPKIN MAN

"A generous man will prosper; he who refreshes others will himself be refreshed" (Proverbs 11:25).

THE CHILDREN OF COLORADO SPRINGS LOST A BIG-hearted friend when Nick Venetucci, age 93, died after a massive stroke. Every year, Nick grew hundreds of pumpkins so schoolchildren could run excitedly through the field and select their very own pumpkin—free! According to Nick, making so many children happy was a big enough reward to satisfy his generous heart. Although he and his blind wife Bambi were childless, Nick once commented, "I've got more children than anybody in this town."

Nick's entire adult life was one of giving to make others happy. He gave up a promised career as a catcher in the New York Yankees minor league baseball system because his dad needed help maintaining the family farm just south of Colorado Springs. The Great Depression had hit and life was tough. Eventually, Nick's parents became ill and their care fell on his shoulders.

But he didn't complain. He even joked that he was better off as a farmer than a professional baseball player. Two years before his death, he quipped, "You don't see too many 91-year-old baseball players."

Thinking motorists passing his farm should have something beautiful to look at, Nick planted a field of marigolds but he is best remembered for the pumpkins. Nearly every child in Colorado Springs has picked a pumpkin at his farm.

Such generosity has been duly noted by a grateful community. Several years ago, an elementary school and a street were named in his honor, and soon a bronze statue of the pumpkin man will stand at the city's Pioneer Museum.

Each of us passes through this life only once. Therefore, we should make the most of the days and years the Lord gives to us. If we spend them pursuing selfish interests and/or worrying about what will happen to us, we dishonor the Lord who taught us to trust Him and to give of ourselves on behalf of others. Children need our love and generosity, whether they are our grandkids or kids in the neighborhood or kids half a world away. We may not be able to give a child a pumpkin, but we can offer a smile, read a Bible story, toss a ball, or send a donation to a children's relief mission. We may not be able to plant a field of marigolds for motorists to enjoy but we can show adults we know and meet a beautiful life that reflects our Savior's love.

"HELP ME, Lord, to focus on the needs of others and to be a generous person. You gave your all at Calvary. May I give my all to share Your love with others."

22

AN ALMOST PAINTED HOUSE

"Suppose one of you wants to build a tower. Will he not first sit down and estimate the cost to see if he has enough money to complete it?" (Luke 14:28)

ON OUR WAY TO CHURCH GLORIA AND I (JIM) PASS A house that is almost painted. The painting project began almost two years ago to transform the house's exterior from yellow to blue. Three sides became blue rather quickly but, for a year and a half, the painting of the last side has moved at a snail's pace. A ten-by-ten patch of yellow surrounded by blue caught our attention for months. Then the yellow patch started to grow smaller as the painting inched toward completion. This month, the yellow patch has shrunk to a five-by-five square. Perhaps—just perhaps—the project will be complete, the house will be blue on all sides, and the owner can step back and admire the metamorphosis.

If you are like most homeowners, you want improvements to start on time and move quickly to completion. Who wants to live indefinitely with an-almost-painted house or a partly remodeled bathroom or kitchen? We want things done on time and professionally so we can be satisfied that our money and efforts were well spent.

EVERY CHRISTIAN HAS a responsibility to invest his or her spiritual gifts, energy, and time into the building of the Church. Our work is never done as long we live on this side of heaven. We cannot excuse ourselves by claiming we are too old or too tired. We may move slower than we did when we were younger but we can still move, can't we? And we can make steady progress in whatever task the Lord assigns us.

In his letter to the Colossians, the apostle Paul offered a challenge for Archippus: "See to it that you complete the work you have received in the Lord" (4:17). This challenge is appropriate for us too. Someday Jesus will inspect the work He assigned us. Let's not leave anything *almost* finished.

"HELP ME, *Lord, to finish every task you assign, and may I do it well and joyfully.*"

23

RETIREMENT ISN'T IN THE BIBLE. SO?

"Teach us to number our days aright, that we may gain a heart of wisdom" (Psalm 90:12).

"Retirement isn't in the Bible. So, I don't plan to retire." The 40-year-old teacher told his adult Sunday school class. Stay tuned. Twenty-five years from now he may change his mind.

The teacher was right about one thing, though; retirement isn't in the Bible. But neither does the Bible mention health insurance, automobiles, vacations, or hot fudge sundaes. Yet, most of us carry health insurance, buy automobiles, take vacations, and enjoy an occasional hot fudge sundae. You haven't heard anyone say, "No hot fudge sundae for me, thank you; the Bible doesn't mention hot fudge sundaes. But, if you happen to have some locusts and wild honey..."

The issue of retiring comes down to a personal decision based on circumstances. More of us are postponing retirement. We recognize that improved medical care—clear diagnoses, safe surgical procedures, and new drugs—is extending human life. If we retire at 65 but live to be 85 or 90, our previously anticipated retirement income need would not carry us through those extra years. Also, if we enjoy good health, we reason that we might get bored after a few years of fishing or lounging beside a pool. So, we opt to stay in the work force a while longer. Then, too, shrinking 401Ks make it hard to retire as early as many of us had planned.

Post-retirement-age workers pose a problem, though, to their companies because they cost more in wages and health benefits. Many firms, therefore, encourage employees to retire by offering them an attractive severance package. But, if aging workers love their jobs or feel no one can replace them, they may choose to stay until they are carried out in a pine box.

The Bible doesn't indicate whether it is right or wrong to retire but it makes it clear that we ought to serve the Lord as long as we live. What happened to the apostle John affirms this fact. The Roman emperor had banished—retired—John to the obscure island of Patmos. Surely, at the age of 90 and living far from the mainland, John would pose no threat to the empire. How could he spread Christianity from Patmos? He might as well kick back, wait for Gabriel to blow his horn, and take his last breath.

But John wasn't the retiring type. He kept on worshiping and serving the Lord and, one day, he received a visit from Him. There, at Patmos, Jesus commissioned John to write Revelation, the last book of the Bible. Revelation has given believers through the centuries a glimpse of Jesus as our glorified Lord, King of kings, and Lord of lords. John's brightest day and perhaps greatest ministry arrived nearly three decades after his 65th birthday.

Your best day, too, may lie ahead.

"LORD, the end of a productive life is not 65. It is the last moment of a lifetime of serving You. Whether that moment comes when I am 70, 80, 90 or 100, may I be able to say, 'I have fought the good fight, I have finished the race, I have kept the faith.'"

24
KEEP ON KEEPING ON!

"Here is the perseverance of the saints who keep the commandments of God and their faith in Jesus" (Revelation 14:12).

SOME POLITICIANS USE CHRISTIAN LINGO FOR THEIR OWN advantage, Ronald Reagan was a true Christian who used politics to further the cause of Christ.

Ronald Reagan became President of the United States at the ripe old age of 69. While many his age were chasing golf balls or catching fish, Reagan was beginning eight of the most difficult, yet rewarding, years of his life. Vibrant and energetic, he displayed a relentless attitude to accomplish his lofty goals—the most important were to restore pride and patriotism to America and to defeat communism in the world. Whether you agreed with him or not, you always knew where he stood on the issues, especially the ones closest to his heart.

His ongoing hatred of communism stemmed from a solid Christian upbringing in Dixon, Illinois. His mother, Nellie, was a committed Christian and young Ronald learned by her words and deeds the power of the Christian message. Many times, in his later life, her words of wisdom and the source of her faith gave him the determination and perseverance to continue, especially to realize his primary goal of defeating communism.

Reagan saw communism as an ungodly ideology that for decades had brought despair and degradation upon the Soviet people. It was the antithesis of freedom, especially freedom of religion, which to Reagan was intolerable. One disappointing venture after another would have discouraged most but Reagan continued to persevere. Then came the words that changed it all. During a speech, Reagan referred to the Soviet Union as the "Evil Empire." Many in our own government thought that this was going too far and the result would be disastrous. But Reagan never wavered and for the first time the Soviet leaders began to realize that Reagan's evaluation, although hard to swallow, was to a large degree, true. Things began to change. The East and West began to agree instead of squabble with each other. Communism began to crumble all over Eastern Europe, thanks in large measure to the courage, conviction, and perseverance of Ronald Reagan.

There are many examples of perseverance in the Scriptures. One of my favorites is the story of the little old lady described in Mark 5:25-34. This poor senior had spent the last twelve years of her life dealing with a devastating condition and had been bounced around until she had run out of money and options—that is until she saw Jesus. The problem was that He was in a huge crowd and, because she was old and weak, she didn't stand much chance to actually tell Him about her problem. But she thought if she could just get close enough to touch His garment that would do the trick. She finally battled through the throng and managed to touch the hem of His garment and immediately was healed. At this point, Jesus asked, "Who touched me?" Imagine, with the crowds pushing in from all sides Jesus could still distinguish between the touch of faith and the indiscriminate press of a mob. In the end, it wasn't the perseverance that healed her but it was what got her there.

Seniors must remember that perseverance displays true faith. Many times, we feel like we want to give up, and even think we have the right to do so. We must realize our Savior loves us and bids us continue to show His love to others.

"LORD, help me to persevere in the faith."

25

STOP ME IF YOU'VE HEARD THIS BEFORE

" . . . the fool multiplies words" (Ecclesiastes 10:14).

MEET ILA JABBERON, OR YOU MAY HAVE MET HER ALREADY. She's the person who talks on and on and on. If she calls on the phone when you are busy, you may tell her you must run to meet an appointment or you should get a load of clothes out of the washer or your house is on fire, but she simply says, "I'll just take a minute of your time." Somehow, the minute stretches close to an hour. Ila Jabberon can't seem to find the OFF button. Worse still, she repeats the same personal stories she has told you a hundred times.

"My father wasn't a religious man but he didn't care if my mother took my three sisters, two brothers, and me to church every Sunday. So, my siblings and I attended church every week. One of my brothers didn't like church, though, so one Sunday . . .

"Reverend Long was the pastor and his name fit him well. He must have been six-and-a-half-feet tall. His sermons were long too. One Sunday, he preached longer than an hour. When we finally got home, Dad was waiting for us, and we could tell he was mad because Sunday dinner would be late. He took Mom aside and we kids heard him tell her ...

"When Harry and I were newlyweds, I thought he was a lot like my dad. Harry would ..."

"Sometimes I wonder how I have survived all these years. One time Harry tried to fix the washing machine but he forgot to shut off the water. You should have seen the mess he made. Water went everywhere. It even flowed into ..."

You know Ila's stories so well you could write her biography if you had the time and interest to do so but you have neither. Ila has stolen your time and her stories became boring a long time ago.

You may not know Ila Jabberon, but you know someone like her, don't you? We all do. Unfortunately, some seniors may jabber on and repeat stories because they are lonely or have a poor memory or both. We want to ease their loneliness and show them respect and patience but we should not let them bore us and embarrass themselves. A gentle, "Oh, yes, I remember that story," may save the day. Or we may redirect the conversation by asking the caller's opinion about an interesting news event. Or insist in a soft but firm voice, "I'm sorry. I really don't have time to talk now. Let me return your call when I find some free time."

We can learn a valuable lesson from the Ila Jabberons of the world. Run-on repetitious talk is about as appetizing as horseradish mixed generously into a root beer float. Let's recall we have two ears but only one mouth. Apparently, the Lord created us to do twice as much listening as talking.

"May the words of my mouth and the meditation of my heart be pleasing in your sight, O LORD, my Rock and my Redeemer" (Psalm 19:14").

26

WHO SAYS YOU CAN'T DO IT?

"I can do everything through him who gives me strength" (Philippians 4:13).

EIGHTY-YEAR-OLD BOB BOWLS TWICE A WEEK.

In his late 80s, George still plays golf. What's even more impressive is the fact that a few years ago he bought a motorcycle, earned his motorcycle driver's license, and joined a "Geysers" motorcycle club. Later, he biked to Sturgis, South Dakota, for a national bikers' rally.

If someone had told these seniors they couldn't do what they do, they might have replied, "Just watch me!"

No one should sell seniors short! We can do astonishing things if we muster courage and trust the Lord for strength.

My (Jim) Scottish grandmother suffered a stroke when she was about 70. The doctors predicted she would die in a few weeks but she recovered and lived several more years. Although she had never dabbled in art, she took up painting by numbers and then graduated to fine-art painting. Her work was outstanding, much to the surprise and delight of all the family members.

If you want to take on a new project, activity, or ministry, don't let anyone discourage you. When Fred Smith turned in a paper proposing reliable overnight delivery service, a Yale University management professor said the concept was interesting and well-formed but, in order to earn better than a "C," the idea must be feasible. Not deterred, Fred Smith went on to found Federal Express Corporation.

Of course, seniors can't do everything they want to do. The hockey skates I strapped on in my youth have been hanging by a strap in the garage for a long time. I won't be trying out for the Chicago Black Hawks. But I can attempt new things like learning Spanish and walking three miles a day and, with the Lord's help, I can realize these goals.

What new endeavor lies in your future? If someone says you can't do it, just say politely, "Watch me!"

"HELP ME, Lord, to embrace new challenges confidently by relying on You."

27

CARL, A LIGHT IN CHICAGO

"... in the midst of a crooked and perverse generation among whom you appear as lights of the world" (Philippians 2:15).

FOR MANY YEARS I (JOE) SERVED AS A BOARD MEMBER FOR an inner-city ministry located in Chicago. This ministry that began in 1906 as a street mission provided light and hope to the struggling, indigent people of the neighborhood. Later, it relocated to a much more dangerous area —one controlled by drug-dealing gangs. Here the light was to shine for many years.

Carl, one of my fellow board members, had a long association with the organization. He was a devoted servant who at one time served as Night Superintendent at the street mission. Many nights police would bring needy men and women to the mission instead of to jail because they knew the mission gave better care. The facility housed homeless people, vagrants, and battered women, many with children. Carl would faithfully demonstrate the light of the Lord as he lovingly provided hot meals, clothes, and a clean bed until arrangements could be made for a more permanent solution.

Carl always supported himself by working as a janitor in as many as ten apartment buildings. He and his wife Drusilla had quite a family. In addition to their own children, they were foster parents, bringing the light to more than 50 youngsters over the years. At their fiftieth wedding anniversary, many of those foster children, now grown up, recalled the loving Christian care they received while living with Carl and Drusilla.

When Carl was well into his eighties and living in the suburbs, his heart was still with the children of the inner city. Every Sunday afternoon, he would board a commuter train, transfer to a bus and walk a couple of blocks to lead a Sunday school class. Carl didn't think what he was doing was extraordinary. He felt he was just doing what the Lord wanted him to do.

Up to this time, Carl and Drusilla hadn't traveled much beyond their immediate surroundings. Deciding that it was time for a real trip, they began planning a major excursion to Europe. They carefully counted the cost and made all the necessary arrangements, including the purchase of their tickets. It was then that Drusilla came down with a devastating illness that eventually hospitalized her. Soon, it was obvious she wasn't going to be well enough to travel. They would have to cancel their dream trip. Disappointed, Carl went downtown to get his refund before attending a board meeting. At the meeting the Treasurer's Report was read and, as usual, there was a huge number of bills to be paid. We decided to bring the matter to the Lord in prayer. When we opened our eyes after praying, we saw the Lord's answer in the middle of the table. Carl had quietly endorsed the travel refund check to the mission, thus enabling us to pay our bills and keep the light shining. Carl's selfless act displayed a heart totally committed to the Lord.

Seniors should realize there are many opportunities only they can embrace. We need to be sensitive to situations where we can be light to those in darkness.

"FATHER, help us to look for ways to reflect Your eternal light, Amen."

28
HERE COME THE SENIORS!

"But my God will meet all your needs according to his glorious riches in Christ Jesus" (Philippians 4:19).

ACCORDING TO THE CENSUS BUREAU, THE NUMBER OF America's seniors will double by the year 2050. In 2004, there were 36.3 million adults, aged 65 and over, which represented 12 percent of the population. In 44 years, that number will explode to 86.7 million and represent 21 percent of our citizens.

There are many reasons for this phenomenal potential growth. Nearly 8,000 "baby boomers" are turning 60 each day, which means that by 2020 there will be a huge wave of retirees. There is also the health factor. Today's elderly are living longer with lower rates of disability. They are wealthier and have a greater understanding of proper diet and exercise. Life expectancy for males is up 4.1 years from 1950 to 74 years. For females, the current figure is 79.5 years.

So much for statistics.

What concerns many seniors reaching retirement

age is the question of whether there will be enough in the Social Security and Medicare funds to meet these upcoming numbers. You can get varied opinions which range from gloom and doom to a brighter outlook regarding the financial shape these programs are in. Most agree that with proper management and prudent budget restraints, they can remain strong through generations to come.

For believers (whatever their ages) God has promised to supply all their needs. Time and again, throughout human history, He has proven Himself to be faithful to His Word by providing for His people. The children of Israel, for example, survived 40 years in the wilderness by eating the manna God sent to them. In the Sermon on the Mount (Matthew 6:25-34) Jesus alluded to flowers, grass, and birds as examples of the heavenly Father's care for His creation. He condemned worry and encouraged His followers to establish their priorities according to God's will.

For senior believers, it boils down to a matter of personal faith. Can we trust our tomorrows to the God of eternity? The answer is yes!

"FATHER, Thank You for Your consistent supply from the beginning of Creation. Help me not to worry but to trust Your Word."

29

CAN WE BRING BACK THE YO-YO?

"Your statutes are forever right; give me understanding that I may live" (Psalm 119:144)

MOST OF US SENIORS OWNED A YO-YO WHEN WE WERE kids. We could buy a good one for 35 cents at any five-and-dime store (Remember the five-and-dime?). We carried our yo-yos to school and practiced neat tricks at recess. After school, we tried to perfect our skills while trying out a new trick Johnny or Sally had demonstrated. Occasionally, we got to watch a yo-yo expert work his magic.

Did you master the Sleeper? How about Walking the Dog, Around the World, or Rock the Cradle? A kid could really get wrapped up in his hobby with Rock the Cradle.

Yo-yos were introduced by Donald Duncan in1928 and made popular when hundreds of yo-yo men toured America and wowed us with their tricks.

When did the yo-yo go the way of the dinosaur? Did

we become so sophisticated that a 35 cent-toy could no longer entertain us? Did electronic toys kill the yo-yo?

Kids today go wild over "hot" video games and iPhones. You never see a yo-yo string on a kid's finger but you often see a flurry of thumbs massaging handheld video games or a wire running from a hip to a plug in an ear. Many kids like their music loud and their games—well, violent and sexually graphic. Is it any wonder violent crime infects our schools and communities? The yo-yo may never return to its glory days, nor will our schools and streets return to the safety and innocence that accompanied the yo-yo era. But seniors may find the yo-yo string pulling their hearts back to the simpler life.

Like the yo-yo, a simple faith may be in danger of passing away. Secularism, skepticism, egoism, and materialism vie for people's allegiance in the postmodern age. An avalanche of anti-Christian books, TV programs, and movies attack the Bible and morals. But we can withstand every attack on our faith, if we cling to the basics: The Bible is God's Word, Jesus is the living Son of God, and He is the only way to heaven.

If you haven't "walked the dog" recently, why not dust off that old yo-yo and give it a good try? And if you haven't read the Bible recently, why not dust it off and give it a good reading?

"LORD, modern life is so complicated, but you have made the truly good life so simple! Help me to enjoy the good life today by simply trusting You."

30

TIRED OF SELF-SERVICE?

"And I will ask the Father, and he will give you another Comforter to be with you forever" (John 14:16).

I HAD BRONCHITIS FREQUENTLY WHEN I WAS A KID BUT good old Dr. Harness was only a phone call away. He knew how to get me well. Moderns might consider him old-fashioned but he was just right for me. He answered Mom's phone calls personally and came to our house within hours of receiving a call. Medical attention has changed since Dr. Harkness toted his black bag from one patient's house to another. Today, we visit the doctor's office—an arrangement that may be best for us but not as convenient as the doctor-to-home visit of long ago.

Does it seem to you that service isn't what it used to be? When gas was 19 cents a gallon, a service station attendant would fill the gas tank for you. He would also pop the hood and check the oil, check tire pressure, and wash the windshield. Not bad for 19 cents a gallon!

Today, gas costs almost 3 dollars a gallon and you pump it yourself. You may find a bucket of water and a squeegee at the pump in case you want to wash the windshield. If you need to put some air in your tires, you can drop quarters into an air compressor and attach an air hose to each tire valve. However, at my age, getting back up from a crouched position to pump air into a tire may lead to another visit to the doctor.

Self-service has arrived at the grocery store too. I prefer a checkout clerk's voice to that of the automated voice at the self-service counter but my wife likes the self-service feature. She enjoys talking back to the automated voice but I don't think the machine scans her items any faster because she talks back. Of course, you bag your own items at self-service. And have you noticed how extinct baggers have become?

Big box stores epitomize self-service. Don't look for an employee if you want to know if a certain item is available. Your guess is as good as the employee's. And don't expect an employee to check the inventory in the stock room to see if an item has arrived. It isn't going to happen.

Did you watch the TV show, "The Apprentice"? After each show, a fired contestant would stride out of an elegant high-rise office building and walk to a cab. The cab driver remained behind the wheel while the passenger opened a rear door and loaded his or her luggage into the back seat before hopping aboard. When did cabbies stop helping passengers with their luggage? Apparently, self-service has reached the taxi business.

Fortunately, we don't have to take a do-it-yourself approach to Christian living. If we did, we would fail,

Jesus said plainly, "Apart from me you can do nothing" (John 15:5).

Knowing we need help to be what we ought to be and to do what we ought to do, God has given us the Holy Spirit. As the name "Comforter" implies, the Holy Spirit is alongside to equip, encourage, and exhort us to lead a productive life.

Now here is an amazing truth: The Holy Spirit is even more readily available than old-fashioned Dr. Harkness. He is in us and with us forever (John 14:16, 17).

"LORD, I can't lead an effective Christian life without Your help. Thank You for the faithful ministry of the Holy Spirit."

31

PROVIDENCE VERSUS COINCIDENCE

"So do not fear, for I am with you; do not be dismayed, for I am your God. I will strengthen you and help you; I will uphold you with my righteous right hand" (Isaiah 41:10).

HOW OFTEN HAVE WE USED THE TERM "COINCIDENCE" TO describe a situation that couldn't be described any other way? Most Christians realize what seems to be coincidental is in reality "providential." Providence (over life) is a concise description of the eternal and sovereign God ruling over every aspect of His creation in a loving and orderly manner. Sometimes, however, providence does seem like coincidence.

Take, for example, the incident that occurred just after the birth of Jesus. On the surface, it might have seemed coincidental but, on closer examination, it became obvious that God's hand of providence was evident in every detail. The "incident" happened amid all the hustle and bustle of a typical day's activities at the temple in Jerusalem. Mary and Joseph had brought baby Jesus to be dedicated as the law required. As they began ceremoniously offering the sacrificial turtle doves, two senior saints—Simeon and Anna— joined them. God had been preparing the two for this specific moment in history.

The righteous and devout Simeon was the first to reach Mary, Joseph, and the baby. Being promised by the Holy Spirit that he would live until this moment, he gently gathered up tiny Jesus in his arms and declared He was the fulfillment of Messianic prophecy. Can you picture faithful Simeon holding Eternity in his wrinkled arms and proclaiming to all that this was the Savior of both Jews and Gentiles?

Anna was an 84-year-old widow whose husband had died after only seven years of marriage. She had made temple service her life's vocation. A recognized prophetess, she confirmed Simeon's words by declaring that Jesus was indeed the Redeemer.

Was it coincidence? After all, what were the chances of all of these individuals meeting at the temple at exactly the same time? No, it wasn't coincidence; it was providence! God was working out His perfect purpose in His precise timing, resulting in His Son being proclaimed publicly as the One and only Redeemer.

As seniors, we need to be sensitive and aware of the providence of God in our personal lives. As we devise our "master plan" for the future, let's be sure that we're in agreement with the Master's plan. If we are not, we can be sure He will make some necessary adjustments... providentially.

. . .

"Father, it gives me such peace and joy to know that You reign supreme in my life."

32

A HEAVENLY NEIGHBORHOOD

"But our citizenship is in heaven. And we eagerly await a Savior from there, the Lord Jesus Christ" (Philippians 3:21).

DURING THE SECOND WORLD WAR, WHEN I (JOE) WAS growing up, we didn't have a telephone. If we wanted to call someone we had to go to Mazor's Drug Store, down the street, and use the payphone. Mr. Mazor watched that phone like a hawk, especially if the caller was a teenager.

Mazor's store along with various other establishments made up one of the numerous neighborhoods in my native Chicago. Many families did not own a car and those that owned a car had to deal with rationed gasoline, so neighborhood living provided a way to survive those difficult war years. Neighborhoods became micro cities, with everything within walking distance. Various churches and synagogues were sprinkled throughout each area that also included supermarkets, dry cleaners, movie theaters, and schools. Since we didn't own a car, my father walked a mile each day to manage his barbershop.

Many neighborhoods reflected strong ethnicity. Numbers of people who migrated to America at the beginning of the twentieth century found it easier to be with their own countrymen, at least until they learned English. These groups formed the basis for many of the neighborhoods that still exist in Chicago. In fact, various nationalities continue to reflect the cultural diversity that has made Chicago's neighborhoods unique and popular places to visit.

My neighborhood was composed of many immigrants, some of whom had fled from Europe when the Nazis came to power. I grew up in a three-story apartment complex, consisting of 24 units. The common backyard we shared provided quite an education in social studies as we children got to know each other.

The people were wonderful. Our next-door neighbors, Mr. and Mrs. Reinheimer had barely escaped Nazi Germany. Mrs. Reinheimer loved to bake, and would often bring over a plate of hot prune klotchkys, which we devoured in minutes. I couldn't help but notice the small blue numbers imprinted on her forearm. It wasn't until I was older that I understood the significance of that brutal branding.

I loved the different accents: German, Swedish, Romanian, Yiddish, and Italian. Those dialects have stayed with me for more than 60 years and I still enjoy respectfully using them when recalling my youth.

I guess, in a real way, my neighborhood was sort of a preview of what heaven will be like. Redeemed people from every tribe and tongue will glorify the Lord together, forever.

"FATHER, thank You for the promise of eternal life in a perfect place of worship and rest."

33

BROTHER, CAN YOU SPARE A TWENTY?

"For you yourselves know how you ought to follow our example. We were not idle when we were with you. Nor did we eat anyone's food without paying for it. On the contrary, we worked night and day, laboring and toiling so that we would not be a burden to any of you" (2 Thessalonians 3:7,8).

IN THE OLD DAYS, A PERSON "DOWN ON HIS LUCK" MIGHT ask, "Brother can you spare a dime." A dime doesn't go far today, so a person "down on his luck" might ask for a twenty.

Nearly 40 years ago, I (Jim) served as pastor of a church in Indiana. The National Highway, Route 40, passed right through our town. Interstate 70 bypasses the town now. Because our parsonage lay only a couple of blocks off Route 40, frequently a transient knocked on our door and requested financial assistance. The transients' faces were distinct but their stories were often strikingly similar. "My car ran out of gas just outside town and I need about twenty dollars for gas so I can visit my dying mother in Columbus, Ohio."

Occasionally, I would smell alcohol on a transient's breath and assume he would spend whatever I gave him on booze. "What's that I smell on your breath?" I would ask.

"Medicine!"

I was positive medicine didn't smell like Jack Daniels, so I didn't shell out any of the church's money to support a non-medical habit. But I often asked a transient if he would mow the church's or parsonage's lawn for ten dollars. That question always separated those who were truly "down on their luck" from those who were simply freeloaders. Freeloaders backed away from work like it was bubonic plague.

Most seniors I know didn't go through life looking for a handout. They learned early on that the world doesn't owe anyone a living. They worked hard for what they acquired. If times were tough, they survived on less. When times were good, they saved as much as they could. Stretching plastic money beyond the limit was out of the question. They bought only what they could afford.

A strong work ethic is part of the biblical code that society respected when we were growing up. We learned idle hands are the devil's tools. We also learned to help a needy neighbor.

A dollar doesn't go far in retirement, does it? A fixed income can't always fix a financial problem caused by spiraling gas prices and medical expenses. Nevertheless, we will watch our expenditures carefully and look to the Lord for the supply of our daily needs. He has never let us down. He never will.

. . .

"THANK YOU, Lord, for daily provisions. At times, I may live from hand to mouth, but it is Your hand and my mouth!"

34

NINETY-NINE AND STILL WALKING

"When Abram was ninety-nine years old, the LORD appeared to him and said, 'I am God Almighty; walk before me and be blameless" (Genesis 17:1).

WALKING IS A SIGNIFICANT FORM OF EXERCISE. It improves our cardiovascular system, combats depression, reduces weight, and builds muscle tone. Also, it is affordable. We may have to purchase a comfortable pair of walking shoes occasionally but we don't have to buy any hard-to-assemble gym equipment or the kind you fold and store under a bed. Some seniors stride up and down shopping mall corridors before stores open. The location allows them to avoid bad weather and the early time allows them to avoid shoppers.

But as we get older, walking becomes more difficult. Some days just getting out of bed is a chore. When we start the day, our muscles and bones are about as limber as a steel beam. It takes a while to get mobile.

Abram, at age 99, must have felt stiff and sore, nevertheless, he received a command from the Lord to walk.

If you and I live to the ripe old age of 99 and can stand, we will be happy, won't we? But if we can walk, we will be hilariously happy. Walking at 99 is an outstanding feat.

But the Lord commanded Abram to do more than walk. He told him to "be blameless." This was a tall order but, for the most part, Abram exercised the kind of faith in the Lord that enabled him to maintain a sterling reputation. He did slip, however, soon after receiving the command to walk before the Lord and be blameless. He laughed when the Lord told him his 89-year-old wife Sarah would give birth to a son (Genesis 17:15–17).

How would our faith survive under similar circumstances? Don't worry; it isn't going to happen. But can we trust the Lord to keep all the promises He has made to us in His Word? Will we walk before Him and be blameless?

What test of faith will you pass today?

"LORD, help me to walk by faith and to live in such a way that my reputation as a Christian will be beyond reproach."

35

OUR RESIDENT DECODER

"Now we have received, not the spirit of the world, but the Spirit who is from God, so that we may know freely given to us by God" (1 Corinthians 2:12).

LIKE MOST SENIORS WHO GREW UP IN THE FORTIES, I (JOE) used to listen to a lot of kid shows on the radio. Those pre-TV years gave youngsters plenty of opportunity to use their imaginations as they listened intently to programs like Superman, Tom Mix, Jack Armstrong, and one of my favorites, Captain Midnight.

Captain Midnight was a fifteen-minute program about a World War II pilot who, along with his "Secret Squadron," performed clandestine missions designed to thwart the enemy's strategies and bring down the bad guys. There was a lot of action and adventure as Midnight's assignments took him all over the world.

Young listeners were given the opportunity to be members of the Captain's extended squadron by sending in the wax seal from the sponsor's product,

Ovaltine, and twenty-five cents. For this, you received a membership card, a pin and the "Official Secret Squadron Decoder." The hard part was getting your mother to purchase yet another jar of the malt-flavored Ovaltine. Our pantry shelf was filled with jars without seals and cereal boxes without tops, all because of premium offers. If you could somehow convince Mom that you would eat or drink the product, you were on your way.

I'll never forget how excited I was the day my decoder arrived in the mail. I eagerly listened as the Captain began. "Okay, gang, set your decoders at G equals 9." Then he delivered the message, using corresponding numbers. I copied all the numbers down, set my decoder and began deciphering the message. D, the first letter is D. R–I–N–K–O–V–A–L–T–I– N–E.

Why, it was nothing more than a commercial! I was so disappointed, I never used it again.

Although the message wasn't very thrilling, it was only after I decoded it that I found out what it said.

We believers also have a special decoder who came to live in each of us when we received Christ. He is the Holy Spirit and, among His other wonderful ministries, He gives us the ability to understand and apply God's Word. That's why we can read a Scripture passage and see eternal truth non-believers can't see. First Corinthians 2:14 teaches spiritual truth is nothing but foolishness to those who are devoid of the "decoder," the Holy Spirit.

So, when the Captain of our salvation sends us a special message through His Word, we can always rely on our resident decoder to guide us into the truth.

. . .

"*FATHER, thank You for the great honor of knowing You by the indwelling Holy Spirit.*"

36

MEMORY BANK DEPOSITS

"Your statutes are my heritage forever; they are the joy of my heart. My heart is set on keeping your decrees to the very end" (Psalm 119:112).

A small sign in my office reads: "When the memory goes, forget it!" I must confess I don't remember as much as I would like to. What is the name of that couple I met at church recently? The medical information form asks me to list surgeries and the dates of those surgeries. Let's see, was it 1988 or 1999 when I had my first back surgery? When did I have a deviated septum repaired? I don't want to confuse the time of that repair with the date of the transmission repair to my Dodge Spirit.

Our son Brian enjoys a remarkable memory. Although he is almost fifty, sometimes he will resurrect memories of people and events from his preschool years. When he was four, he participated in a memory study conducted by the Psychology Department of Denver University. He received 25 cents for every series of pictures he remembered in sequence. He came home a rich boy. When he is a senior citizen, he should be able to remember the things his dad frequently forgets in his senior days: *Where did I put my car keys? I know the cashier gave me a receipt but what did I do with it? I have to go back to the restaurant; I forgot my hat. You mean I forgot to take the trash out again? Did I close the garage door?*

Although we all have memory lapses occasionally, we shouldn't think our ability to memorize and retain Scripture left us when our hair became gray or "invisible."

Ninety-year-old Pearl memorizes Scripture regularly in Awana's, "Take It to Heart" program. But she also maintains an individual memorization schedule. She has been doing so for years. Right now, she is memorizing the entire book of Hebrews—not an easy task! Pearl finds great joy in making regular deposits of Scripture to her memory bank.

If our memory bank receives regular deposits of Scripture, we will be able to withdraw promises for times of testing and apply principles for successful living. If you haven't opened a savings account, why not do so today?

"Lord, Your Word is more precious than gold and silver. Help me store generous portions of it in my memory bank."

37

A TEMPORARY SITUATION

"I have learned the secret of being content in any and every situation" (Philippians 4:12).

WHEN CHUCK GOT HIS ORDERS TO REPORT FOR MILITARY duty, he knew it was going to be tough. He had been married only three months when he received word that he was going to be a father. Now, he was sorry he had enlisted and wondered if there was any way out of his commitment. After all, he rationalized, we weren't at war with anyone and his wife certainly needed him more than Uncle Sam did. Nothing he tried worked and, after saying his good-byes, he found himself on a train along with dozens of other young men, bound for an army base.

The first week was a disaster. Chuck and hundreds of other raw recruits were herded from one station to another. There followed inoculations, uniform distributions, more shots, classes to learn how to wear the uniform properly, more shots, and then the ultimate humiliation—the two-minute GI haircut!

Chuck wanted out! On the way back to the barracks from the barbershop, he stopped by an army chapel in search of a chaplain. He thought a cleric might be able to help him wrangle some sort of hardship discharge. The place was deserted as Chuck sat patiently waiting in a back-row pew. Finally, the frustration got the best of him. He cried out loud to God, asking Him to get him out of this seemingly impossible situation. The answer he received was silence and, in that quiet moment, Chuck began to get the message that this was indeed where God wanted him. Now, he knew he should accept the inevitable. But how to deal with it, that was the question.

As he walked along he concluded he had to approach this situation one day at a time. Each morning, he would prayerfully prepare for whatever he was scheduled to do that day. Some days he found himself on KP and working in the kitchen. Guard duty was another detail that Chuck performed during basic training. Whatever the assignment, Chuck would take it in stride, always looking forward to the day when his military obligation would end and he would return home. When Chuck saw his situation as temporary he could cope with the anguish and loneliness that separation from the one he loved most had brought.

Chuck's approach to army life can be applied to the life of every believer. The apostle Paul reminds us that although we spend a lifetime on planet Earth, our eternal citizenship is in heaven. Peter called us aliens and strangers (1Peter 2:11).

Because of health and financial problems, seniors can become vulnerable to depression and despair. It's then that we need to step back and see the big picture.

We must realize that, bad as it may be, this situation is only temporary. There's a place being prepared for us right now and, when it's completed, we'll be going home.

"FATHER, help me not to get bogged down by situations that are at best temporary. Help me see my situations from Your eternal perspective."

38

THE HIGH VALUE OF A COMPLIMENT

"A word aptly spoken is like apples of gold in settings of silver" (Proverbs 25:11).

"How are you?" I (Jim) asked Tony, a newcomer to our church.

"Pretty good. How are you?" Tony replied.

I responded in my usual manner. "Not too bad for an old guy."

Tony smiled. "Wait 'til you get to be my age."

"How old are you, Tony?"

"Sixty-two."

"Well I'm older than you. I'm seventy," I answered.

Tony smiled again. "Looks like you take good care of yourself."

I don't get many compliments, so I will remember Tony's remarks. They made my day.

Empty flattery irks our souls but honest compliments lift our spirits. A kind word about how we look or what we do encourages and energizes us. It serves as a gentle motivation to continue our journey through a day. And seniors know how getting through some days can be challenging.

In his New Testament writings, the apostle Paul often complimented his readers. You can't read the final chapter of Romans without discovering some very nice compliments he paid to Phoebe, Priscilla, Aquila, Epenetus, Mary, Andronicus, Junias, and to several other fellow-believers. In his letter to the Corinthians, he complimented his readers' giftedness (1 Corinthians 1:5–7). He told the Ephesians and the Colossians he gave thanks continually for their faith and love for all the saints (Ephesians 1:15; Colossians 1:3, 4). The Philippians, too, received a compliment from Paul because they had faithfully partnered with him in the gospel "from the first day until now" (1:4).

Let's lift someone's spirit today by paying him or her a sincere compliment. We can say something like, "Joan, what a nice outfit. You look so nice." "Bill, your Bible teaching is always interesting and helpful." "Marge, you bake the best angel food cake." "Ray, your singing always ministers to me." "Mark, you look far too young to be a great-grandfather."

Paying others compliments is like showering them with roses but compliments cost nothing. Also, roses eventually fade, whereas compliments may stay in bloom for years.

"HELP ME, Lord, to remember to compliment others every day."

39
ZOOM!

" . . . you do not even know what will happen tomorrow. What is your life? You are a mist that appears for a little while and then vanishes. Instead you ought to say, 'If it is the Lord's will, we will live and do this or that" (James 4:14, 15).

MY (JIM) CAR HAS 265 HORSEPOWER. THAT'S MORE POWER than I need but, occasionally, all that power comes in handy, especially when I enter an interstate highway and must accelerate rapidly to keep from getting run over. *Zoom!*

But time zooms faster than my car. This fact became extremely clear when I spoke at the 50th anniversary of Bible Baptist Church in Williamson, New York. I had served as the church's first full-time pastor until 1964. The intervening years of absence seemed so brief! So, I expected to find everyone I had left in Williamson to look the same as he or she did in 1964. Wrong! In 1964 the church's leaders were in their early 40s. In 2005, they were in their early 80s. Somehow, their energy had plunged, their walk had slowed, and their faces had wrinkled. (Their bright smiles were still bright, though.)

When I left in 1964, the youth group was overflowing with vivacious teenagers. Much to my delight, a few were on hand for the 50th anniversary. "Glenn, how old are you now?" I asked one of the former teenagers."

"Fifty-nine, and I retired from Kodak," Glenn responded.

Turning to another former teenager, I asked, "How old are you, Terry?"

"Sixty-one."

Zoom! Where had the years gone?

I'm sure you, too, have wondered where the years have gone. You can close your eyes and see yourself in high school or learning to drive or at your first job or at your wedding or holding your first baby, whose hair is beginning to turn gray. It's hard to believe the past passed so quickly.

The apostle James compared life to a mist that evaporates rapidly, so he counseled us to make the most of whatever future remains by living according to God's will.

When I was in my late teens, I heard the words, "Only one life. 'Twill soon be past. Only what's done for Christ will last." None of us know how much time remains to do God's will, so let's make today count—for eternity.

"I COMMIT this day and all that I am to you, Lord. I want to do Your will now and forever."

40

BEYOND THE SUNRISE

"The city does not need the sun or the moon to shine on it, for the glory of God gives it light, and the Lamb is its lamp" (Revelation 21:23).

"BEYOND THE SUNSET" MAY BE THE HYMN MOST frequently played or sung at funerals, although "Amazing Grace" seems to be running a close second. The words of "Beyond the Sunset" are okay but I think the title should be changed to "Beyond the Sunrise." After all, what lies beyond a sunset? Night and darkness! A sunrise, on the other hand, introduces a new day with a fresh slate of opportunities and activities. Light follows a sunrise. So, does renewed energy. We feel invigorated in the morning but tired—perhaps exhausted—after sunset.

When a Christian dies, he enters heaven and enjoys eternal life. His energy level there is unprecedented and his joy is unrivaled by anything on earth. Trouble, pain, and sorrow cannot touch him in heaven, where glory and beauty surround him. Nighttime never falls in heaven and God's eternal day never ends. Best of all, in heaven, the departed Christian beholds his glorious Savior, a glory that outstrips the glory of the sun.

The apostle John looked back on his relationship with Jesus during Jesus' earthly ministry and recalled, "We have seen his glory, the glory of the One and Only, who came from the Father, full of grace and truth" (John 1:14). Years later, John caught a glimpse of Jesus in the heavenly New Jerusalem and testified the Lamb [Jesus] is its Lamp (Revelation 21:23). Our cities on earth may experience blackouts but the New Jerusalem draws its light from an unfailing Source. The Lamp will never flicker or fail!

Christianity is not drab because Jesus is glorious. Because He purchased our redemption and we believed on Him, we will spend eternity in glorious light, not darkness. So, shouldn't we start singing "Beyond the Sunrise"?

"HEAVENLY FATHER, thank You for the bright hope of spending eternity in heaven with Jesus, Your glorious Son."

41

A STREETCAR NAMED DALHOUSIE

" . . . 'Not by might nor by power, but by my Spirit,' says the Lord" (Zechariah 4:6)

STELLAR! STELLAR! THAT'S MY OPINION OF THE outstanding way in which streetcars moved people.

Connected by a pole on its roof that extended to an overhead power line, each streetcar whirred along city streets at a good pace and emitted zero pollution. Their high efficiency was marred only when the pole became disconnected. The streetcar came to a halt and passengers waited for the conductor to prop the pole back into place.

My (Jim) favorite streetcar was named Dalhousie and traveled from downtown St. Catharines, Ontario, to Port Dalhousie, a Lake Ontario resort, about four miles away. The ride cost only a nickel but it journeyed past Martindale Ponds, my favorite fishing spot, and several productive fruit farms.

Back then, Ralph Bell, now retired from the Billy Graham team, was my riding companion. In the good old summertime, we headed for the beach and midway rides Port Dalhousie offered. After a swim and a few rides on the Tilt-A-Whirl, Carousel, and Bumper Carts, we boarded the streetcar again and rode home. An occasional stall simply gave us additional time to talk about the day's fun.

Of course, stalling was never the power line's fault. The power was always available but the streetcar had to stay connected. Similarly, the Christian must stay connected to God's power in order to move forward. Progress stalls instantly if the Christian fails to stay in vital union with Christ.

By obeying the Scriptures, yielding ourselves to the Holy Spirit's control, and confessing our sins we experience God's power to move forward toward the successful completion of His will. And all along our journey to heaven, we enjoy an unforgettable ride.

"FATHER, I need your power for daily progress in the Christian life. May I stay connected and thereby serve You well."

42

DISARMING THE ENEMY

"Resist the devil, and he will flee from you" (James 4:7b).

RALPH AND MARLA HAD BEEN MARRIED FOR MORE THAN forty years. They loved the Lord and they loved each other. Their neighbors and friends held them in high regard. They had always been active in church and their newfound retirement had given them great availability to serve in various capacities. With more time on their hands, they also enjoyed special moments together—nothing elaborate or expensive, just simple pleasures, like mornings together on their patio. These were wonderful times, especially in the summer. The soft breezes brought refreshment; the summer sun brought warmth and the birds brought delight.

One morning, however, brought something else. An uninvited, invisible intruder had joined them. It all started innocently enough. Ralph had just opened a book about the Civil War. Marla had been relaxing on the chaise, quietly surveying the many trees and plants that adorned their large backyard. Her words broke the silence.

"Ralph, I've got a job for you."

"Hmmmm?" came his detached reply.

"I have a little job for you," she repeated. "It won't take long."

Without missing a word in the book, Ralph asked, "What is it?"

"I'd like you to take the pruning shears, go around the yard, and snip off those ugly shoots that have grown around our trees."

With his attention still riveted to his book, Ralph replied, "Yeah, I'll take care of it."

"When?" Marla asked.

Annoyed, Ralph looked up from his reading and shot a glance at his wife. "I said I'd get to it but it can't be today! Today, I've got to play golf."

After a moment, Marla answered, " I just thought you might want to help me."

"What's that supposed to mean?" Ralph snorted. " ... that I never help you? I said I'd do it but not today! Today I'm busy!"

Marla knew she should've dropped it, but couldn't resist. "Yeah, busy reading your books and playing golf!"

They glared at each other for a split second before both broke out in huge smiles. Almost in unison, they said to each other, "I'm sorry, will you forgive me?" Immediately, the tension was relieved and the conflict dissolved. Those six simple words had disarmed the enemy.

The apostle Peter wrote that the devil prowls about like a roaring lion seeking whom he may devour (1 Peter 5:8). We must be aware of his tactics, no matter how innocent they may seem. At the first instant we sense his subtle assault, we must activate our greatest resource—God's Word. That's what Jesus did.

When Satan tried to tempt Jesus in the wilderness, he failed miserably because each of his three attacks met Jesus' powerful use of eternal Scripture (Matthew 4:1–11). We, too, can ward off the devil's attacks by studying, memorizing, and applying Scripture. And don't forget those six simple words. They will send the enemy packing every time.

"DEAR FATHER, thank You for Your precious Word. Help me to know it and use it when confronted by the enemy."

43
A LITTLE RESPECT, PLEASE!

"Rise in the presence of the aged, show respect for the elderly and revere your God. I am the LORD" (Leviticus 19:32).

COMEDIAN RODNEY DANGERFIELD WAS FAMOUS FOR HIS lament, "I tell you, I get no respect." But he wasn't the only one to be disrespected. Senior citizens have felt the sting of disrespect. Age discrimination hurts whether it occurs in the job line or in the grocery checkout line or the telephone line. It is about as hard for a senior to get a job as it is to do cartwheels. We know the law prohibits age discrimination in hiring, but an employer can hide the real reason he turns down a sixty-year-old job application. "Over-qualified" camouflages age discrimination really well. So does, "We plan to interview several more applicants before deciding."

If you relocate, you may find it difficult to connect with a doctor. Some do not accept Medicare patients. Others are not accepting new patients. Be prepared to fight through your pain and stay off ladders until you find a new doctor.

Even phone surveys end abruptly when you give your age. You know how they start, "May I take just a couple of minutes of your time. I'm not selling anything. I'm just conducting a brief survey." A few routine questions follow: "Are you the head of the household?" "What kind of car do you drive?" "Which radio station do you listen to most often?" "What make of vacuum cleaner do you own?" "Which age group do you fall into —20-30? 30-40? 40-50? 50-60? Older than 60?" When you respond, "Older than 60," you hear a quick, "Thank you for your time" and a click.

But the cheapest shot may come at a big box store or at a restaurant. A hired guy at the door greets you with, "Hi, young man—or young lady!" if your spouse is with you, you may hear, "Hi, kids. Welcome to Del Mart!" The salutation is demeaning, a veiled way of saying, "Your old age is showing." The greeter would never tell twenty-year-olds, "Hi, old timers, welcome to Del Mart."

Sure, we have acquired a few wrinkles and age spots along life's highway. And we don't walk as spryly as we did thirty or forty years ago but we have contributed to society. By and large, our generation worked hard, raised good sons and daughters, and upheld basic values like honesty and kindness. Our grandchildren think we are pretty special. We never hear them call us "kids."

The Bible teaches each generation to respect its seniors. Leviticus 19:32 even links such respect with reverence for God. Job 12:12 credits old age with understanding and Proverbs 16:31 describes gray hair as "a crown of splendor ... attained by a righteous life."

You may not want to confront the disrespectful greeter at Del Mart but don't let his inappropriate greeting damage your self-respect. Your life is a tribute to God's loving care and purpose for your life. He has brought you this far—and He will continue to perform His will in your life until you are safely Home.

"LORD, *may I never forget that You love me now as much as when I was young. May my love for You grow deeper as I grow older.*"

44

OUR FAITHFUL COMPANION

"Never will I leave you; never will I forsake you" (Hebrews 13:5b).

I loved the Lone Ranger.

I, along with thousands of others, listened intently to his adventures on the radio three times each week. The mysterious mask, silver bullets, and great white stallion, Silver really appealed to me and to the imagination of youngsters of all ages. The program that originated in Detroit in 1932 quickly became one of the most popular shows ever to play on the radio. It made a successful transition to television in 1948, with reruns still being shown today. In addition, there were movies, serials, comic books, magazines and a variety of merchandise, all available under the Lone Ranger brand.

In later years, The Lone Ranger's name became synonymous with being a "loner," an individual totally independent and self-reliant. Although this type of individual may appeal to our spirit of independence, it isn't likely many men or women have existed without some support and encouragement from others.

Not even the Lone Ranger was that independent. The word "Lone" in his title came from the fact that he was the sole survivor of a fierce ambush that wiped out five other Texas Rangers. In fact, if it hadn't been for Tonto, the Indian who witnessed the attack and carefully tended the Lone Ranger's wounds, he too would have died. Tonto would later become the Ranger's "faithful Indian companion" and ride side by side with the masked man for decades, proving the Lone Ranger was not the "Alone" Ranger.

When Jesus' time on earth was coming to an end, He began to prepare His faithful companions—His disciples, for His imminent departure. He began by assuring them that He was going to prepare a place for them in Heaven. Sensing their anxiety, He promised that at the proper time, He would return for them. In the meantime, as a pledge of His constant presence with them, He promised to send the Holy Spirit to abide with them until His return. Fifty days after His resurrection, during a feast called Pentecost, the Holy Spirit came and took up residence in every follower of Christ. From that moment until the present, the Holy Spirit has lived in every true Christian. He ministers to and through us in a myriad of ways. He gives us special gifts and the opportunities to use them to serve one another. It is because of Him that we can have a proper understanding of God's Word. The Holy Spirit guides us and gives us special insight as we grow in the Christian life. All this and so much more, from the One who promised never to leave us or forsake us. He is indeed our most faithful companion!

"Dear Father, thank you for the power and presence of your blessed Holy Spirit."

45

BEWARE OF SMILING SWINDLERS!

"A friend loves at all times, and a brother is born for adversity" (Proverbs 17:17).

Judas Iscariot betrayed Jesus with a kiss and did so for thirty pieces of silver. Nevertheless, a theory being advanced today portrays Judas as Jesus' friend. It alleges he simply carried out Jesus' wishes. With a friend like Judas, who needs an enemy?

We seldom, if ever, meet anyone named Judas, but we may encounter a "Judas" nonetheless.

In her prime, Rita was a vivacious celebrity in the entertainment industry. Her success brought her plenty of money and friends. An extremely generous person, Rita hosted elaborate parties, donated sizable sums to charity, and treated her friends to breakfast buffets and lunches at a four-star hotel.

In her seventies and still unmarried, Rita was experiencing rapidly declining health. She was too weak to leave home. Her mind was no longer sharp. Her memory was almost gone and her speech was often incoherent. Because she had no living relatives, she depended entirely upon others to care for her. However, most of her friends dropped out of her life when she became too ill to lavish money on them.

Rita ended up with very little money. A former friend—a "Judas"—whom she trusted with her credit cards and bank accounts, bilked her out of $285,000. This "friend" almost stole Rita's home out from under her but a true-blue friend uncovered the fraud and hired a lawyer to protect Rita's interests.

Rita missed the former social times, but she valued the few friends who truly cared about her. Most important, Rita was a believer. In her halting way, she talked about how good her best friend Jesus is. She knew He is a trustworthy and constant companion.

As we age, we need to depend upon others for things we routinely handled in our younger years. However, we should not be deceived by a phony smile into committing our financial affairs to a swindler. No one wants to distrust everyone but we must choose our friends wisely. True friends care about us, not our possessions. And we will never have a better friend than Jesus!

"Lord, may I wisely discern who is truly a trustworthy friend; and I thank You for being my best friend."

46

PAIN RELIEF AND AIRPORT SECURITY

"Dear friend, I pray that you may enjoy good health and that all may go well with you, even as your soul is getting along well: (3 John 2).

SOME THINGS DON'T MIX WELL! SALT IN COFFEE IS definitely a no-no. Grapefruit and blood pressure medicine can produce bad side effects. Sugar in a gas tank cripples a car. A sympathy card sent to newlyweds is another no-no. In June 2006, security agents at the Tallahassee, Florida's airport found what it thought was a hazardous mix in a food editor's carry-on luggage. They evacuated the airport for three hours and used a robot to open the suspicious luggage. What they found was recording equipment, a special kind of honey, oyster shell, and seasoning rub. The editor was visiting the area to do a story about the food of Apalachicola, Florida's oyster capital.

It's a wonder seniors' carry-on luggage doesn't unleash a battalion of robots. After all, we carry such exotic mixtures of pain relievers and prescriptions. We have rub-ins for arthritic joints, rub-ons for aching backs, and rub-outs for aging skin spots, not to mention daily pills nestled neatly in Sunday-through-Saturday compartments of pill boxes. A container of Metamucil and a bottle of Geritol only heighten the appearance of hazardous material. Security agents must respect old age; otherwise, none of us would pass through Security without having our luggage undergo a robotic search. Worse still, we might get strip-searched. Kind of makes you consider bus travel, doesn't it?

Growing old is, definitely, not for sissies and it isn't cheap either. Those ointments and pills cost a lot of money but if we didn't hurt in the pocketbook, we would surely be hurting in the lower back, hips, feet, shoulders, knees, elbows, sinuses, stomach, and a few other regions. So, we swallow our pills, apply the pain-relief ointments, and do whatever else is necessary to soothe our pain and ward off whatever has invaded our body.

But, as we age, our soul can escape what our body must endure. Because the Savior took our sins away and grants perfect peace for every day, we can enjoy top-notch spiritual health. Complete forgiveness of sins and close fellowship with the Lord are priceless gifts bestowed on us by grace.

Another good thing about top-notch spiritual health: our souls will never set off alarms at airport security.

"Lord, I am aware of the aging process. My medicine cabinet keeps me informed that I'm not as young as I used to

be. But I am thankful I can enjoy top-notch spiritual health as I walk close to You."

47

THE DOOMSDAY CLOCK IS APPROACHING MIDNIGHT

"And they sang a new song: 'You are worthy to take the scroll and to open its seals, because you were slain, and with your blood you purchased men for God from every tribe and language and nation. You have made them to be a kingdom and priests to serve our God, and they will reign on the earth'" (Revelation 5:9, 10).

ARMAGEDDON! MANY BOOKS HAVE BEEN WRITTEN ABOUT it. Sermons have been preached about it. Movies have been filmed about it. And, since 1947, the hands of a clock have pointed out the time remaining until this alleged nuclear doomsday occurs. The clock, called the Doomsday Clock, was conceived and constructed by atomic researchers at the University of Chicago to warn of approaching nuclear disaster. Midnight signals Armageddon. Originally the hands were set at seven minutes to midnight.

As world tensions increased, the clock's guardians—

the Board of Directors of the Bulletin of Atomic Scientists—occasionally moved the hands forward. They have also moved them back when tensions decreased. In 1991, with the United States and Soviet Union's signing of the Strategic Arms Reduction Treaty, the hands were moved to seventeen minutes to midnight. But India's and Pakistan's testing of nuclear weapons in 1998 sent the hands to nine minutes to midnight where they remained until 2002.

Breakdown of international relations and the threat of terrorism in 2002 persuaded atomic scientists to move the hands once again to seven minutes to midnight.

What will happen when the Doomsday Clock announces midnight? Perhaps nothing. The Clock is simply a human invention subject to human speculation about the threat of nuclear disaster. But the Bible does predict Armageddon, a global battle that will take place in the Tribulation.

But Armageddon will not blow the world to smithereens. Its destruction will be immense but not terminal. Sometime after Armageddon, Jesus will return to earth in a blaze of glory to establish His kingdom. At that time, He will destroy every bellicose bully and subdue evil. With evildoers out of the way, He will restore nature to Edenic conditions. Peace, purity, righteousness, reverence, longevity and productivity will characterize His reign (see Psalm 72:1–8).

Now, here's more good news to offset the Doomsday Clock's bad news. Jesus will evacuate Christians from the earth before the Tribulation and Armageddon blanket the earth in unprecedented violence, villainy, and vileness. We will be going up in the Rapture before

Doomsday Clock strikes midnight (see 1 Thessalonians 4:16, 17; 5:4–9).

Of course, we may die before the Rapture occurs. In that case, we will enter our Lord's presence immediately and the glories of heaven will delight us forever.

Regardless of how we meet our Lord, our best day lies ahead and may occur soon.

"I AM THANKFUL, Lord, that history is in Your hands. Help me make every moment count and anticipate the time I shall see You face to face."

48

WHAT PART OF "ALL THINGS" DON'T WE UNDERSTAND?

"O Lord, you have searched me and you know me" (Psalm 139:1).

ABOUT 2,000 YEARS AGO, ASAPH THE PSALMIST, musician, and choir director was almost at wits' end. He had puzzled long and hard to understand why wicked people prospered. Life just didn't seem fair. He wrestled with a heavyweight question, "Does the Most High have knowledge?" (Psalm 73:11b).

Asaph finally discovered the answer in "the sanctuary of God" (verse 17). Not only did God know the wicked were prospering while His people were suffering, but He also knew He would punish the wicked someday. He would destroy the wicked, sweep them away, and "despise them as fantasies" (verses 19, 20).

Maybe you have stood in Asaph's sandals or you are wearing them right now. You look at unfair personal situations and wonder if God really knows what is going on in your life. If He knew your troubles, wouldn't He fix them—make them go away?

What Christian hasn't been tempted to think God doesn't know everything? Sure, He knows all about the composition of outer space but does He know all about the bills piling up on my kitchen table? Does He know how badly I am hurting from the loss of my spouse? Does He know my son hasn't contacted me for weeks? Does He know how lonely I feel? And what about those nagging joint pains that keep me from doing things younger people do so easily? Does He know?

"Open theism," A new twist to theology (a twisted theology) insists God doesn't know everything. If correct, this theology can't put its arms around us when we hurt and assure us God understands and cares. It leaves us quite alone and helpless to see God at work in our dark days.

But the Bible is still the best theology book and it still teaches us that God is all knowing. Nothing escapes His knowledge, not even that recent utility company's rate increase or that sudden stiffness of the right knee.

The apostle Peter often put his foot in his mouth, but he spoke wisely in response to Jesus' third interrogation, "Do you love me?" He responded, "Lord, you know all things" (John 21:17).

Let's side with Peter in the open theism debate. The Lord does know all things. If we know He knows all things, we can trust Him to use all things for our good and His glory.

"LORD, nothing takes you by surprise. You know all about my aches and pains and the situations that seem unsolvable. I trust You for grace to wait patiently for You to perfect Your work in my life."

49
SHEPHERDS

" I will place shepherds over them who will tend them . . ." (Jeremiah 23:4a).

SHEPHERDS, LOCATED IN SOUTHERN WISCONSIN, IS HOME to nearly two hundred adults with mental disabilities. These special individuals receive the finest in Christian care along with the opportunity to reach their personal potential in every area of life. There's really no place quite like Shepherds.

The ministry began nearly fifty years ago in an adult Sunday school class in the Milwaukee area. One of the couples had a child with Down syndrome and were so occupied with his care they seldom got any relief. Class members decided to take turns babysitting each week to give these dedicated parents some time to themselves. As the years passed, this class project expanded to include friends and neighbors who were also parents of mentally challenged youngsters. As the number grew, the need for a care facility became obvious.

Shepherds was born to meet that need. Eventually,

concerned Christians purchased land and constructed buildings. Today, more than one hundred staff people give loving, compassionate care to each individual.

In recent years, Shepherds has had to adjust its focus. Because its residents have aged considerably (the average age is now beyond fifty), new programs have been developed to accommodate the elderly. For example, the "Crowns of Splendor" program provides seniors with a variety of activities precisely geared to their interests.

The residents at Shepherds have always occupied a special place in my (Joe) heart. At first, I was a bit apprehensive about visiting Shepherds because I wasn't sure how I should act around a mentally challenged person. However, the moment I arrived, all my fears dissipated immediately. Each resident greeted me with such warmth and genuine love that I soon forgot my anxieties and just enjoyed each new friend I met. I was deeply impressed with the ability each showed in memorizing lengthy Scripture passages and with the glow that emanated from all who told what Jesus meant to them. Here were people who probably had every reason to be despondent and discouraged. But their cheerful spirit reflected a joy and a bright testimony of the presence of Christ in their lives.

I'm sure you would be similarly impressed if you visited Shepherds.

Local senior groups have always been a vital part of Shepherds' ministry. Each month, many help with mailings and other special projects. Others volunteer in various areas of service, including helping in the kitchen and the greenhouse. Some would rather get involved more personally by reading stories to the residents, playing table games, and helping them with crafts. These activities have had a residual effect as well. Seniors have found they have special resources that meet vital needs while the residents have found fresh and delightful experiences with their new friends.

Seniors have so much to offer, in so many ways. Just look around. There are probably plenty of opportunities for you to use your special gifts and talents right in your own neighborhood. Go for it! It may just change your life.

"DEAR FATHER, Thank you for wonderful ministry of Shepherds and the important part that seniors play in it. Use me where You want me to serve today."

50

THE PURSUIT OF PEACE

"And the peace of God, which transcends all understanding, will guard your hearts and your minds in Christ Jesus" (Philippians 4:7)

A RECENT SURVEY AMONG SENIORS REVEALED THAT OVER 85% of those polled felt peace was the most important single issue in their lives. Whether personal, national, or family related, the impending possibility of turmoil and conflict poses a grave concern to the elderly. It's obvious that as we age we become increasingly cautious about perilous conditions.

Of course, this is nothing new. The pursuit of peace has been the most sought-after element of every generation, society, or culture in the history of the world. The quest for peace has consumed every nation, resulting in billions of dollars spent to develop and maintain a degree of security and stability. However, history teaches us that human effort has never produced genuine lasting peace. Although peacekeepers and other agents of government work to establish a tranquil environment, sooner or later violations occur that eventually result in turmoil and devastation.

Peace talks go on constantly in various parts of the world. Peace treaties are being devised, argued, signed, and broken. The cycle repeats itself. We applaud the dedication of those who work diligently to find solutions because we know the horrible alternative. Yet, these countless hours of energy and debate seem so futile when agreements have proven to be at best, tenuous. Therefore, it's clear that this is not just an old age issue but an age-old tragedy.

So, what's the answer? Will we ever know true peace?

The bad news is that as a society we will never attain ongoing genuine tranquility. However, the good news is that in Jesus Christ we can experience the true and lasting peace that passes all understanding. The better news is that this kind of peace comes to us absolutely free when we receive Jesus Christ as Savior. Believers enjoy an ongoing peace, deep in the soul, that transcends every difficult situation. Even when confronted with tribulation and various trials, we can rely on an inner security based on the lasting peace God brings to those who have placed their trust in Christ, no matter what their age.

"Dear Lord, We are so grateful that you are The Prince of Peace and that You bring eternal peace and joy to Your children."

51

LEARNING A NEW LANGUAGE

"I will extol the LORD at all times; his praise will always be on my lips" (Psalm 34:1).

INCLUDED IN A LONG LIST OF CLASSES OFFERED AT SENIOR centers in the Colorado Springs area are language classes. A senior can choose Arabic, Japanese, or Spanish. Tough choice! With so much news coming out of the Middle East these days, wouldn't it be neat (a more senior-friendly word than "cool") to be able to read those Arabic inscriptions we see on TV? Of course, Japanese would be handy. So many computer-related instructions come in Japanese. Perhaps they are easier to understand than the English ones, that is if we knew Japanese. Understanding Spanish would be wonderful and practical, especially with millions of Spanish-speaking immigrants entering the United States. If we knew Spanish, it would be a whole lot easier to order a sandwich at a fast-food restaurant. And wouldn't a correct pronunciation of burrito or enchilada wow the person taking our order? *Si!*

I (Jim) studied French for five years and German for four years, and thoroughly enjoyed the experience. However, I have rarely had an opportunity to use either language, so my French and German vocabularies have dwindled significantly. I think I should wade into a new language while my brain waves are still somewhat active. Spanish seems to be the right choice.

Have you noticed that every English-speaking senior is fluent in either the language of praise or the language of lament? One senior looks beyond his or her trials and says, "Praise the Lord." Another fails to look beyond his or her trials, and exclaims, "Woe is me!" I know seniors who see only thorns in their circumstances but, thankfully, I know others who see the roses. Frankly, the thorn-seers aren't any fun to be around. Their personalities jab like thorns. The rose-seers, on the other hand, display a pleasant personality. Their beautiful spirit attracts me and shows me they have been lingering in the presence of Jesus, the Rose of Sharon.

David, the psalmist, employed the language of praise. He had experienced numerous trials, including those he endured in caves and ravines as a fugitive from King Saul. Through it all, David focused on God's sovereignty instead of Saul's savagery. Because he trusted in God, he expected to emerge from trials as a victor and not a victim. He wrote in Psalm 33:20, 21: We wait in hope for the LORD; he is help and our shield. In him, our hearts rejoice for we trust in his holy name."

If you know someone who ought to learn the language of praise, why not share Psalm 33:20, 21 with him or her? You might just help that person stop saying, "Woe is me!" and start saying, "Wonderful is He!"

. . .

"LORD, help me focus on Your plan and power. May I become fluent in the language of praise!"

52

WHO CAN YOU TRUST?

"Watch out that no one deceives you" (Matthew 24:4).

GROWING UP IN THE 1940S MEANT HAVING TO MAKE SOME serious sacrifices. World War II had become the primary consideration for products and services, which meant people had to do without many conveniences, including automobiles.

Our (Joe's) family never owned an automobile. We lived in a neighborhood on the north side of Chicago and could easily walk to stores, schools, and churches. After the war, economic conditions began to improve and new cars rolled off the assembly lines once again. Many of our friends and neighbors purchased brand-new cars... but not us.

During my teen years, I longed for a car. I wanted the independence and attention that having "my own" car would bring. I had even picked out the one I wanted. A black, shiny 1954 model that didn't have one scratch or mark on its sleek body. It even had a dual exhaust system that guaranteed a certain level of "noise status" that appealed to the teens of the '50s. Although the purchase lay far beyond my budget, I did, eventually, with my parents' consent and a lot of financial wrangling, get the car! I felt like one liberated teen as I drove my black beauty off the lot.

Two weeks later, things began to go wrong until it seemed I had replaced every part under the hood. Repair bills quickly gobbled up my weekly paychecks from the local A & P store. After a year of frustration, I finally got rid of my black beauty. I recall the day I sold it (at a loss, of course). It was as shiny and loud as the day I bought it. I've come to refer to it as my "Pharisee Car," bright and loud on the outside but empty and dead under the hood.

One of the things Jesus taught when He was on earth was the need to look at the heart of a matter. On subjects such as murder and adultery, He continuously considered the motives that prompted outward acts. His greatest antagonists were the Pharisees, the religious leaders of the day, who paraded about, proudly displaying their spirituality for all to see. However, Jesus saw right through them, past their proud exterior, and right into their deceptive hearts. He rebuked them for their superficial manner of giving, fasting, and praying. Eight times in Matthew 23, He called them hypocrites. In verse 27, He called them "whitewashed tombs."

We are sometimes surprised and disappointed to find that someone we trusted turned out to be deceptive and insincere. At times, our trust has been betrayed to the point of costing us dearly. The bottom line is that we must be very careful when dealing with people. Those who seem to have our best interests at heart may really be after all our interests. However, there is One who does have your eternal interest at heart. Jesus Christ, the sinless One, proved His genuineness by becoming the sacrifice God required for sin. That act of perfect love provided forgiveness of sin and the promise of everlasting life for those who will place their trust in Him.

"DEAR LORD, we thank you for your great sacrifice that enables us to have forgiveness of sins and eternal life. Help me to follow You sincerely and devotedly."

RETHINKING POPULAR BELIEFS

ABOUT THE END TIMES

Dedicated to the memory of Betty Rahm, who loved the Lord and prophecy. At age 90, Betty typeset parts of this study and published them in the form of a booklet.

and

to the memory of Dr. John L. Benson, a gifted Bible teacher who was my good friend and associate. John and I enjoyed many stimulating conversations about the end times.

and

to all who seek to determine God's plan for the future by an honest interpretation of Scripture.

1
THE STUDY OF PROPHECY HAS NO PRACTICAL VALUE

CAN YOU PICTURE YOURSELF PURCHASING TICKETS FOR YOU and your wife to take that well-deserved vacation you have dreamed of for such a long time? It's going to be a ten-day Caribbean cruise. Finally, the day arrives when you board ship. You hug each other as the luxury liner pulls out of port but then you learn the ship lacks a guidance system. The captain has chosen not to be concerned about where the ship is going. He just cares about where it is today. Your dream vacation has turned into a nightmare!

Traveling through life, people want to know where the world is headed. Of course, we accept the fact that we cannot know the specifics but knowing the broad sweep of the future has definite benefits. We no longer have to ask: What is this world coming to? Nor do we need to wonder if God will let injustice, violence, and suffering continue forever? Prophecy supplies this broad sweep of the future and assures us God is in control. As the once-popular song proclaimed: "He's got the whole world in his hands."

An essential question related to prophecy relates to what theologians dub "the millennium," a future period of 1,000 years in which Christ presumably will reign over the earth. Those who believe he will establish his kingdom on earth for 1,000 years are called millennialists. Those who reject the concept of a 1000-year reign of Christ on Planet Earth are called amillennialists (no millennium). A divided thinking among millennialists leaves us with premillennialists—those who believe Jesus' coming to earth precedes the millennium—and postmillennials—those who believe he will return after the millennium. Postmillennialists see the millennium as a period in which conditions on earth have evolved into an unprecedented period of peace and prosperity.

Some Christians, even some pastors, avoid studying what prophecy has to say about the future. They classify themselves as panmillennialists, stating with intended humor that they believe everything will pan out in the end. Unfortunately, they and all who cop out of the study of prophecy are missing out on the practical value prophecy carries.

The book of Revelation brims with prophecy but many believers fail to read its message. Yet, when Jesus delivered the book of Revelation to the apostle John, he spoke of the value of reading and obeying its words. He promised: "Blessed is the one who reads the words of this prophecy, and blessed are those who hear it and take to heart what is written in it" (Rev. 1:3).

Let's consider samples of the value prophecy offers.

Anticipation of heaven and Jesus' presence:

Jesus prophesied that after returning to heaven and preparing a place for his followers, he would come again and receive them unto himself to be with him forever (John 14:1-3).

Comfort and Encouragement:

Paul informed the Thessalonian believers that someday living Christians will see their departed Christian loved ones and friends again. There will be a grand reunion when Jesus comes for his church (1 Thess. 4:16-17). The bodies of dead Christians will be raised and glorified and the bodies of living Christians will be translated. The perishable (bodies of departed Christians) will be clothed with the imperishable, and mortality will be clothed with immortality (1 Cor. 15:53).

Grief will always attend the death of a loved one but we do not grieve like those who have no hope. The prophecy about Jesus' return to gather all Christians together and the prophecy about the reception of new bodies at his return make our tears lighter and our hope stronger. Strengthened by these prophecies, we are motivated to work steadily, faithfully and optimistically for the Lord (1 Cor. 15:58).

Purification:

The apostle John prophesied that a marvelous future awaits Christians. He wrote: "Dear friends, now we are the children of God, and what we will be has not yet been made known. But we know that when he appears, we shall be like him, for we shall see him as he is" (1 John 3:2). Now the practical application—the prophecy's value: John wrote: "Everyone who has this hope in him purifies himself, just as he is pure" (v. 3). Knowing Jesus will return motivates us to be at our best every day. We long to be pure as he is pure. So we endeavor to resist temptation, avoid compromising circumstances, disdain evil, and obey God's Word.

Triumph over Suffering:

Paul's body carried the marks of persecution and suffering (2 Cor. 11:23-29; 12:7-9). Yet, Paul regarded his suffering as only temporary and looked beyond this temporal life to an eternity when his body and the bodies of all believers would no longer experience suffering. He prophesied in 2 Corinthians 5:1-2: "Now we know that if the earthly tent we live in [the body] is destroyed, we have a building from God, an eternal house in heaven, not built by human hands. Meanwhile we groan, longing to be clothed with our heavenly dwelling." Because of what lies ahead, we see our affliction as "light and momentary troubles" precursors to eternal glory. Therefore, we focus on the eternal instead of on the temporary (4:17-18).

Confidence That God Will Put an End to Evil:

To be sure, we are tired of injustice and inhumane acts of violence and we ask, "How long, O Lord? How long?" Nevertheless, the wheels of justice grind slowly although they do grind surely. Prophecy assures us God will someday execute justice upon evildoers. Second

Thessalonians 1:6-9 promises: "God is just: He will pay back trouble to those who trouble you and give relief to you who are troubled and to us as well. This will happen when the Lord Jesus is revealed from heaven in blazing fire with his powerful angels. He will punish those who do not know God and do not obey the gospel of our Lord Jesus. They will be punished with everlasting destruction and shut out from the presence of the Lord and from the majesty of his power." Jude 14 predicts: "See, the Lord is coming with thousands upon thousands of his holy ones to judge everyone and to convict all the ungodly acts they have done in the ungodly way ... "

Revelation 19:11-18 portrays Jesus' return to earth in a display of power and glory. He strikes down the nations and treads the winepress of the fury of the wrath of Almighty God. Payday is coming!

Optimism:

It is easy to grow pessimistic as crime, corruption, and civil unrest erupt. It is hard to be optimistic when brave soldiers die in the defense of freedom but prophecy gives us a sense of optimism. When Jesus is King over all the earth, our planet will undergo dramatic changes. Peace, prosperity, productivity, and pure worship will characterize his reign. Read, for example, Isaiah 9:6-7; 11; 25:8; 35:2, 5-7; 42:7; 52:7; 60:3, 18; 65:21-22, 25; Joel 2:24-26; 3:12; Mic. 5:4; Zech.14:16-21; Rev. 22:2.

These are just a few of the benefits that accrue from a study of prophecy.

Back to the analogy of a cruise! Wouldn't you be shocked to find a passenger eating only the cheese and crackers he had packed for the voyage? When you ask why he doesn't visit the dining room and enjoy the plenteous food there, you learn he didn't know the food was included in the cost of the cruise. The Lord has given us a prophetic feast in His Word so don't neglect what he has provided. Dig right it!

2
POPULAR BELIEF: JESUS MUST BE COMING SOON
—LOOK AT ALL THE SIGNS!

AN EARTHQUAKE RUMBLES IN THE MOUNTAINS OF IRAN, destroying villages and killing thousands. Famine blights North Korea and the Sudan, causing many men, women, and children to die of starvation. China suffers a SARS epidemic. Ebola devastates parts of Africa. The Zika virus targets Brazil but also penetrates other areas, including southern parts of the USA. Scientists scramble to find a repellant to ward off the mosquitoes that carry the virus. AIDS afflicts more than 21 million victims in Africa. Believers endure persecution around the world. Christian martyrs lie dead at the hands of ISIS. False prophets deceive thousands.

North Korea and Iran pursue a reckless course of developing far-reaching nuclear capability. Iraq and Afghanistan reel from the effects of war and terrorism. The United States came under terrorism's vicious attack on innocent civilians on 9/11, and other acts of terrorism have maimed and ended other American lives since then. Religious apostasy, crime, and immorality run rampant like a three-headed monster.

The sanctity of marriage and the family are under siege. Torrential floods, severe storms, and vast forest fires rage in Australia and the USA. Weird weather patterns puzzle meteorologists and we are supposed to attribute much of it to global warming. Troubled teenagers gun down fellow students in school classrooms and hallways.

Are these alarming events signs that we are living in the last days? Do they signal the return of Jesus to planet Earth? Is Jesus poised in heaven, ready to come in the clouds and snatch his church from the earth?

Let's put our newspapers aside for a few minutes, turn off the TV news, and pick up our Bibles. The answers to our perplexing questions await us there.

Are we living in the last days? Yes! Are we living near the end of the last days? Maybe yes. Maybe no.

Let me explain.

Writing in the first century, the apostles pointed to events occurring in their lifetime as characteristic of "last days" or "last times" or "last hour." They observed:

"In the past God spoke to our forefathers through the prophets at many times and in various ways, but in these last days he has spoken to us by his Son, whom he appointed heir of all things, and through whom he made the universe" (Heb. 1:1-2).

"He was chosen before the creation of the world, but was revealed in these last times for your sake" (1 Peter 1:20).

"Dear children, this is the last hour .... This is how we know it is the last hour" (1 John 2:18).

"But, dear friends, remember what the apostles of our Lord Jesus Christ foretold. They said to you, 'In the last times there will be scoffers who will follow their own ungodly desires.' These are they who divide you" (Jude 17-19).

Christians from the first century to the present have lived in the last days. We are certainly closer to the rapture now than first-century Christians were but we cannot assert dogmatically that the end of the last days is upon us.

But what about the signs of the times?

Let's look at the signs Jesus gave in Matthew 24, Mark 13, and Luke 21. Where do they belong in what might be called a prophetic jigsaw puzzle? He gave these signs to the disciples in response to their questions about the temple's destruction and the timing of Jesus' coming at the end of the age. "Tell us," they said, "when will this happen [the destruction of the temple], and what will be the sign of your coming and of the end of the age" (Matt. 24:3). "Tell us, when will these things happen? And what will be the sign that they are all about to be fulfilled?" (Mark 13:4). "Teacher," they asked, "when will these things happen? And what will be the sign that they are about to take place?" (Luke 21:7).

As we scan these passages that unfold what has been called the Olivet Discourse, here are the signs we find:

- False messiahs
- Wars and rumors of wars
- International strife
- Famines
- Earthquakes
- Persecutions and martyrdoms
- Apostasy
- Religious deception

- Increase in wickedness
- Gospel of the kingdom to be preached worldwide
- Abomination of desolation
- Counterfeit signs and miracles
- Solar and lunar eclipses
- Stellar disturbances
- Pestilences
- Jerusalem surrounded by hostile armies
- Oceanic upheaval
- Panic

According to Jesus, the generation that witnesses these signs will also see "the Son of Man coming on the clouds of the sky, with power and great glory" (Matt. 24:30). Matthew 25:31-45 expands on this glorious appearance of Jesus by describing the Judgment of the Nations that follows it immediately on the earth. This judgment separates the sheep (righteous Gentiles) from the goats (unrighteous Gentiles). The sheep receive an inheritance in the Messiah's kingdom (v. 34), whereas the unrighteous are consigned to eternal fire "prepared for the devil and his angels" (v. 41). King Jesus presides at this judgment (vv. 34, 40).

Several aspects of this event distinguish it from the rapture.

1. The rapture occurs in the air. Jesus does not return to the earth when he catches up Christians to himself. The apostle Paul described the rapture in 1 Thessalonians 4:16-17: "For the Lord himself will come down from heaven ... and the dead in Christ will rise first. After that, we who are still alive and are left will be caught up

together with them in the clouds to meet the Lord in the air."

2. The rapture features Jesus' arrival in the air as the Bridegroom who takes his bride (the church) to his Father's house. He promised in John 14:2-3, "In my Father's house are many rooms . . . I am going there to prepare a place for you, And if I go and prepare a place for you, I will come back and take you with me that you also may be where I am." When Jesus takes his bride to heaven, he will present her to himself as a radiant church, without stain or wrinkle or any other blemish, but holy and blameless" (Eph. 5:27). At the end of the tribulation, he will return to the earth in a blaze of glory as King of kings and Lord of lords and will execute judgment on his enemies (Rev. 19:11-16).

3. The title, Son of Man, used 81 times in the Gospels, is a messianic term that relates Jesus to Israel. Jews would have associated the title with the picture in Daniel 7:13-14 of a heavenly end-times figure who comes with the clouds of heaven and is vested with authority, glory, and sovereign power, and has an everlasting dominion and invincible kingdom. At his second coming, not at rapture, Jesus the Son of Man will seize the reins of government from the nations and establish his glorious kingdom rule.

4. New Testament writers treated the rapture as an imminent event. They believed it could take place at any time and they longed for it to happen in their lifetime. They did not teach that a series of signs would have to be fulfilled before the rapture could occur. Paul wrote:

"The Lord is near" (Phil. 4:4). James wrote: "The Lord's coming is near" (James 5:8), and "the judge is standing at the door" (v. 9). Further, John recorded Jesus' promise: Yes, I am coming soon" (Rev. 22:20).

5. One sign of Jesus' coming involves the worldwide preaching of the gospel of the Kingdom (Matt. 24:14). Some zealous Christian leaders suggest that Christians must proclaim the good news of salvation to the ends of the earth in order to hasten the coming of Christ. Their zeal is admirable but our commission to preach the gospel to all nations issues from Matthew 28:18-20, not from Matthew 24:14. The Gospel of the Kingdom was never committed to Christians. We find many references in the Epistles to preaching the gospel but none involve the gospel of the kingdom. See, for example, "the gospel of his Son" (Rom. 1:9); "the gospel" (v. 16; 11:28; 1 Cor. 1:17; 9:16; 15:1; Gal. 2:2; Phil. 1:5; Col. 1:5; "my gospel" (Rom. 2:16; 2 Tim. 2:8); "the gospel of God" (Rom. 15:16; 1 Thess. 2:9); "the glorious gospel of the blessed God" (1 Tim. 11); "our gospel" (2 Cor. 4:3. 2 Thess. 2:14); "the gospel of the glory of Christ" (2 Cor. 4:4); "the gospel of Christ" (Gal. 1:7; 1 Thess. 3:2); and "the gospel of your salvation" (Eph. 1:13).

John the Baptist preached the gospel of the kingdom. He summoned his fellow Jews to "repent, for the kingdom of heaven is near" (Mat. 3:2). Indeed, the kingdom was near, because Jesus, the Messiah, had been born. He held the title deed to the throne of Israel and was about to begin his ministry.

Jesus, too, preached the gospel of the kingdom. Matthew 4:23 reports that "Jesus went throughout

Galilee, teaching in their [the Jews'] synagogues, preaching the good news of the kingdom." Mark 1:15 states that he said, "The kingdom of God is near. Repent and believe the good news!" On one occasion, Jesus announced, "The kingdom of God is within you (Luke 7:21), meaning it was present in the person of the King. Jesus formally presented the kingdom to Israel but, as we know, Israel rejected the King and His kingdom.

Jesus' disciples preached the gospel of the kingdom. Responding to Jesus' command to do so (Luke 9:2), "they set out and went from village to village, preaching the gospel [of the kingdom, see v. 2] and healing people everywhere" (v. 6). Their message, like that of John the Baptist and Jesus, was intended to persuade Israel to repent and receive her King.

The message about the Messiah's kingdom was appropriately designed for the Jews. It struck a responsive note in the hearts of faithful Jews who anticipated the arrival of their Messiah. They believed the Old Testament promises about an earthly theocratic kingdom of peace and prosperity and, therefore, they waited for "the consolation of Israel" (Luke 2:25). This hope was running high in the disciples' hearts after Jesus' resurrection. They asked him, "Lord, are you at this time going to restore the kingdom to Israel?" (Acts 1:6).

The gospel of the kingdom, then, is a Jewish message about the imminent messianic kingdom. Christians have not been commissioned to proclaim this gospel because the kingdom is not imminent. The King is absent and we do not know when he will return to earth to establish his kingdom.

But the gospel of the kingdom will be proclaimed in

the whole world in fulfillment of Jesus' prediction in Matthew 24:14. It will happen after the rapture when the kingdom is imminent. Saved Jews of the tribulation period will be the preachers. Indeed, all the signs given in Matthew 24, Mark 13, and Luke 21 will be fulfilled in the tribulation.

The book of Revelation unfolds three series of judgments that God rains down upon the earth before Christ returns and establishes his kingdom. They are the Seal Judgments, the Trumpet Judgments, and the Bowl Judgments (Rev. 6—18). These judgments fulfill the signs given in the Olivet Discourse but, before we identify them, we need to see what takes place before they begin.

The first chapter of Revelation pictures Jesus as the risen, glorified, eternal Son of Man, who holds the keys of death and Hades. Jesus appears to the apostle John and instructs him to write a letter to each of seven churches in Asia Minor (modern-day Turkey).

Chapters 2 and 3 record the seven letters Jesus dictated to John. Each letter uncovers the receiving church's distinct characteristics and ministry track record. Many Bible teachers point to parallels between the characteristics of the seven churches and the characteristics of periods of church history. They suggest the church at Ephesus, the first church addressed, prefigures the first-century church, and the seventh church, Laodicea, prefigures the final period of church history.

Chapter 4 of Revelation begins, "after this" (v. 1), and indicated that the writing of the seven letters was concluded. However, if we see the seven churches prefiguring periods of church history from Pentecost to the rapture, we can take "after this" to mean after the entire church age. Subsequent events described in Revelation occur after the church age.

At the end of the church age, the rapture is pictured by what happened to the apostle John. According to Revelation 4:1-2, John looked up, saw a door standing open in heaven, heard a voice like a trumpet summoning him to "come up here" and promising to show him "what must take place after this." Immediately, John found himself in heaven.

Chapter 5 reports that John saw a Lamb (Jesus) in heaven. The Lamb received a scroll with seven seals from the occupant of heaven's throne (presumably God the Father). This transaction elicits from heaven's population "praise and honor and glory and power forever and ever" to the Lamb.

What follows in chapters 6 through 18 is the unleashing of tribulation judgments upon the earth. John witnesses these judgments from his vantage point in heaven. If we view John's "rapture" (Rev. 4:1-2) as picturing the church's rapture, we can anticipate that Christians will be in heaven when the tribulation rages on the earth.

The similarities between John's "rapture" and the church's rapture are striking.

<u>John's Rapture (Rev. 4:1-2)</u>
Hears a voice like a trumpet.
Caught up to heaven

<u>The Church's Rapture (1 Thess. 4:16-17)</u>
Voice and Trumpet
Caught up to heaven.

Now we return to our discussion about the timing of the signs given in the Olivet Discourse. The judgments that unfold in Revelation 6-18, after the rapture but before the glorious return of Christ to establish his kingdom, fulfill those prophesied signs.

Signs of the Times:

<u>Prophesied in the Olivet Discourse:</u>

1. False messiahs (Matt. 24:5; Mark 13:6; Luke 21:8)
2. Famine, pestilence, earthquakes (Matt. 24:6-7; Mark 13:7-8; Luke 21:11)
3. Wars (Matt. 24:6-7; Mark 13:7-8; Luke 21:9)
4. Persecution of the righteous (Matt. 24:9; Mark 13:9; Luke 21:12-19)
5. Worldwide preaching of the gospel of the kingdom (Matt. 24:14; Mark 13:10)
6. Abomination of desolation (Matt. 24:15; Mark 13:14)
7. Religious deception (Matt. 24:24; Mark 13:22; Luke 21:8)
8. Solar and lunar blackouts, stellar disturbances (Matt. 24:29; Mark 13:24-25; Luke 21:25-26)

<u>Fulfilled in the Tribulation:</u>

1. Rev. 6:2; 13:11-15
2. Rev. 6:5-6; 8:5; 16:18-20
3. Rev. 6:6-8; 16:2-14
4. Rev. 6:9; 12:13-17; 13:15
5. Rev. 7:1-10; 14:1-6
6. Rev. 13:14-15
7. Rev. 13:11-14
8. Rev. 6:12-14; 8:12

Just a few concluding remarks about signs:

Although no signs have to be fulfilled before Jesus raptures his church, we cannot say dogmatically that the current phenomena some Christians identify as signs are not stage dressing for the drama that will unfold in the tribulation. We simply don't have Biblical authority to say that they are.

Further, some students of eschatology (the study of last things) do not identify two phases of Jesus' second coming. They believe he will rapture the church and immediately return to earth with his church. These Bible teachers believe Christians will be alive on earth during the tribulation.

Other Bible teachers insist that the church will experience the first half of the tribulation and be raptured before the second half (the great tribulation) begins.

I take the view of pretribulational dispensationalism that God will remove the church from the earth before the tribulation and then resume his prophetic program for Israel (see Rom. 11:25-27). The tribulation will serve as a purging force for Israel. Many Jews will repent and believe in the Messiah during that period. After the tribulation, they will enter the long-awaited messianic kingdom, The 144,000 servants of God mentioned in Revelation 7:4 comprise a core group of saved Jews. While respecting other views, I believe the dispensational view honors the distinction drawn in 1 Corinthians 10:32 between Jews, Greeks (Gentiles), and the church.

Israel can expect dreadful persecution in the tribulation period but it can also anticipate spiritual cleansing and deliverance. The prophet Zechariah promised: "And I will pour out on the house of David and the inhabitants of Jerusalem a spirit of grace and supplication. They will look on me, the one they have pierced, and they will mourn for him as one mourns for an only child, and grieve bitterly for him as one grieves for a newborn son" (Zech. 12:10).

Zechariah 13:1 predicts: "On that day a fountain will be opened to the house to the house of David and the inhabitants of Jerusalem, to cleanse them from sin and impurity." Verses 8 and 9 state: "'In the whole land,' declares the LORD, 'two thirds will be struck down and perish; yet one-third will be left in it. This third I will bring into the fire; I will refine them like silver and test them like gold. They will call on my name and I will answer them; I will say, 'they are my people,' and they will say, 'The LORD is our God.'"

Speaking to Jews, in Matthew 24, Jesus offered hope to the generation that would witness the signs of the times. It cannot know the day of the Lord's coming but it can know he is coming. Therefore, the saved should be watchful. Like wise virgins, they should be ready for their Master's return (Matt. 25:1-13); and like faithful servants, they should invest their talents in the Master's service (vv. 14-30).

If we believe Jesus could come for us at any time, and we do not have to wait for signs to be fulfilled, we surely ought to lead the kind of life that honors our Savior and attracts the lost to him. We cannot say we have at least tomorrow to honor and serve him. If we need to reconcile with an offended brother or sister in Christ, now is the time to do so. If we need to pray for a loved one's salvation, now is the right time. If we need to perform a charitable deed or talk to a neighbor about Christ, we should not procrastinate. If we need to rid

Rethinking Popular Beliefs

ourselves of enslaving bad habits, we should do so today. An any-moment anticipation of Jesus' coming in the air for his church should lead to an every-moment dedication to him. According to 1 John 3:3, our hope of seeing Jesus inspires pure living. The verse states, "Everyone who has this hope in him purifies himself, just as he is pure."

3

POPULAR BELIEF: THE ANTICHRIST IS THE HEAD OF THE REVIVED ROMAN EMPIRE

BIBLE TEACHERS HAVE WRITTEN NUMEROUS ARTICLES AND books about the Antichrist. Hollywood has produced movies about him. Pastors have preached countless sermons about him. And he has been the topic of numerous group sessions and conversations. Yet, no one knows his actual identity. Speculation has run high for ages, though. Many centuries ago, Christians believed Nero was the Antichrist. He surely was a psychopathic villain but time proved he was simply that and not the Antichrist. Many sermons and writings of Reformation vintage identified the pope as the Antichrist. With the passing of time, other men fell under suspicion. Much like pinning the tail on the donkey, believers blindly pinned the name Antichrist on such infamous characters as Napoleon, Kaiser Wilhelm, Hitler, and Mussolini. More recently the name has been attached respectively and ridiculously to John F. Kennedy, Henry Kissinger, Moshe Dayan, Ronald Reagan, and even Santa Claus.

Although no one can name the Antichrist, almost

everyone agrees that he will be the head of the Revived Roman Empire in the tribulation period. This identification dominates the prophetic thinking in evangelical seminaries and Bible colleges and is perpetuated by the vast majority of their alumni. But does the Bible assign a political role to the Antichrist? Can we take for granted that he will rule the world from a European capital?

Have you read or heard even one verse of Scripture that specifically mentions the Antichrist as the head of the Revived Roman Empire? I haven't. Nor have I read any verse that specifically mentions him in any other role. So it seems to me no one can say dogmatically that the Antichrist is this person or that. Although I do not believe he will be the head of the Revived Roman Empire, I respect those who do.

Here's why I reject the popular view:

First, every Scripture passage having the word "antichrist" relates to religious apostasy, not political power. The word doesn't appear at all in the Old Testament and appears only five times in the New Testament. Further, all references to "antichrist" are huddled together in John's epistles. Here they are:

"Dear children, this is the last hour; and you have heard that the antichrist is coming, even now many antichrists have come. This is how we know it is the last hour" (1 John 2:18).

"Who is the liar? It is the man who denies that Jesus is the Christ. Such a man is the antichrist—he denies the Father and the Son" (1 John 2:22).

"But every spirit that does not acknowledge Jesus is not from

God. This is the spirit of the antichrist, which you heard is coming and even now is already in the world" (1 John 4:3).

Many deceivers, who do not acknowledge Jesus as coming in the flesh, have gone out into the world. Any such person is a deceiver and the antichrist" (2 John 7).

If we examine the context in which John wrote about the Antichrist, we observe that the Antichrist is the culmination of many purveyors of false religious teaching (1 John 2:18). He is *the* liar (v. 22). He denies that Jesus is the Messiah, whose Father is God (v. 22; 4:3. He is *the deceiver* (2 John 7).

The Greek word translated "antichrist" can indicate a counterfeit Christ. *Anti* can mean either *against* or *instead of*, and *christos* (Christ) means messiah or anointed one. The Antichrist is the one Jesus spoke about when he commented: "I have come in my Father's name, and you do not accept me; but if someone else comes in his own name, you will accept him" (John 5:43). Jesus was speaking as the Messiah to the Jews, and the Antichrist will pose as Israel's Messiah.

Two diabolical powerful figures appear in the tribulation. The seven-year period I believe stretches from the rapture to the return of Christ to establish his kingdom. This viewpoint absents the church from the tribulation and places Israel in the central focus of God's attention as he pours out three series of judgments onto the earth. They are (1) the Seal Judgments, (2) the Trumpet Judgments, and (3) the Bowl Judgments. During the tribulation, God will discipline and purify Israel. This "time of Jacob's trouble" (Jer. 30:7) will bring salvation to Jews who acknowledge Jesus as Israel's Messiah (Zech. 13:1). Two-thirds of the Jews will perish but one-third will be saved. The Lord promised: "This third I will bring into the fire; I will refine them like silver and test them like gold. They will call on my name and I will answer them; I will say, 'They are my people,' and they will say, 'The LORD is our God'" (Zech. 13:9).

The first diabolical figure to emerge in the tribulation period is the "beast" that rules out of the sea (Rev. 13:1). The description that follows his introduction indicates he is a powerful political figure in control of the Revived Roman Empire, symbolized by the seven heads (Rome's seven successive forms of government). Dispensational interpreters see the ten horns as rulers of the empire until the "beast" emerges as the uncontested ruler. Another reason to believe he is the head of the Revived Roman Empire stems from the fact that he arises from "the sea." The sea from a Biblical perspective would be the Mediterranean Sea. The Roman Empire primarily encompassed the Mediterranean world, and the Revived Roman Empire probably approximates this same area. The beast from the sea is so powerful that his subjects ask: "Who is like the beast? Who can make war against him?" (v. 4) He is so blasphemous that he slanders God, heaven, and those who dwell in heaven (vv. 5-6). He makes war against the saints, and unbelievers universally worship him (vv. 7-10).

Once in uncontested power, the Roman prince, the beast of the sea, rules "for a time, times, and half a time" (three and a half years or 1,260 days. See Revelation 11:2-3; 12:14; 13:5). His reign of terror extends from the middle of the tribulation until the end of the tribulation.

As malevolent as the Roman prince is, it does not

appear that he is the Antichrist, although much popular prophetic teaching calls him the Antichrist. For one thing, he does not pretend to be Israel's Messiah. For another, he does not perform any miracles. The true Messiah established his credentials by performing miracles. Doesn't it seem logical to expect a false messiah, someone posing in the stead of the true Messiah, to perform miracles? Further, Jesus the Messiah functions as High Priest but the Roman prince does not cast himself in the role of a priest.

The second beast described in Revelation 13:11-18 seems to match John's identification of the Antichrist as a religious apostate, a liar, and a deceiver. He rises from the earth (v. 11), which must surely represent Israel, the land of Bible times. Israel, after all, is central to Bible geography.

This second beast, also known as the false prophet (16:13; 19:20; 20:10), is even more diabolical and dangerous than the first beast. A religious deceiver is always more dangerous than an overtly wicked person. He is what Jesus called a wolf in sheep's clothing (Matt. 7:15).

The false prophet imitates Jesus Christ in several ways. First, he has "two horns like a lamb" (13:11). Jesus came to Israel as the Lamb of God, the one who would die for the people's sins. Isaiah 53 depicts the Messiah as being "led like a lamb to the slaughter" (v. 7) and being "cut off from the land of the living; for the transgressions of my people was he stricken (v. 8).

Jesus spoke words of life, whereas the false prophet speaks "like a dragon" (v. 11). Energized by Satan, called "the great dragon" in Revelation 12:9, the false prophet speaks Satan's lies and opposes the truth.

Second, the false prophet performs "great and miraculous signs" (v. 13). Like Pharaoh's wicked magicians, the false prophet puts on a spectacular show of supernatural wonders. The Jewish leaders did not respond in faith to the miracles Jesus performed to demonstrate he was the Messiah but numerous Jews in the tribulation will believe the false prophet is the Messiah based on his signs and wonders. Not all of his show-stopping wonders are designed to deceive and those who accept him as the Messiah are grossly deceived (v. 14).

Third, the false prophet directs worship to the Roman prince (v. 14). In consort with the Roman prince, he sets up an image in honor of the Roman prince, animates it, and commands everyone to worship it (vv. 14-15).

At the beginning of "the times of the Gentles" (Luke 21:24), Nebuchadnezzar, King of Babylon, created an image in his own honor and commanded everyone to bow down and worship it (Dan. 3:1-6). Near the end of "the times of the Gentiles", the false prophet (Antichrist) duplicates the event. However, he commands everyone to bow down and worship the image of the Roman prince (Rev. 13:14). All who refused to worship Nebuchadnezzar's image faced execution. Similarly, all who refuse to worship the Roman prince's image experience the same fate.

The prophet Daniel predicted that this horrible act of idolatry would occur in the middle of the tribulation. He wrote: "In the middle of the seven he will put an end to sacrifice and offering. And on the wing of the temple he will set up an abomination that will cause desolation, until the end that is decreed is poured out on him" (Dan. 9:27).

Jesus pointed to this despicable act as a sign to righteous Jews to flee to the mountains for refuge. In the Olivet Discourse, he said, "So when you see standing in the holy place 'the abomination of desolation that causes desolation,' spoken of through the prophet Daniel—let the reader understand—then let those who are in Judea flee to the mountains" (Matt. 24:15-16).

Because they were suffering intense persecution, the Thessalonian Christians thought they were already living in the tribulation period. Paul helped clear up this misconception by pointing to two features of the tribulation. It would reveal the Antichrist (the false prophet), whom Paul described in 2 Thessalonians 2:4 as "the man of lawlessness.

The tribulation would also feature "the rebellion" (vv. 1-3). This rebellion likely refers to Israel's rebellious act of turning her back on God and capitulating to the false prophet's demand to worship the Roman prince's image.

In the tribulation period, the false prophet controls not only Israel's religious life but also her economic life. He forces everyone to receive a mark on the and on the forehead, perhaps a laser ID. Without this mark, which is 666, the number of the prophet's name, a person can neither buy nor sell. This number appears in only one other place in Scripture: Ezra 2:13. This verse reports 666 descendants of Adonikam accompanied Zerubbabel from captivity in Persia to Jerusalem. Adonikam means "the king who rises up," so we may wonder if the name of the beast that rises from the earth is Adonikam. Of course, this is merely interesting conjecture.

Many ingenious methods have been applied to disclose the false prophet's name. Those who are converted to Christ in the tribulation—the 144,000 Jews and their converts (Rev. 7:1-9)—will know his identity and be cautious. The wicked, too, will know his identity, but they will be deceived.

It does seem highly unlikely that the Antichrist is a Gentile. Because he poses as Israel's Messiah, he must surely be a Jew. Perhaps he belongs to the tribe of Dan. Revelation 7:4-8 lists the tribes of Israel to which the 144,000 sealed Jewish believers of the tribulation belong. The name of the tribe of Dan is conspicuously absent, although the tribe of Dan will participate in the kingdom the Messiah establishes after the tribulation (Ezek. 48:1).

Dan was the first tribe in Israel's history to practice idolatry. The Antichrist leads Israel into idolatry in the tribulation. Further, when Jacob blessed his sons, he prophesied: "Dan will be a serpent by the roadside, a viper along the path, that bites the horse's heel so that its rider tumbles backward" (Gen. 49:17).

The second beast of Revelation 13:11-18 imitates the three offices held by Jesus: prophet, priest, and king. As a prophet, he speaks like a dragon and performs lying wonders. As a priest, he directs worship to the Roman prince. As a king, he rules in Israel and does whatever he wants.

Why would the false prophet in Israel direct worship to the Roman prince, the head of the Revived Roman Empire? I believe the answer is this: A treaty between Western Europe and Israel is suddenly broken (Dan. 9:27). This leaves Israel vulnerable to attacks from every direction. She must, therefore, placate the Roman prince and do precisely what he demands. Israel believes an alliance with the Roman prince will save the day and gain her security. At that time, the people of Israel live in unwalled villages and are "peaceful and unsuspecting" (Ezek. 38:11).

However, Israel's idolatry invites God's wrath. When Israel practiced idolatry in Old Testament times, God unleashed armies from the north to punish her. Assyria invaded Israel in 721 B.C. and led many Jews into captivity. Judah, the southern kingdom, was less idolatrous than her sister to the north and, therefore, survived longer. Ultimately, however, Judah fell into the hands of a northern army. The Babylonians led a large contingent of Jews from their homeland to Babylon in 597 B.C.

Israel's idolatrous worship of the Roman prince in the tribulation evokes similar divine judgment. The "king of the south" (like Arab states) attacks Israel and then the Lord brings "the king of the north" into Palestine.

Daniel 11:40-49 supplies the details:

At the time of the end, the king of the South will engage him [the Antichrist] in battle, and the king of the North will storm out against him with chariots and cavalry and a great fleet of ships. He will invade many countries and sweep through them like a flood. He will invade the beautiful land. Many countries will fall, but Edom, Moab, and the leaders of Ammon will be delivered from his hand. He will extend his power over many countries; Egypt will not escape. He will gain control of the treasures of gold and silver and the riches of Egypt, with the Lybians and Nubians in submission. But reports from the east and the north will alarm him, and he will set out in a great rage to destroy and annihilate many. He will pitch his royal tents between the seas at the beautiful holy mountain. He will come to his end, and no one will help him.

According to Ezekiel 38:18-23, the sovereign Lord will destroy the northern invader in the mountains of Israel. He will shake the aggressor with a mighty earthquake. Landslides will crush the invader while panic causes the soldiers to turn on one another. Further, rain, hailstones, and burning sulfur will pummel the troops. Ezekiel 39:4 describes the slaughter as a provision of "food to all kinds of carrion birds and to wild animals."

Where is the false prophet, the Antichrist, when the northern invader strikes Israel? He leaves Israel and hides out until the coast is clear. Zechariah 11:17 tells us: "Woe to the worthless shepherd, who deserts the flock! May the sword strike his arm and his right eye! May his arm be completely withered, his right eye totally blinded!" Perhaps Jesus alluded to the false prophet's desertion when he contrasted an uncaring shepherd with the Good Shepherd. He warned: "The hired hand is not the shepherd who owns the sheep. S when he sees the wolf [the northern aggressor] coming, he abandons the sheep and runs away. Then the wolf attacks the flock and scatters it. The man runs away because he is a hired hand and cares nothing for the sheep" (John 10:12-13).

With the demise of the northern invader, the Roman prince occupies Palestine, overruns Jerusalem, and desecrates the temple area and Jerusalem. Jesus predicted a Jewish dispersion when this occurs: "They shall fall by the sword and be taken prisoners to all nations. Jerusalem will be trampled on by the Gentiles until the times of the Gentiles be fulfilled" (Luke 21:24). This same disaster is described in Revelation 11:2: "But exclude the outer court [of the temple]: do not measure it, because it has been given to the Gentiles." The Gentiles will trample on the holy city for 42 months (the second half of the tribulation period). At this time, the Antichrist cooperates fully with the Roman prince at the expense of the Jews. Daniel 11:38-39 reveals that "he will honor the god of fortresses, a god unknown to his fathers he will honor with gold and silver, with precious stones and costly gifts . . . and will distribute the land at any price."

The alliance of the Roman prince and the Antichrist will not go uncontested. Armies from the east will cross the Euphrates and march against the Roman prince's forces at Armageddon (Rev. 16:12-16). At this time, God will intervene to destroy the Gentile powers. He will unleash an earthquake of unprecedented magnitude and simultaneously rip the skies with lightning, rumblings, and thunderclaps. Hailstones weighing 100 pounds will fall on men (vv. 17-21).

These dramatic occurrences precede the most dramatic event in history. Revelation 19:11-21 portrays the return of Jesus to earth in a blaze of glory. Accompanied by the armies of heaven, he captures the Roman prince and the false prophet (the Antichrist) and casts them alive into "the fiery lake of burning sulfur (v. 20). He also kills the armies gathered at Armageddon. When the judgment concludes, birds of carrion feast on the dead, The Roman prince and the Antichrist's kingdom may have been powerful but it ends as *something for the birds*.

This study of the identification of the Antichrist would not be complete without stressing once again that the Bible does not assign the name "Antichrist" specifically to any end-time figure. The identification, therefore, is a matter of conjecture. However, it seems to me that the weight of scriptural evidence supports the position I have expressed in this chapter. In the final analysis, we do not have to know who the Antichrist is and an inordinate curiosity may distract us from our main task of sharing the Good News with lost and bewildered men and women.

If this chapter has accomplished anything, I hope it has shown that we must not be dogmatic about matters the Bible leaves open to interpretation. Saying dogmatically, this is this" and "that is that" can be divisive. Each of us is free to speculate about matters not clearly defined in the Bible. If we disagree, we ought to do so agreeably.

We may not be able to pin an antichrist nametag on an individual but we can plainly detect the spirit of the antichrist. Its mark is on every religious teaching that contradicts the Bible's portrayal of Jesus Christ. Jesus is the virgin-born Son of God. He led a sinless life, performed real miracles, shed his blood for our sins, arose bodily from the grave, was seen by many witnesses, ascended to heaven, and is coming again. He deserves our deepest love and our undying loyalty.

4

POPULAR BELIEF: WHATEVER WE DO FOR THE POOR WE DO FOR JESUS

POVERTY BLIGHTS OUR PLANET. IN SOME THIRD-WORLD countries, children live in cardboard boxes and rummage through garbage dumps in search of scraps of food. Some parents sell their daughters as prostitutes in order to support their families. Homeless people in the United States live in their cars or under bridges or alongside creeks. Homeless camps are not uncommon. Panhandlers beg at busy intersections or on downtown streets.

A town where I ministered in the 1960s included several streets of rundown houses that lacked indoor plumbing and central heating. Outhouses served as bathrooms. Most residents burned their trash in a backyard trash pit. For two or three dollars, a driver of a beat-up car would empty the contents of a trash pit into what used to be the back seat of his car and haul the trash to the dump. Many kids didn't eat well but lice did. Periodically, the schoolteachers combed through students' hair for signs of infection.

According to the U.S. Census Bureau report, the official poverty income level for a family of four in the United States in 2016 was $24,300. Of course, some people live at poverty level or below because they refuse to work. Others work hard at a pay rate that doesn't keep pace with the rising cost of living. Some are seniors on a fixed income like Social Security that doesn't cover the increasing costs of utilities, taxes, groceries, health care, and other necessities. Some live in poverty because of ill health.

Some poor families attend our churches. Becoming believers did not solve their financial problems but it did solve their sin problem and brought them into a close relationship with our loving heavenly Father. They can access supernatural peace and support as they struggle to get from the red to the black.

Perhaps you have heard a pastor conclude the announcement of a freewill offering at Communion by commenting: "Jesus said, 'I tell you the truth, whatsoever you do for one of the least of these brothers of mine, you did it unto me.'"

Is it true that the poor are the least of Jesus' brothers? Let's examine Matthew 25:31-46, in Jesus' famous Olivet Discourse. The Discourse, you may recall, was prompted by the disciples' request, "Tell us when will this happen, and what will be the sign of your coming and of the end of the age?" (Matt. 24:3) The question came in response to Jesus' assertion that every stone of the temple would be thrown down (v. 2).

Jesus answered the disciples' curiosity about end-time events by identifying a number of signs that would precede his coming in glory to establish his kingdom. The following verses describe his coming and the inauguration of his kingdom:

At that time ["immediately after the distress of those days" (Matt. 24:29)]"the Son of Man will appear in the sky, and all the nations of the earth will mourn. Thy will see the Son of Man coming on the clouds of the sky, with power and great glory" (v. 30).

When the Son of Man comes in his glory, and all the angels with him, he will sit on his throne in heavenly glory (25:31). Then the King will say to those on his right, "Come you who are blessed by my Father, take your inheritance, the Kingdom prepared for you since the creation of the world" (v.34).

It is in regard to the inauguration of his kingdom in the end time, after the "distress" (the tribulation), that King Jesus says, "I tell you the truth, whatsoever you did for one of the least of these brothers of mine, you did it for me" (v. 40).

Zeroing in on the inauguration of Jesus' kingdom, we find it occurs after history's darkest period, the tribulation. During that horrendous time, religious deception and global disasters rise to unprecedented levels. Jesus predicted religious deception, international conflict, famines, pestilences, astrological wonders, and earthquakes. He prophesied that believers would be persecuted and even martyred. Wickedness will abound, the love of many will grow cold, and the gospel of the kingdom will be proclaimed to all nations. Further, the abomination of desolation will stand in the Holy Place (see Matthew 24:4-15). These events signal the imminent arrival of the Son of Man from heaven (v. 30).

In chapter 3, we studied the role the Antichrist plays in setting up the abomination of desolation. He erects an image in the temple in honor of the Roman prince.

He animates the image and imposes the death penalty on all who refuse to worship the image (Rev. 13:13). Also, he forces everyone to receive the mark of the beast on the right hand or on the forehead (v. 16). Without this mark, no one can buy or sell (v. 17).

Jesus instructed believers (both Jews and their Gentile converts) to seek sanctuary in the mountains at first sight of the abomination of desolation. He advised a hasty evacuation (vv. 15-16).

Let no one on the roof of the house go down to take anything out of the house. Let no one in the field go back to get his cloak, How dreadful it will be in those days for pregnant women and nursing mothers! Pray that your flight will not take place in winter or on the Sabbath (vv. 17-20).

Why this advice? Jesus explained, "For then there will be great distress, unequaled from the beginning of the world until now—and never to be equaled again: (v. 21). The distress will be so intense that the days will be shortened; otherwise, no believer would survive (v. 22).

We might wonder: *What's going on here?*

In every period of history, God has preserved a faithful remnant. For example, he preserved Noah and his family in the flood. Those eight souls rode out the storm. They were safe in the ark. God had shut them in!

When idolatrous Ahab and Jezebel ruled Israel, the nation followed their lead by worshiping Baal. But Elijah and 7,000 other Israelites—God's remnant—kept the faith.

Perhaps the most memorable remnant was Daniel and his three friends in idolatrous Babylon. God preserved Daniel's three friends after Nebuchadnezzar had them bound and tossed into a blazing hot fire for refusing to worship his image. They emerged from the roaring flames untied and unscathed. Not even the faintest scent of smoke had settled onto their clothes. Daniel, too, experienced God's preserving power. He was thrown into a lions' den but the lions did not touch him. God had sent an angel to protect him.

When Rome occupied Palestine in the first century, most Jews blindly followed the apostate leadership of the scribes and Pharisees. But a remnant of Jews eagerly awaited the arrival of the Messiah. The gospel of Luke mentions some of the faithful: Zechariah and Elizabeth, Joseph and Mary, Simeon, Anna, and John the Baptist. Revelation indicates that a remnant will shine like lights in the sky out of the inky blackness of the tribulation.

Revelation 7 introduces us to a nucleus of tribulation believers. It numbers 144,000 saved Jews. God seals them—marks them for protection prior to the Great Tribulation, the second half of the tribulation. Throughout the Great Tribulation, the 144,00 serve as evangelists. They preach the gospel of the kingdom and win a multitude to Christ (v. 9; Matt. 24:14). At the end of the Great Tribulation, when Jesus stands on the Earth and prepares to inaugurate his kingdom, he comforts these redeemed saints. The Antichrist had persecuted them relentlessly during the Great Tribulation. They had experienced hunger, thirst, and exposure to the elements but, in King Jesus' kingdom, they will never hunger or thirst or suffer scorching heat (Rev. 7:16). Verse 17 promises: "The Lamb at the center of the throne will be their shepherd; he will lead them to springs of living water. And God will wipe away every tear from their eyes."

It seems many tribulation believers will be

martyred. Having refused the mark of the beast, they will not be able to buy food or water. Nor will they be able to rent or buy a home. They will die of hunger or thirst or exposure to the elements. However, when Jesus returns to earth to set up his kingdom, he will raise the martyrs from the dead. Along with Old Testament saints who experience resurrection at that time, the resurrected martyrs will enter the messianic kingdom, and "the Lamb at the center of the throne will be their Shepherd" (Rev. 7:17).

The kingdom on earth will include resurrected and translated believers from the church age (compare Col. 3:4; 1 Thess. 3:13; 4:16-17; Jude 14-15) and resurrected Old Testament believers (Dan. 12:2-3; John 5:28-29). But tribulation martyrs, too, will experience resurrection at Jesus' return to earth.

Revelation 20:4 explains:

I saw thrones on which were seated those who had been given authority to judge. And I saw the souls of those who had been beheaded because of their testimony for Jesus, and because of the word of God. They had not worshipped the beast or his image and had not received his mark on their foreheads or their right hands. They came to life and reigned with Christ a thousand years.

Since all these saints enter the kingdom in glorified, resurrected bodies and therefore do no procreate, we might ask how earth's population grows to such incredible number by the end of the one-thousand-year kingdom. After all, Revelation 20:7-9 describes a rebellion of massive proportions against Jesus at the end of the 1,000 years. Satan, who has just been released from his thousand-year imprisonment in the abyss (v. 2), leads this rebellion. His followers are described as coming from the four corners of the earth and gathering to battle "like the sand on the seashore" (v. 8).

The reason this anti-God army is so huge brings us full circle to the question: are the poor the least of Jesus' brothers? You see, when Jesus returns to earth, he will gather the nations before him for judgment. All who come before Jesus' bar of judgment do so in unglorified bodies. They are the sheep and goats mentioned in Matthew 25:31-33. He will welcome the sheep into his kingdom (v. 34), but he will consign the goats to eternal fire (v. 41). His criterion for judging will be "whatsoever you did for one of the least of these brothers of mine, you did for me" (v. 40).

But we cannot identify the poor of every period of history as the least of Jesus' brothers. Understanding the distress of Jewish believers of the tribulation leads us to their positive identification as Jesus' brothers and to the conclusion that charitable treatment of even the least of these tribulation believers will capture Jesus' favorable attention.

Hunted and hounded by the Antichrist and his followers, Jewish believers will seek refuge wherever they can find it. Like those kind, brave souls who hid World War II Jews from the Nazis, some individuals will help persecuted Jewish believers in the tribulation. They will give them food, drink, and shelter. Just as believers in every period of history are saved by grace alone through faith, those who aid the persecuted tribulation saints will be saved by grace. Their kindness will demonstrate their acceptance of the gospel of the kingdom preached by the Jewish remnant. Jesus will accept them into his kingdom as his "sheep."

Those who refuse assistance to the saved Jews of the tribulation will demonstrate by their negative treatment that they did not accept the gospel of the kingdom. Therefore, Jesus will identify them as "goats" and exclude them from his kingdom.

You may recall Jesus' words to Saul of Tarsus on the Damascus Road: "Saul, Saul, why do you persecute me?"

When Saul asked, "Who are you, Lord?"

Jesus replied, "I am Jesus, whom you are persecuting" (see Acts 9:4-5). Of course, Saul was persecuting believers before Jesus stopped him on the Damascus Road. Saul was carrying arrest warrants for the apprehension of believers in Damascus and he did not intend to show any mercy. He would arrest women as well as men and haul them off to prison in Jerusalem. Jesus viewed such persecution as persecution against himself.

Similarly, Matthew 25:31-46 shows the oneness Jesus and the saved Jews of the tribulation share. They are his "brothers" (v. 40), and Jesus regards the treatment they receive as the treatment he receives. He tells the sheep, whom he welcomes into his kingdom, "I was hungry and you gave me something to eat. I was thirsty and you gave me something to drink. I was a stranger and you invited me in. I needed clothes and you clothed me. I was sick and you looked after me. I was in prison and you visited me" (vv.35-36). He tells the goats whom he sends into eternal punishment: "For I was hungry and you gave me nothing to eat. I was thirsty and you gave me nothing to drink. I was a stranger and you did not invite me in. I needed clothes and you did not clothe me. I was sick and in prison and you did not look after me" (vv. 42-43).

So the poor are not the least of Jesus' brothers! But we should offer compassionate help to the poor. The Bible commands such treatment.

In preparation for their settlement in the Promised Land, the Israelites received, from the Lord, laws to live by. One law concerned harvest time. It instructed: "When you reap the harvest of your land, do not reap to the very edges of your field or gather the gleanings of your harvest. Do not go over your vineyard a second time or pick up the grapes that have fallen. Leave then for the poor and the alien. I am the LORD your God" (Lev. 19:9-10).

Out of similar concern for the poor, the Lord commanded the Israelites to give their fields, vineyards, and olive groves a rest every seventh year. The produce of the seventh year was to be designated for the poor and the wild animals (Ex. 23:11).

Undoubtedly, righteous Boaz observed the command given in Leviticus19:9-10 concerning the poor. Ruth, a Moabite widow, asked her mother-in-law Naomi, also a widow: "Let me go into the field and pick up the leftover grain behind anyone in whose eyes I find favor" (Ruth 2:2).

After receiving Naomi's permission, Ruth "went out and began to glean in the field behind the harvesters (v. 3). Later, Boaz, the owner of the farm, instructed his workers: "Even if she gathers among the sheaves, don't embarrass her. Rather pull out some stalks for her from the bundles and leave them for her to pick up, and don't rebuke her" (vv. 15-16).

This incident flared into one of the greatest love stories of all time. Boaz married Ruth, and Ruth became an ancestress of our Savior (Matt. 1:1-5).

The New Testament, too, includes teaching about helping the poor. When Jesus stood up and read Scripture in the synagogue of Nazareth, he read from Isaiah 61:1-2: "The Spirit of the Lord is upon me, because he has anointed me to preach good news to the poor (see Luke 4:18). When the apostles I the church in Jerusalem received complaints that the Gentile widows were being overlooked in the daily distribution of food, they told the congregation to choose seven Spirit-filled, wise men to superintend this ministry to the needy (Acts 6:1-3). Later, a council convened at Jerusalem to decide whether Gentile converts must become Jews. The decision was a resounding no but the council urged Paul and Barnabas, representative of the Gentile believers, to remember the poor (Gal. 2:1-10). Faithful to this responsibility, Paul spearheaded a relief fund among Gentile churches for the benefit of poor believers in Judea (see 2 Cor. 8 and 9).

Many Scriptures show God's concern for the poor and commend those who help the poor. Here are a few:

The righteous care about justice for the poor (Prov. 29:7).

Speak up and judge fairly; defend the rights of the poor and needy (Prov. 31:9).

Is not this the kind of fast I have chosen . . . ? Is it not to share your food with the hungry and to provide the poor wanderer with shelter? (Isa. 58:6-7)

Do not oppress the widow or the fatherless, the alien or the poor (Zech. 7:10).

Jesus answered, "If you want to be perfect, go, sell your possessions and give to the poor, and you will have treasures in heaven" (Matt. 19:21).

But when you give a banquet, invite the poor, the

crippled, the lame, the blind, and you will be blessed (Luke 14:13-14).

Listen, my dear brothers: Has not God chosen those who are poor in the eyes of the world to be rich in faith and to inherit the kingdom he promised to those who love him (James 2:5)?

If anyone has material possessions and sees his brother in need but has no pity on him, how can the love of God be in him? Dear children, let us not love with words or tongue but with action and in truth (1 John 3:17-18).

Clearly, the Bible mandates that we help the poor, but how can we fulfill this mandate? Here are a few suggestions:

- *A church pantry and clothes closet.* If your church wants to send a message that it not only talks about God's love but also shows it. A food pantry and clothes closet will help to convey that message.
- *Meals for the homeless.* Even if it is simply a matter of preparing sandwiches and delivering them to the homeless, this ministry is worthwhile. It can include entire families and communicate God's love to many needy men, women, and youth.
- *A Thanksgiving or a Christmas meal.* Some Christians strap on aprons and serve a hot meal to the needy at a rescue mission or soup kitchen at Thanksgiving and/or Christmas. God's love reaches the hungry on a platter!
- *An anytime cookout.* Why not fire up grills in a

Rethinking Popular Beliefs

downtown park and provide hot dogs for the homeless?
- *Job skills assistance.* You can help the unemployed poor by developing their resume-building and job interview skills. Check your community for opportunities to work with the needy!
- *Volunteerism.* Many poor people need transportation to medical facilities and government offices. Some, especially needy elderly and physically challenged, need meals delivered to them. Why not volunteer to help?
- *Fundraising to benefit the poor.* Your family can take on a fund-raising project to benefit the poor. Parents in one neighborhood encouraged their children to operate a lemonade stand on hot Saturdays and give 50% of the profits to a soup kitchen. Perhaps your family can brainstorm similar ways to benefit institutions that serve the poor and needy.

These suggested enterprises are few but they can launch you into a ministry that communicates God's love in tangible ways. You may discover many opportunities by hosting a brainstorming session at church or but hosting such a session at home. Poverty is not going away but if we truly love our neighbors as ourselves, even neighbors on welfare, we will try to improve their lot in life.

5
POPULAR BELIEF: WE ARE BUILDING THE KINGDOM

I DON'T RECALL WHEN THE SHIFT IN TERMINOLOGY occurred. I don't think it happened in the '50s or '60s or even in the '70s, but it happened, took hold, and spread rapidly. Today the old terminology is almost nonexistent and the new seems to be here to stay. I'm referring to the shift from such statements as, "We are doing the Lord's work," and "We are furthering the cause of Christ" to "We are building the kingdom" and "We are doing kingdom work" and "We are working for the kingdom." Although I would not question the sincerity of those who use the new terminology, I do question the terminology's theological accuracy.

The issue is one of definition and timing. If we define the kingdom as the reign of Christ over the church, we believe the kingdom is present on earth now in a spiritual form. If we define the kingdom only as the literal, earthly reign of Christ, we believe the kingdom is future and distinct from the church. The former view leads us to say we are building the kingdom or doing kingdom work or working for the kingdom. The latter view leads us to say we are doing the Lord's work or advancing the cause of Christ.

The latter view is sometimes called the millennial kingdom idea. It is not a contrived theory begun by dispensationalists, although it is inherently dispensational. Archibald Robertson claims this view "prevailed in the Church generally for two centuries and a half, and in the Western Church for four centuries . . . until the time of Augustine."[1] Augustine adopted an allegorical interpretation of Scripture. Alva McClain writes: "Augustine may be regarded as the father of this Church-Kingdom idea."[2]

Not all theologians see the kingdom in the same light, although they all agree that God reigns over all things and, in the broadest sense, his kingdom includes everything and every created being. Usually, they call this domain, "the kingdom of God."

We read about God's universal kingdom in a number of passages of Scripture. Here are a few:

The LORD is in his holy temple; the LORD is on his heavenly throne. He observes the sons of men; his eyes examine them (Ps. 11:4).

But it is God who judges; He brings one down, he exalts another (Ps. 75:7).

The LORD has established his throne in heaven, and his kingdom rules over all (Ps. 103:19).

Your kingdom is an everlasting kingdom, and your dominion endures through all generations (Ps. 145:13).

In the year King Uzziah died, I saw the LORD *seated on a throne, high and exalted (Isa. 6:1).*

The most high God is sovereign over the kingdoms of me and sets over them anyone he wishes (Dan. 5:21).

Many theologians differentiate between the kingdom of God and the kingdom of heaven in some instances but equate the two in certain biblical contexts. For example, Emory H. Bancroft writes:

"The kingdom of heaven" in the first twelve chapters of Mathew has an entirely different force and scope from that which it has in the later chapters. In Matthew, the kingdom, which John announced was "at hand" was the messianic kingdom of Old Testament prophecy, whereas in Matthew 13, etc., the "kingdom of heaven" has reference to the Christian profession. Yet both of these significations of "the kingdom of heaven" are spoken of as the kingdom of God in the other Gospels. It would therefore be as scriptural to say that the "kingdom of heaven" in Matthew 13 is the kingdom of God also but it would not be accurate to say of other Scriptures that the kingdom of God is synonymous with "the kingdom of heaven" except we qualify our words by adding which aspect of "the kingdom of heaven" we are referring to.[3]

If all of this seems confusing, the reason is simple: It is. I believe the confusion clears up if we perceive both terms, "the kingdom of God" and "the kingdom of heaven," as references to the future messianic kingdom (the millennial, earthly reign of Christ), except where the context clearly points to God's universal over all things and all beings. I see no reason to relate the parables of

Matthew 13 to the Christian profession. They were addressed to Jews who anticipated a messianic kingdom. Appropriate to this interpretation is the use of the messianic name "Son of Man in verses 37 and 41. Further, the setting for the parables is the millennial kingdom, not the church age. Notice these expressions: "the harvest" (v. 30); "the harvest is the end of the age" (vv. 39-40, 49); "the harvesters are the angels" (v. 39; cf. 24:30-31; 25:31-33); "will weed out of his kingdom" (13:41); and "will throw them into the fiery furnace, where there will be weeping and gnashing of teeth" (vv. 42, 50; cf. Rev. 20:11-15 [the final judgment]).

Although many excellent Bible teachers explain the coexistence of believers and unbelievers as existing together in a period of explosive growth as Christendom spreads and includes those who merely profess to be believers as well as genuine believers (the weeds and the wheat), these characteristics mark the messianic kingdom. Only saved individuals enter the kingdom. Raptured and resurrected Christians, resurrected Old Testament believers, and resurrected martyrs will enter the kingdom in glorified bodies. They will not procreate. But saved survivors of the tribulation, the sheep on Jesus' right hand (Matt. 25:33-34) will enter the kingdom in natural bodies and they will procreate. So the kingdom will experience a population explosion, and both believers and unbelievers will inhabit the planet under King Jesus' rule.

However, at the end of the kingdom reign, unbelievers who merely gave lip service to King Jesus will side with Satan when he is released from his one-thousand-year confinement in the Abyss (Rev. 20:1-3, 7-8). They surround the kingdom's capital, Jerusalem, and pit themselves against the King. But they are no match for our omnipotent Lord and Savior. They become fuel for fire that falls from heaven (vv. 9-10). Only genuine believers (wheat) remain to enjoy eternal bliss.

John L. Benson writes:

Satan will appeal to the last generation of children born to millennial saints. Evidently, thousands of these children will neglect the time of their probation by refusing to trust Christ as their Savior, Satan will deceive them into thinking they are capable of vanquishing the King and overturning His kingdom of righteousness and holiness. Perhaps under the guise of going to Jerusalem to worship at some annual feast, Satan will lead a countless number of sinners in an attack upon the capital city. Fire from heaven will fall upon the rebel crowd, annihilating them. The devil's final fling over, God will sentence him to everlasting torment in the lake of fire."[4]

Distinguishing between God's universal kingdom and the millennial kingdom answers the question, "Are we building the kingdom?" In the vast scheme of things, we are, because God's universal kingdom encompasses everything. However, I don't think those who use the expression, "building the kingdom," intend such a broad use. They see the church and the kingdom as the same thing. But the Scriptures portray Messiah's kingdom not as the church but as his future reign on earth. Furthermore, we are not building God's universal kingdom because it is already all-inclusive. Nor are working in Messiah's kingdom because it has not arrived.

When John the Baptist heralded Jesus' arrival as Israel's Messiah, he announced: "The kingdom of heaven is near" (Matt. 3:2). This was not wishful thinking on his part, because the kingdom of heaven was near. Jesus, Israel's king, would soon begin His earthly ministry, validate His messianic credentials by performing signs, and offer the kingdom to all who would repent and receive Him.

When Jesus heard that John had been imprisoned, He entered Galilee and "from that time on . . . began to preach, 'Repent, for the kingdom of heaven is near'" (Matt. 4:17).

When Jesus gathered his disciples, He taught them to pray, "Our Father in heaven, hallowed be your name, your kingdom come, your will be done on earth as it is in heaven" (Matt. 6:9-10). When he commissioned his disciples, he told them to "preach the kingdom of God" (Luke 9:2).

Israel rejected the King and His kingdom. Consequently, the nation has been set aside and God is working through the church to glorify Himself and to invite sinners everywhere to trust in his Son as Savior (Rom. 11:112). The church was never commissioned to preach the gospel of the kingdom but she has been commissioned to preach the gospel of Christ's vicarious, expiatory, substitutionary death, His burial, resurrection and subsequent appearances to many witnesses (1 Cor. 15:1-8).

When the church exits the earth and meets the Lord in the air (1 Thess. 4:13-17), God will resume his prophetic program for Israel (Rom. 11:25-27). Many Jews will be saved in the tribulation and will proclaim the gospel of the kingdom to the nations (cf. Matt. 24:14 and Rev. 7). Their message is valid because the kingdom arrives at the end of the tribulation period.

We know from reading the Gospels that Jesus taught many truths about the kingdom and not once did the disciples consider the kingdom anything but the Messiah's earthly rule on behalf of Israel and as the fulfillment of Old Testament prophecy. They failed to understand the need to serve one another humbly and not to covet the most prominent positions in the kingdom (Mark 10:35-45), but they were clear about the fact that the kingdom would arrive. Even after receiving forty days of post-resurrection teaching from Jesus about the kingdom (Acts 1:3), their focus was still on the earthly kingdom promised to Israel. They asked Jesus, "Lord, are you at this time going to restore thy kingdom to Israel?" (v. 6)

Had they flunked the course on the kingdom? Had they failed to learn that the kingdom existed in spiritual form? Why didn't they conclude that the kingdom is the church and vice versa? The answer must be that Jesus never taught that the kingdom existed in a spiritual form in the hearts of his followers who compose the church.

How did Jesus respond to his disciples' question about the kingdom? He did not say, "Look, men, you've got it all wrong. Stop thinking the kingdom will be restored to Israel! The kingdom is the church I am about to inaugurate." Here's what he said, "It is not for you to know the times or dates the Father has set by his own authority" (v. 7). In other words, Jesus assured his disciples that the Father will usher in the kingdom promised to Israel, but he will do so according to his preset timetable.

But how do we explain Colossians 1:13 that tells us, "For he has rescued us from the dominion of darkness and brought into the kingdom of the Son he loves"? Doesn't this verse teach that Christians are already in the kingdom? The word "kingdom" in this verse translates to *baseleia*, a Greek word that can also be translated *royal power, dominion, rule*. The context indicates that the Father has qualified believers for an inheritance in the kingdom and has transferred us from the dominion of darkness to the dominion of Jesus' rule. Someday we will participate in Jesus' rule on earth.

Will conditions be vastly different when King Jesus rules our planet? If newspapers, periodicals, the Internet, radio, and television communicate news items during the millennium, they will issue only good news. Jesus will see that his subjects and nature, too, enjoy the best of times.

Occasionally, men and women appear on TV as candidates for a makeover, usually an extreme makeover They submit to procedures that restructures their faces, improve their smiles, remove their fatty tissue, style their hair, and adorn their bodies with the latest fashions. They may have begun the makeover as unappealing "caterpillars," but they emerge as attractive "butterflies." The whole earth is waiting eagerly for the extreme makeover Jesus will give it when he returns to earth. Romans 8:19-21 tells us, "The creation waits in eager anticipation for the sons of God to be revealed. For the creation was subjected to frustration, not by its own choice, but by the will of the me who subjected it, in hope that the creation itself will be liberated from its bondage to decay and brought into the glorious freedom of the children of God."

Environmental issues will be past issues when Jesus rules the earth. All of nature will return to Edenic conditions because Jesus will roll back the curse imposed on nature when Adam and Eve sinned. Isaiah 35 portrays the desert and wasteland blossoming profusely. Forests will spring up and grasslands will blanket the land. This dramatic beauty and productivity comes about because abundant rain will fall on previously parched ground. Isaiah 35:7 predicts that "the burning sand will become a pool, the thirsty ground bubbling springs. In the haunts where jackals once lay, grass and reeds and papyrus will grow." No one will quarrel over water rights or battle drought in the millennium.

Living water will flow from Jerusalem westward to the Dead Sea (Zech. 14:8). The Dead Sea will become a freshwater fishermen's paradise. Ezekiel foretold: "There will be large numbers of fish, because this water flows there and makes salt water fresh; so where the river flows everything will live. Fishermen will stand along the shore; from En Gedi to En Eglaim there will be places for spreading nets. The fish will be many kinds—like the fish of the Great Sea" (Ezek. 47:9-10).

Longevity and good health will prevail in Jesus' kingdom. Isaiah 65:20 predicts an infant mortality rate of zero and a life span of 100 as that of "mere youth." Perhaps the leaves of the trees in the New Jerusalem (a satellite city during the millennium?), described in Revelation 22:2 as being "for the healing of the nations, will promote outstanding health and stimulate longevity.

Earth's population will enjoy abundant light because Jesus will be its "everlasting light" (Isa. 60:19), and the "sun will never set again" (v. 20). No one will suffer depression from a lack of exposure to light!

Today, medical science is prolonging life so well that the United States Government is scrambling to find a way to protect Social Security for those who live far into retirement. This problem will not exist in the kingdom, because productivity and prosperity will exist without conflict. Isaiah 65:21-22 predicts that everyone will eat well and live secure.

People will not have to lock their doors when they go on a vacation and wonder if they will return to find their possessions stolen. Property rights will be respected (Mic. 4:4). Jesus' kingdom will be free of gangbangers, con artists, scammers, molesters, thieves, murderers, muggers, and robbers. If anyone acts up, Jesus will slay him with "the breath of his lips" (Isa. 11:5). Violence will cease and prisons will be empty (Isa. 60:18).

Mothers will not have to tell their children, "Don't play in the street," because the streets will be safe. Zechariah 8:5 announces, "The city streets will be filled with boys and girls playing there." Children will be safe even around snakes. According to Isaiah 11:8: "The infant will play near the hole of the cobra, and the young child will put his hand into the viper's nest."

Wild animals will abandon their savagery. Former predators and prey will live harmoniously. "The wolf will lie down with the lamb," Isaiah predicts. "The leopard will lie down with the goat, the calf, and the lion and the yearling together; and a little child will lead them. The cow will feed with the bear, their young will lie down together" (Isa. 11:6-7). Previously carnivorous animals will be herbivorous. "The lion will eat straw like the ox" (v. 7).

Nations will no longer build military arsenals. Satellites that kept tabs on nuclear sites will be unnecessary. Nations will enjoy peace administered by Jesus, the Prince of Peace. Isaiah 2:4 predicts: "He [Jesus] will judge between the nations and will settle disputes for many peoples. They will beat their swords into plowshares and their spears into pruning hooks. Nation will not take up swords against nation, nor will they train for war anymore." According to Isaiah 9:7, there will be no end to the peace Jesus establishes as he reigns from David's throne.

The first Adam failed to mediate God's "kingdom" in Eden but the second Adam, the Lord Jesus, will not fail. He "will delight in the fear of the LORD," and he will judge righteously, justly, and decisively (Isa. 11:3-4).

The kingdom reign of Jesus will fulfill all the covenant promises made to the patriarchs and King David. Jesus will dwell among the restored, regenerated, and rejoicing people of Israel. Isaiah 12 records saved Israel's song of praise to the Messiah. The song reflects the joy of his comfort (v. 1), the joy of his salvation (v. 4), and the joy of his presence (v. 6). If we think we have joy now, just wait and see how much joy we will experience when we, like restored Israel, enjoy Jesus' physical presence!

Jesus was rejected when he came to earth the first time but he will be recognized worldwide at his second coming as Lord and King. He will establish Jerusalem as his capital, and he will be "King over the whole earth" (Zech. 14:9). People from around the globe will make an annual pilgrimage to Jerusalem to "worship the King, the LORD Almighty, and to celebrate the feast of tabernacles" (v. 16). Failure to make the pilgrimage will result in the King's withholding rain from the delinquents' land and his bringing the plague on them (vv. 17-19).

Currently, opponents to Christianity are working relentlessly to remove Christian symbols and practices from public places. As a result, city seals that once displayed a cross no longer do so. Invocations at military events used to conclude with the words, "In Jesus' name" no longer do so. School children can sing, "Here Comes Santa Claus" but not "Silent Night." Crosses honoring the memory of the victims of the Columbine High School massacre were removed from a small hillside in a public park. But this hostile attitude will not surface in Jesus' kingdom.

Knowledge of the Lord will pervade the earth during the millennium. Isaiah 11:9 predicts: "The earth will be full of the knowledge of the LORD as the waters cover the sea." The prophet Jeremiah echoed this truth. He wrote: "' This is the covenant I will make with the house of Israel after that time,' declares the LORD. 'I will put my laws in their minds and write in on their hearts. I will be their God, and they will be my people. No longer will a man teach his neighbor, saying 'know the LORD,' because they will all know me, from the least of them to the greatest,' declares the LORD" (Jer. 31:33-34).

Righteousness and holiness will be reflected in even the most unexpected places. Zechariah prophesied: "On that day HOLY TO THE LORD will be inscribed on the bells of the horses, and the cooking pots in the LORD's house will be like sacred bowls in front of the altar. Every pot in Jerusalem and Judah will be holy to the LORD Almighty, and to all who come to sacrifice will take some of the pots and cook in them" (Zech. 14:20-21).

Christians are not working in the kingdom now but

we will work in it when it arrives. The prospect is certain, for 2 Timothy 2:12 promises we will reign with Jesus.

John L. Benson writes:

The glorified saints of all ages will rule and reign with Christ. All who participate in the first resurrection will rule in the kingdom (Rev. 20:6). This will include the Old Testament saints, the tribulation martyrs, and the church saints. Christ is the heir of the kingdom, and the church saints are joint heirs with him.[5]

Tragedies like 9/11, suicide bombings, campus shootings, and other horrendous acts paint a dismal picture of the twenty-first century, and reasonable people question the humanness of the perpetrators. We shake our heads in disbelief of such senseless and heartless crimes against innocent people but we know, from prophecy, that a better day is coming. Jesus will take control of planet Earth someday and turn all that is wrong upside down, shake it out, and discard it. He will reign in righteousness and the world will resound with shouts of joy. There is hope! Let's share the hope with so many who are hopeless!

---

1. "Philo of Alexandria," *New Schaff-Herzog Encyclopedia of Religious Knowledge*, ed. E. M. Jackson (New York: Funk and Wagnalls, 1911). Vol. IX, 39.
2. Alva J. McClain, *The Greatness of the Kingdom* (Chicago: Moody Press, 1968), 9.
3. Emory H. Bancroft, *Christian Theology, Systematic and Biblical* (Grand Rapids: Academic Books, Zondervan, 1976), 287.
4. John L. Benson, *The Future Reign of Christ on Planet Earth* (Denver: Accent Books, 1974), 57-58.
5. Benson, *Truth about Tomorrow* (Denver: Baptist Publications, 1976).

6

POPULAR BELIEF: GOD IS TOO LOVING TO SEND ANYONE TO HELL

NOBODY WANTS TO GO TO HELL. AT LEAST I HAVE NEVER heard anyone say, "I want to go to hell." Have you?

Some who don't want to go to hell raise the argument that God is too loving to send anyone to hell. So they use this reasoning as a kind of security blanket. But if God is too loving to send anyone to hell, why is hell so highly populated? Jesus taught that "wide is the gate and broad is the road that leads to destruction, and many enter through it" (Matt. 7:13).

At least those who view God as too loving to send anyone to hell believe in the existence of hell and apparently think of it as a highly undesirable destination. They are correct on two points: God is loving and hell is a highly undesirable destination. First John 4:16 asserts that "God is love," and Luke 16:23 describes hell as a place of torment.

Sheol is the Old Testament word translated to "hell" thirty-one times, "grave" thirty-one times and "pit" three times. Generally, it refers to the realm of the dead. It is used to refer to the destination of both the righteous (for example: Ps. 16:10; 30:3; Isa. 38:10) and the wicked for example: (Num. 16:33; Job 24:19; Ps. 9:17).

One of the New Testament words for "hell" is *hades*. It refers to the abode of departed unbelievers between death and the resurrection. The word appears eleven times in the New Testament. A second word for "hell" is *gehenna*. It appears twelve times in the New Testament and refers to the place of eternal suffering, the post-resurrection abode of the wicked from all periods of history. Luke 12:5 uses the word in its warning about being thrown into "hell."

Hell is as miserable as heaven is blissful. Jesus told a story about a rich man who went to hell after living a selfish, materialistic life (Luke 16:22-23). Obviously, the rich man was not a believer because he failed to obey God's commands to care for the poor and needy. While he was alive, he wore luxurious clothes and gorged himself on the finest cuisine but totally ignored the needs of Lazarus, a frail, hungry beggar who lay at his gate and longed to eat whatever fell from the rich man's table (vv. 19-21). Dogs treated Lazarus better than the rich man treated him. In hell, the rich man was fully conscious. He experienced torment and agony and was barred from the presence of God (vv. 23-26).

By contrast, when Lazarus died, he went to a place of comfort (vv. 22, 25).

Jesus said the abode of eternal fire was prepared for the "devil and his angels" (Matt. 25:41). Before Jesus inaugurates his earthly kingdom, he casts the head of the Revived Roman Empire and the antichrist into "the fiery lake of burning sulfur" (Rev. 19:20). One thousand years later, the devil meets the same fate (20:10). The doom is one of eternal torment.

Revelation 20:11-15 describes the final judgment—the Great White Throne Judgment—in which unbelievers from all periods of history and from all walks of life stand before God. We learn that "death and Hades gave up the dead that were in them" (v. 13). They are judged according to their works but condemned for one reason only: Their names are not found in the book of life (v. 15).

Obviously, God is not too loving to send anyone to hell. Multitudes will spend eternity there and the agony is endless. Of course, God does not rejoice in the eternal doom of unbelievers but he is too just to let them go unpunished. The eternal state does not amend the sinfulness of sinners (Revelation 22:11).

Let's look back to the Garden of Eden. It was there that God tested our first parents, Adam and Eve. He provided a perfect environment for them but he told them not to eat the fruit of the tree of knowledge of good and evil (Gen. 2:17). If they disobeyed God, they would die.

Sounds like an easy test, doesn't it? After all, they could eat from any other tree in the garden. So how did they do? They flunked the test (Gen. 3:6). Aren't we just like our first parents? We step beyond the limits of what God has put off limits. We transgress the Ten Commandments. We profane God's name, lie, steal, covet, commit adultery, and despise our neighbor. And like our first parents, we are under the penalty of death.

Adam and Eve did not die physically the day they sinned but they died spiritually; that is, they were separated from God. Eventually, they died physically. Because of our sin, we receive the "wages of sin," which is death (Rom. 6:23). This sentence of death is threefold:

(1) spiritual death (separation from God now), physical death ultimately (Heb. 9:27: separation of the soul from the body), and eternal death (separation from God for eternity; Rev. 20:14).

But here's really good news: God is so loving that He provided a way for you and me to avoid hell and enjoy the assurance that heaven is our eternal home. In His great love, He provided His Son Jesus to take our punishment (John 3:16). On the cross, Jesus voluntarily paid the penalty of our sin. If we believe in Jesus as our Savior, God forgives us and gives us eternal life. Romans 6:23 tells us "the gift of God is eternal life in Christ Jesus our Lord." John 3:36 promises: "Whoever believes in the Son has eternal life."

When Jesus died for our sins, he offered a perfect payment for them. He called out from the cross, "It is finished" (John 19:30). This statement translates the Greek word *tetelestai* that literally means, "It stands finished." The Greeks used *tetelestai* to mark a bill as paid in full. Artists used it when they viewed what they painted and were satisfied that nothing need to be added to it. So nothing needed to be added to the payment Jesus made for our sins and God accepted Jesus' sacrifice on our behalf by raising Jesus from the grave (Rom. 4:25).

At the time of the crucifixion, a rebellious crowd urged Governor Pilate to set a criminal Barabbas free. Barabbas, whose name means "the father's son," was supposed to die on the cross with two other criminals on their crosses. He deserved to die but the crowd set him free and, in his place, they called for the crucifixion of Jesus (Matt. 27:15-26). So it was that one "father's son" was set free while another, Jesus the Son of the heavenly

Father, died in his place. Like Barabbas, we sons of our first father Adam deserve to die for our sins but Jesus the Son of God died in our place. Isaiah 53:5-6, written several centuries before the crucifixion, prophesied concerning Jesus: "But he was pierced for our transgressions, he was crushed for our iniquities; the punishment that brought us peace was upon him, and by his wounds we are healed. We all, like sheep, have gone astray, each of us has turned to his own way; and the LORD has laid on him the iniquity of us all."

Why not affirm God's love right now by trusting in Jesus as your Savior, believing he died for your sins and arose from the grave? He will welcome you to heaven someday and right now put a little bit of heaven in your soul that will give you peace for the rest of your earthly life.

IF YOU LIKED THIS, YOU MAY ENJOY: THE GULAG P-PA DIARIES
BY PRESTON LEWIS

As new empty-nesters Harriet and Preston next looked forward to becoming grandparents. Their journey to assuming the names of Mema and P-Pa, however, took a tragic and unexpected turn.

The Gulag P-Pa Diaries tells a bittersweet story of anticipation, loss and sorrow counterbalanced with hope, faith and a butterfly on the path to grandparenthood.

OUT NOW

ABOUT THE AUTHOR

James Dyet, Senior Curriculum Editor for Accent Publications, Bible teacher, and author, is an avid golfer and member of the U.S. Golf Collectors Society. He was born in Scotland, the country that originated golf. At age three he moved to Canada with his parents and older brother. When he was six, he began caddying at St. Catharines Golf Course in St. Catharines, Ontario.

By sixteen Jim was scoring consistently in the 70s and was regarded locally as a golfer with a promising future. However, his conversion to Christ that same year turned his life in a different direction. Believing that God had called him into the ministry, two years later Jim sold his golf clubs to help fund his way to Moody Bible Institute. He was graduated from Moody in 1957 as senior class president.

In addition to his Moody training, Jim holds a B.A. from Houghton College and the M.A., Th.D., and D.Lit. degrees from Baptist Christian University. He also has taken graduate studies at Indiana State University and the Denver Seminary. He and his wife, Gloria, reside in Colorado Springs, Colorado.

www.ingramcontent.com/pod-product-compliance
Lightning Source LLC
Chambersburg PA
CBHW010429190426
43201CB00047BA/2332